INSIDE THE FIRM

INSIDE THE FIRM

The Inefficiencies of Hierarchy

HARVEY LEIBENSTEIN

Harvard University Press
Cambridge, Massachusetts, and London, England
1987

This book is printed on acid-free paper, and its binding materials
have been chosen for strength and durability.

Library of Congress Cataloging-in-Publication Data

Leibenstein, Harvey.
  Inside the firm.

  Bibliography: p.
  Includes index.
  1. Industrial organization (Economic theory)
2. Competition, Imperfect. 3. Industrial
management—Japan. I. Title.
HD2326.L45 1987   302.3′5   87-8426
ISBN 0-674-45515-0 (alk. paper)

To Marge

Preface

This book may be viewed as a contribution to the theory of the firm, especially under conditions of imperfect competition. Earlier writers on monopoly, monopolistic competition, and imperfect competition did not ask what new behavioral possibilities arise in firms once the constraints imposed by a perfectly competitive environment are loosened. This book examines how the behavior of firm members differs when firms are sheltered from the rigors of competition. It shows how internal inefficiencies develop as a result.

The theory presented can also be seen as a contribution to the new institutional economics. Institutional economics depends to a considerable extent on the formalized concepts of conventions (inside the firm) and institutions (conventions outside the firm). These concepts are critical to the theory of the firm underlying this book.

The volume provides the essentials of an organizational theory of the firm. Many of the concepts and basic ideas are applicable to other types of organization, as well as to management problems. Thus, the book should also interest readers who are concerned with questions of organization and management.

The main concerns of the book are the components of the intrafirm behavior of firm members and how these components interact in response to market pressure. These matters require examination of such institutional concepts as conventions, employment relations, and hierarchical organizational structures. These and related elements are involved in the nonmarket, interdependent relations between firm members that play a role in the market behavior of the firm. The book focuses on such interdependencies of firm members. The connecting strand is the search for sources of X-inefficiency, or internal inefficiency (terms that are used interchangeably).

The comment and controversy engendered by my previous book, *Beyond Economic Man* (Cambridge, Mass.: Harvard University Press, 1976), served as a stimulus to this work. Some of the ideas contained herein were presented earlier, under severe constraints of time and space, in conference papers, responses to critics, and symposia. It seemed desirable to develop the argument further in the less constrained format of a book.

For the most part this study deals with different elements of the theory of the firm from those that were discussed in *Beyond Economic Man*. These new elements are: view of the firm as an entity that faces *hidden* multiperson Prisoner's Dilemma problems, which it solves by the adoption of intrafirm conventions; consideration of the theory of hierarchy to help explain intrafirm behavior and *internal inefficiencies;* examination of the "theory" of the large Japanese firm in connection with latent Prisoner's Dilemma problems and the role of hierarchy; and reconsideration of the theory of entrepreneurship and its relation to microeconomics. Throughout, the focus is on an explanation of X-inefficiency, especially within hierarchies.

Since the publication of *Beyond Economic Man,* two occasions for extended reflection and uninterrupted study have influenced my thinking. I spent the academic year 1978–79 at the Institute for Advanced Study, Princeton, where I became aware of the theory of conventions or social norms developed by philosophers such as David Lewis, which employs a theory of games approach to coordination problems. Conventions viewed in this manner turn out to be solutions to Prisoner's Dilemma problems. In 1982 I spent six months in Kyoto University in Japan, where I worked with Japanese colleagues on the nature of the large Japanese enterprise. It struck me at the time that the Japanese firm represents a different view of how a firm operates, how it should be run, and what are the forces within it. It appeared to me then, as it does now, that any theory which attempts to deal with internal inefficiency has to be able to explain how such ideas apply to the Japanese firm.

The firm faces two problems simultaneously: size of the pie and division of the pie. The size and the division are closely related. The connections generally involve a *multifaceted* Prisoner's Dilemma-like situation—a dilemma that is usually hidden but which surfaces from time to time. The conventions for many aspects of internal organization having to do with creation and division of the pie help to solve intrafirm Prisoner's Dilemma problems.

Hierarchy is a ubiquitous and complex phenomenon. There are too many possible connections and relations between members of a hierarchy to allow anything like a complete treatment. The book deals only with some aspects of hierarchy, especially the more important vertical and horizontal relations between firm members, and it attempts to show how these relationships contribute to internal inefficiency. In recent years a number of approaches have been tried to understanding hierarchies. The one emphasized here examines hierarchy in terms of vertical interpersonal relationships and certain presumptions about the nature of such relationships. It also looks at the simple or intricate horizontal relations that may exist at the same time between workers on the same level. In addition, vertical relations influence the nature of the horizontal relations, and vice versa. Hierarchy has implications for the internal efficiency of the different types of vertical and horizontal relations that arise in specific contexts.

As for the Japanese firm, the book focuses especially on internal hierarchical relations and the contrast between such relations and their counterparts in Western enterprises. In this connection it analyzes how the Japanese firm solves its latent Prisoner's Dilemma problems and how their particular hierarchical structure facilitates avoiding standard Prisoner's Dilemma solutions. The contrast between American and Japanese firms is a means of highlighting aspects of the theory of hierarchy.

Entrepreneurship plays a role in relations not only between firms but also inside the firm. The book examines why entrepreneurship does not fit into standard micro theory and how micro theory can be reformulated so that entrepreneurship plays a critical role in microeconomic analysis. This reformulation is handled through the concept of a "loose equilibrium," in contradistinction to the tight equilibrium of standard theory.

The most difficult part of writing this book involved addressing the controversy raised by relaxing the maximization postulate. To non-economists, the idea of allowing for occasional nonoptimizing behavior seems obvious and readily acceptable. But to many economists any relaxation of utility maximization arouses strong objections. Debates connected with substituting one postulate for another interfere with the job of explaining the nature of the theory and drawing out its implications. Important linguistic aspects are involved in "the possibility of nonmaximization" debate. Although the issues of this debate must be addressed, they are not an integral part of the story that follows. Hence, all linguistic, terminological, and related matters appear in an appendix.

It is impossible to express fully one's intellectual indebtedness. Ideally one would write a history of the ideas put forth in a book and then proceed to suggest new analytical elements. Needless to say, nothing of the sort is attempted here. The problem of indebtedness is simplified in fields with a recognized research frontier, such as physics or microbiology, since in those cases readers can easily tell whose work the author is building on. In fields without a frontier, such as economics, it is frequently impossible to know whether any body of work contributes ideas that go beyond the frontier of the subject, and thus it is almost impossible to indicate one's intellectual debts adequately. I envy those who are able to include in their books a set of references that represents a *Who's Who* in the field. At the same time I regret any unintentional lapses in expressing my indebtedness to others.

I am grateful for permission to include in this volume portions of papers that were published earlier as follows: "Intrafirm Effort Decisions and Sanctions: Hierarchy Versus Peers," in *Handbook of Behavioral Economics: Behavioral Microeconomics,* ed. Benjamin Gilad and Stanley Kaish (Greenwich: JAI Press, 1986), pp. 213–231; "On the Economics of Conventions and Institutions: An Exploratory Essay," *Journal of Institutional and Theoretical Economics (Zeitschrift für die gesamte Staatswissenschaft)* 140, (March 1984): 74–89; "Entrepreneurship, Entrepreneurial Training, and X-Efficiency Theory," *Journal of Economic Behavior and Organization* 8 (June 1987); "On Relaxing the Maximization Postulate," *Journal of Behavioral Economics* 14 (Winter 1985): 5–20.

It is not possible to thank explicitly all who were helpful in this endeavor, such as the anonymous referees for Harvard University Press. Members of audiences for the lectures dealing with topics in this volume were helpful either by raising challenging questions or by making useful suggestions. Daniel Bell helped choose the title and provided an apt story for a point made in the appendix. Others who reviewed the volume in whole or in part or who were helpful in other ways include David Bloom, Roger Frantz, Jeffrey James, Shlomo Maital, David McClelland, Paul Streeten, and Klaus Weiermair. I am especially indebted to my research assistant, Louise Fredericksen, who helped in a variety of ways throughout the production of this manuscript.

Contents

INSIDE THE FIRM

CHAPTER 1

Organization and the Procedural Perspective

Much of the productive economic life of individuals is carried out through or within organizations, yet the theory of organization is not part of standard economic analysis. The focus of this study is the relations of the components of economic organizations to internal efficiency. We will look at organizations from several viewpoints: that of individuals making decisions as agents for the organization; that of individuals facing, in their work, decisions that entail their own personal interests; and that of the various elements of organizational structures that constrain and influence the decisions made by individuals.

In studying such connections we will look at both formal contractual relationships and the seemingly invisible informal connections between different individuals. Also possibly important are the relations between individuals or groups who work in isolation from each other but who are inside the same organization. While our main interest is the firm, that is, privately owned or government-owned economic organizations, many of the ideas will apply to organizations whose main purpose is not necessarily economic. All of these matters will be looked at directly or indirectly with the purpose of finding sources of internal inefficiency.

In part, we will be concerned with the influence of various types of hierarchies on decisions, but there is much more to understanding this than simply understanding the relations of individuals to the organization. What is critical is to understand the relations of individuals to each other and the effects of these relations on organizational behavior. This will involve examining the relative interests of those at different levels (for example, employees versus the hierarchy), as well as examining different factions which may be united along vertical lines. We will be concerned with the bonds or the absence of bonds between individuals, either along horizontal lines (peer-group influences), or along vertical lines. Again, all of these matters will be related to efficiency.

Is this area of inquiry important? It would be almost banal to point out that for most of us in Western economies the organization we work in and its influence on us are among the most important aspects of our lives. In some cases they are the most important. Whether we are happy or not may depend to a large extent on how we fare in the organizations we belong to, especially those in which we work. Organizations impose rules on our daily lives. We cannot avoid such rules, regulations, and customs and their influence on us. They may facilitate what we want to do, but frequently they are sources of irritation and frustration. To many of us some of these procedures, rules, and the like may appear arbitrary. In most cases, whatever the rationale, they are not of our own making, yet we cannot escape them. Some may not only influence us adversely, but we may believe that they are not in the interest of the organization, that they are essentially inefficient.

Clearly, all of this must be important since many of us spend most of our waking hours under organizational control, frequently more waking hours than we spend under our own personal control. In addition, many people feel they cannot escape organizational controls because their livelihood depends on fitting into an organization. Although there are choices, most involve being in either one organization or another rather than escaping organizational involvement. All of this is not to suggest that employment, even in large organizations, is necessarily inferior to being self-employed, but it does suggest the importance of organizational influences on our lives, as well as the importance of trying to understand how organizations function, and how well they function.[1]

This last point is especially significant when we take into account the fact that there appears to be an inexorable growth in the average size of organizations, in the depth of their hierarchies, and in the remoteness of those who make decisions that affect others. Furthermore, a steadily growing proportion of the economy is being dominated by large organizational structures and the internal bureaucracies that control them. This appears to be a worldwide trend. Is this trend in the interest of efficiency? Would we be better off if some limits were placed on the growth of organizations? Is smaller in some sense better than

---

1. While sociologists, anthropologists, and industrial psychologists appear to study such matters, they do not examine the efficiency aspects simultaneously. The study of efficiency is clearly the province of the economist.

larger, or are there other characteristics that are more important? Is it the structure that really matters?

If all firms were relatively small, then we could argue that efficiency depends on the nature of the market. However, when many firms are large and some dominate their industries, then clearly market considerations are not the only determinants of the efficiency of specific organizations. A great many economic activities, which under a regime of very small outfits are under market discipline, under a regime of large firms are partly determined by internal nonmarket decisions. For the moment let us refer to all such nonmarket decisions as bureaucratic. Under what circumstances would such bureaucratic decisions be efficient, or more rather than less efficient? It seems clear that we must study the mixture and interaction of both internal decisions and market forces in order to make assessments about inefficiency.

The fact is that standard economics contains very little to help us understand organizational phenomena. Microeconomics is not concerned with the internal workings of the organization. The problem of internal efficiency is assumed away by postulating the existence of a production function, combined with the maximization postulate. Once we imagine that the firm knows the relation between inputs and outputs, and can magically get the best results, then nothing more need be said. Although such a simplification of reality is useful for some types of theory construction, at present it seems desirable to try to develop theories on a more realistic basis. To do so it is necessary to relax both of these basic microtheory postulates. A possible procedure is first to try to understand how organizations function, including sources of inefficiency, and then use the model of the organization arrived at in this manner to build up more macroanalysis, such as the study of industries and sectors.

A basic question: What is the relation between the environment external to the firm and what goes on inside? Three elements of this question can be distinguished: the nature of environmental pressures and the perception of them; the transmission of external pressure to the inside; and the response of the entities inside the firm to the transmitted pressure. In a sense, all these influences occur more or less simultaneously. Inefficiencies can arise either because of misperceptions of the environment, incorrect translations, or inadequate responses. We shall see that gaps and obstacles to the appropriate transmission of signals, and to carrying out effective responses, can arise at every juncture of the process. Part of the problem of trying to understand organizational behavior will be to identify what goes on in organizations that can create such gaps and obstacles. This will suggest sources of internal inefficiency.

Once we focus on the internal workings of the organization we will see that formal employment contracts, or what may be interpreted as such contracts, are almost trivial in helping to explain how people behave in work contexts. The presumed formal contract cannot by itself tell us what it is that we want to know about intraorganizational behavior. The main elements affecting behavior are not usually the relation between the individual and the enterprise, but rather the almost invisible bonds and other relationships between individuals. In other words, the firm is not simply a collection of isolated, visible contractual relationships between each employee and the enterprise. The informal connections between individuals in the organization are critical to our understanding of how efficiently a firm operates.

A related theme is the divergence between the private interests of employees and company interests. What is the interplay between such diverging interests? If they exist, how do they affect the outcome of the firm's operation and the degree of internal inefficiency? This is part of the larger question, which is the extent to which firm members in their roles as firm representatives may have private agendas that differ from company objectives. Can such differences be eliminated, and if not, what are their consequences?

The nature of a hierarchy and the established structure underlying it can also be sources of inefficiency. Here, too, both visible and invisible connections are of paramount significance, and both types of relations need to be analyzed.

Underlying some of these ideas is the view that organizations do not necessarily have to be efficient. Even the survival of an economic enterprise does not depend on efficiency in an absolute sense. At most, all that matters is the *relative* efficiency of firms vis-à-vis each other. Furthermore, there are a variety of sheltering mechanisms, and various ways in which an organization can operate under sheltered circumstances. Some organizations can themselves contribute to increasing the degree of shelter from competitive forces. Hence, stability, survival, and *inefficiency* can all persist for long periods of time. We will consider in some detail this critical question of whether inefficiency and equilibrium can coexist.

Certain policy questions are suggested by these considerations. Should firms be limited in size? Should hierarchical structures be limited in depth, or in degree of remoteness from those they control? The answer to such questions probably depends, at least in part, on the relations between size, hierarchical structure, and inefficiency. Here, too, it is likely that both visible and invisible elements are significant and require careful analysis. These problems are clearly important, but at present have no solutions.

The answers to some of the questions we have raised are clearly very important in determining the relative efficiencies of different systems. For instance, what is the difference in efficiency between socialism and capitalism? This is a question that cannot be answered simply by examining the extent to which markets operate in different economies. Both privately and publicly owned enterprises can operate within market systems. However, beyond a certain size the organizations will operate, to some degree, in terms of nonmarket components. As a result, the answers to this broad question must depend on how organizations are likely to operate within different environments, and what aspects of the environment are likely to affect internal efficiency. Clearly, motivational aspects and incentive structures are two of the elements that will influence internal efficiency, but the question that arises is how such things differ in different systems. These questions by themselves suggest the extreme importance of undertaking an analysis of the relations between organizations and internal efficiency.

Finally, certain questions that may not appear to be directly connected with efficiency may be viewed from a similar intellectual framework. For example, these chapters were written at the time that the Challenger space shuttle and Chernobyl nuclear power reactor disasters took place. Serious writings about these matters suggest that they were partly instances of organizational failure. Such failures can readily be interpreted as a type of inefficiency since inefficiency involves a deviation between intended attainable results and the actual outcome. If a different organizational framework, or one with some different components or characteristics would have avoided the accidents, then we could interpret the existing organizations as inefficient. Undesirable accidents are part of the quality aspect of production. It is interesting that almost no organizational analysis seems to have been used in the investigation and interpretation of the causes of these accidents. Certain organizational deficiencies were discovered by the investigators (for example, blocked communication arteries in the Challenger case). However, a question that did not seem to have been raised was whether correcting these particular aspects would be sufficient to eliminate or reduce future organizational deficiencies of a similar (or different) type. The value of an organization theory with a focus on inefficiency can be seen in the consequences of inefficiencies, which in some instances may be a percentage reduction in profit, while in others may involve significant loss of human life.

The Procedural Perspective

An important and ubiquitous aspect of organizational behavior is an emphasis on procedures, both formal and informal. We may view procedures simply as ways of doing things—they may be efficient or inefficient. Part of our appreciation of organizational behavior involves understanding the nature and consequences of the procedures used. What are they, and how do they influence efficiency? Once the focus is on procedures it becomes clear that it is important to consider the ways in which procedures are constrained. That is to say, in what ways do we constrain ourselves, and in what ways do we constrain each other? I will argue that the procedural analysis is a desirable complement to other approaches; it will pervade, directly or indirectly, the analytical discussions that follow.

Herbert Simon, in a well-known paper, distinguished between procedural rationality and substantive rationality (1978).[2] Essentially, the substantive approach does not indicate the details of how individuals or groups go about doing whatever it is that they do. A substantive maximizing decision theory, for example, simply indicates the end result, maximization; it does not indicate the procedures used to achieve this end. In contrast, the procedural approach asks, What are the procedures that have to be carried out in order to achieve this end? and What are the procedures actually used in particular situations? We can extend this distinction in various directions. For instance, we can speak of a procedural decision theory versus a substantive decision theory. On a broader scale, we can speak of a procedural analysis versus a substantive analysis. Also, we can look at various problems from a procedural viewpoint or a substantive viewpoint.

Using the term "nonprocedural theory" rather than "substantive theory" probably makes it easier to visualize what we mean. We are

2. Simon speaks of "process" rationality. As far as I can judge, the terms "procedures" and "processes," are used approximately interchangeably. I shall employ the terms "procedures" and "procedural perspective," since they suggest more clearly what it is that I have in mind.

primarily concerned with the fact that many economic theories, including standard microeconomic theory, are *nonprocedural* in nature. The point is that the procedural perspective may suggest important ideas that have not been obtained from the nonprocedural approach.

It is important to distinguish between open and constrained procedures. By open procedures we have in mind a situation in which there is no limitation on the procedures that can be used. Since we see a procedure as simply a way of doing things, an open procedure set would include all of the possible ways of doing something, whereas in a constrained procedure set some ways of doing things would not be allowed. In the extreme case of a constrained procedure only a single procedure is permitted from a variety of possible ways of doing things.

Standard economics is concerned primarily with exchange and with decisions as they relate to exchange. For the most part it is not concerned with a thorough analysis of the underlying, potentially diverse ways of doing things. Also, it is not concerned with constraints imposed on ways of doing things. Standard economics visualizes constraints only as parameters somehow coming from the state of nature. Thus, standard theory discusses budget constraints, income constraints, and so on, but rarely visualizes constraint creation as an individual and group activity. But, it will be argued below and in various places throughout this book that constrained ways of doing things are a very significant aspect of intrafirm behavior, organizational behavior, and economic life generally. Analyses of procedures and constraints are likely to be fundamental for getting a realistic handle on the nature of economic activities and problems. For the most part this also holds for organizational analysis. Thus, an important part of economic activity usually left uninvestigated is the variety of ways in which we constrain ourselves and others. A procedural perspective fills this gap by raising questions about procedures and constraints, where applicable, and examining whether the answers fit relevant nonprocedural theories.

A procedure may be constrained by ourselves or by others. It may be constrained by ourselves in terms of our past history, ambitions, affiliations of various sorts, ethical views, religious views, and so on. It may be constrained by others when limitations are imposed by the groups or organizations to which we belong. The point is that part of the procedural approach is to determine if procedures are constrained, the nature of the constraints, and their consequences. I shall argue that the procedural perspective is especially important in studying the internal operation of firms and other types of organizations, since such organizations are, by their very nature, forced to constrain the procedures available to individual actors.

The fact that in normal economic life the ways of doing things are constrained almost immediately suggests a possible source of inefficiency. It is possible that the procedures *allowed* are the optimal way of doing things. On the other hand, it is possible that the best way of doing something is one of the procedures *disallowed*. In that case the allowed procedures would be a source of inefficiency. While this seems obvious once stated, it is rarely a question that is examined in the economic theory of the firm, or in other forms of organizational analysis. In fact, it is frequently assumed away by some of the basic postulates of microtheory, including the notion that constraints and constraining behavior are given without any further questions being asked.

Essentially, we view the procedural perspective as a partial research program. Whenever one is dealing with a nonprocedural theory it may be useful to examine the underlying procedures as well. It may lead to insights about what goes on in the object of study. It may help elucidate the complexity of the world, which otherwise may be excessively simplified in substantive theory. It may help us to find gaps in substantive theory, as well as special cases, and possibly contradictions. More specifically, since the world of organizations is largely a constrained procedural world, it is of great interest to see what can be learned from examining the procedures that take place within organizations.

However, I do not necessarily advocate a *detailed* procedural approach. Attempts to enumerate all procedures involved or possible in a given type of behavior could become too cumbersome—one could get needlessly and endlessly bogged down in detail. Nevertheless, we can derive useful information when we categorize procedures into a limited number of subsets and then look for any interesting implications. This will be the approach used in this book. For instance, in a later chapter we shall classify decision procedures into various components, and then see how suggestive they are of insights into economic decisions.

The procedural perspective will be applied to a number of areas, such as the problems surrounding decisions and decision making. Later we will use it to examine intrafirm Prisoner's Dilemma problems. Then we will show that conventions may be usefully viewed as constrained procedures, and that this is important for understanding the role of conventions in firms and their relation to internal inefficiency. Finally, we shall try to show that the question of hierarchy can also be usefully examined from a constrained-procedural viewpoint, and that different types of procedural asymmetries exist within hierarchies.

A variety of practical problems can also be attacked from the procedural perspective. In essence, we shall look at inflexibilities that may be introduced into economic behavior (such as price inflexibilities or quantity inflexibilities) as being, in part, a consequence of the way individuals and enterprises constrain the procedures of their members.

The Connections of the Various Components of the Book

For some readers it may be useful to provide a map of sorts to suggest where we are going. The remarks that follow are intended only as a rough guide to show how the various elements we will discuss are related to each other. In the last chapter we will review this overall scheme and use it to summarize the details explored in the intervening chapters.

In the chapters that follow we will try to present a coherent view of the internal behavior of the firm, and the relation of that behavior to inefficiencies of various types. The overall structure can be viewed in terms of the following scheme.

$$\text{EPr} \longrightarrow [\text{HPr}] \longrightarrow [\text{E}] \longrightarrow [\text{Per}] \longrightarrow [\text{PR}]$$

The external pressure (EPr) determines or influences the hierarchical pressure (HPr), which in its turn determines effort (E) of various kinds. The sum of the effort determines performance (Per), which in its turn determines the pressure reaction (PR). The pressure reaction is then related in a feedback loop to the hierarchical pressure at the outset.

In this scheme external pressure (EPr) is transmitted internally where it becomes translated into hierarchical pressure (HPr). This, in turn, directly or indirectly results in two types of effort (E): Effort that transmits pressure further down the hierarchy, and effort that adds value to the output (by providing a service or helping to create the commodity sold by the enterprise).

Pressure is related to the various decision procedures that are used by firm members. We will see that the pressure determines the extent to which decisions are optimal or depart from optimality. A considerable part of this book is concerned with the various ways in which transmitted pressure determines effort decisions and effort itself. Especially important are the ways in which responses to pressure are connected to various motivations felt by individuals. We will see that there are situations commonly found inside firms that give rise to motivations that could result in a Prisoner's Dilemma outcome, where individual maximizing behavior results in a highly suboptimal outcome. However, we will also show how the Prisoner's Dilemma problem is frequently avoided through the use of effort conventions. Furthermore, we will examine how these conventions may be supported by sanctions imposed by firm members.

We will then examine why hierarchy exists, and analyze the hierarchical system. This analysis will look closely at pressure in the sense that a hierarchy has to transmit information to those at lower levels, including the degree of urgency for those receiving the information to react. We will see that the response to pressure depends on a variety of usually invisible relations between firm members. These can be usefully divided into vertical and horizontal relationships. The significant relations are what we will refer to as the enlarged commitments of individuals to others, either vertically in the hierarchy, or horizontally, or both. Horizontal commitments may be for vertically adversarial objectives or for cooperative, productive objectives. By examining the various types of commitment structures we will be able to draw conclusions about the relationships between hierarchy, effort, and various types of inefficiencies.

The final effort produced by the effort transmitted through the hierarchy will determine the performance characteristics (Per) of the firm. Performance determines the pressure reaction (PR), which is counterpoised to the internal pressure at the outset. We shall be especially concerned with the stable situation where external pressure and the translated internal pressure turn out to be the same as the pressure reaction that results from performance. The chapters on the Japanese Management System may be viewed as an example of the relationship between hierarchy, pressure, effort, and degree of efficiency. Later we look at the details of the various possible interrelationships of these components, and present some suggestions as to why the overall picture presented helps us to analyze various types of inefficiencies inherent in the hierarchical characteristics of firms.

CHAPTER 2

Decision Occurrences

This chapter sets out the main aspects of the decision theory to be employed in the rest of the book. The theory allows for *both* suboptimal and optimal decisions. The basic idea is that almost no one makes optimal decisions all the time. The mix of optimal and nonoptimal decisions will depend on circumstances, in particular the pressures people face. By examining the procedures that constitute a decision we will be able to define suboptimal decisions in a convenient and straightforward manner.[1]

The focus, to a considerable degree will be on effort decisions, but the theory to be developed is general, and is applicable to all types of decisions. We will largely avoid terms such as choice, or decision making, and emphasize instead "decision occurrences." The reason for this is to get away from the image of decision making being necessarily active, and to include decision by default or "passive" decision making, that is, decisions that occur because nothing is done. The various sections of this chapter and the next are connected roughly as follows. We start by postulating that an inner preference ordering exists for each individual. However, we avoid the concept of revealed preference. What people *do* is not necessarily what they *prefer*. But inner preferences exist so that there is some way of ascribing optimality or suboptimality to a decision. We then consider the procedures that enter into decision processes and distinguish between optimal versus nonoptimal procedure sets. Next we turn to the Yerkes-Dodson Law which relates pressure and performance. Looking at decisions as a type of

1. See Weiss and Ilgen (1985) for an excellent review of the psychological literature in this area. Also see the excellent discussion of low-level procedures as a significant aspect of economic behavior in the chapter on "routines" in Nelson and Winter (1982, pp. 99–136).

performance we are able to connect the degree of suboptimal performance to pressure. The postulate of inert areas allows us to understand the continued use of formerly optimal procedures, some of which become suboptimal as a consequence of environmental changes.

This chapter and the one on the anatomy of decisions suggest the possibility and likelihood that some decisions will be suboptimal, and this supports the relaxation of the maximization postulate. Finally, not all decisions are exchange contract decisions. Some are *intra*contract decisions; and we shall argue later that some of the most important decisions that take place in organizations are of this type.

The Inner Preference Set

We begin with a set of preferences such that these preferences are available, or known in some sense, or knowable before a decision is made and after it is made. It is immaterial whether we start with the idea of a preference ordering, or whether we associate ordinal utilities with every set of options of commodities or effort bundles. For the time being, it is easiest to assume that the "inner preference set" has all the usual properties of being completely ordered and of being transitive. The point is that we assume there is some way of an individual knowing what his preferences are, and that he can in some sense state them. Once we have such an inner preference set, then we are able to tell whether actual decisions are in conformity with this inner preference set or not.

It is extremely important to note that we separate inner preferences from observed behavior. We need to settle inner preferences in order to assess the optimality or lack of optimality of behavior. Thus, there is a clear-cut distinction between preferences which are assumed to be given *within* the personality of the individual, and what the individual does or how he or she behaves. This allows for *both* the possibility that (1) behavior will be consistent with inner preferences, or (2) observed behavior can be, in part, and at times, inconsistent with inner preferences, that is, it allows for the possibility of suboptimal decisions. Where it is consistent we have optimal behavior, and where it is inconsistent we have less than optimal behavior. Such a scheme really permits us to consider both maximizing and nonmaximizing behavior. As we will see, decision behavior will depend on the selection procedures. These procedures are, at least in part, observables external to the individual. An individual "chooses" through the use of a procedure, or set of procedures, and hence decision behavior is separable from the internal preference set.

Later, we will distinguish between those preferences immediately known to an individual and those that are somewhat deeper in his consciousness, so that he may have to search inside to know what he really prefers. Some preferences are somewhat complex and some cogitation is necessary to determine whether Bundle A is preferred to Bundle B or not. Nevertheless, for present purposes what is important is that a clear-cut set of inner preferences is assumed to exist.

Decision Procedures

Herbert Simon argues that standard microeconomics basically makes a substantive assumption about choice; it does not indicate how people make choices that maximize utility or profits, but simply that they choose so that the end result is what would occur if utility or profits were maximized. Real choices involve intermediate steps in which procedures are employed. These decision procedures may or may not be consistent with the substantive theory (Simon, 1978).

The two basic elements for each decision are a context signal, and a response in accordance with that signal. Thus, the individual is viewed as someone who perceives a context, is able to interpret the signal, and responds accordingly. By this last, we have in mind the use of an appropriate procedure.

Consider the following two categories of possible procedures: calculated and noncalculated. By calculated procedures we have in mind those in which an individual searches for all the information necessary and then actually attempts to make whatever necessary calculations have to be made in order to arrive at a choice. In other words, this involves a search for the options, a search for information that enables one to evaluate the options, and to make whatever calculations are necessary in order to choose the best options. These procedures may be correct, or faulty, or incomplete. Clearly a correct procedure will lead to an optimum result, but there is the possibility of calculating and yet having the procedures be faulty or incomplete. That is, in the latter case, certain necessary steps have been omitted. Faulty or incomplete procedures do not necessarily involve mistakes in the sense of arithmetical errors, but rather the sort of situations in which, because of haste, or pressure, or emotional factors, an individual leaves out certain steps in the calculation, hazily or fully aware that such steps have been left out.

Among noncalculated procedures are those that involve some sort of noncalculated reaction to circumstances. For instance, decisions made on the basis of:

1. habit,
2. conventions,
3. the emulation of others,
4. a response to commands or regulations,
5. a response to an ethical or moral imperative,
6. uncalculated acts of cooperation or noncooperation,
7. following a standard procedure or standard rule of thumb,
8. nonresponsive reactions such as an uncalculated failure to react to some request or to some other decision possibility that results in a decision as a consequence of the passage of time and the lack of a response.

We want especially to emphasize nonoptimal procedures. Now, many procedures can, under some circumstances, be optimal. Furthermore, various procedures may initially have been optimal, but at some later date, if circumstances change, may turn out to be nonoptimal. Thus, simply by knowing the nature of the procedure, one cannot necessarily determine whether it is or is not optimal. The point is that there is a large variety of routinized procedures which are frequently nonoptimal for the circumstances and which, under "normal conditions," are not reconsidered. It is in this sense that we are concerned with, and will use the concept of, a nonoptimal procedure set.

Some procedures are clearly individualistic. That is, they do not depend on others. Most habits are of this kind. Thus responses to situations on the basis of habit, where the procedures do not involve others in any sense, are individualistic procedures. We will not be much concerned with such procedures although they enter as part of our list of nonoptimal procedures.

Within the firm the interesting types of procedures we want to consider are those which are constrained in some way, directly or indirectly, either by superiors in the hierarchy, or by peers in the area in which people work. Here we have in mind: (1) conventions, (2) the emulation of others, (3) rules of thumb generally used, (4) standard operating procedures developed by higher levels in the hierarchy, and so on. Here we will assume that in most instances these are nonoptimal procedures. There is certainly no reason why many of these should be superior to procedures that are tailor-made for a particular context. All we are concerned about here is the fact that such procedures can be nonoptimal, and that when individuals make choices in a particular context on the basis of these procedures, such choices are nonoptimal.

A type of procedure that is very important, although frequently not considered, is the "nonresponse." An example of the nonresponse decision developed for commercial purposes are book clubs (or record clubs) that require you to return a postcard if you do not want the book or record in question. If you do not respond you have automatically purchased the book or record; thus some sales are made as a consequence of individual neglect. There may be a variety of situations where optimal behavior, or even sensible behavior, would require a response of some sort, but where the individual or organizational reaction is not to react to the circumstances or the signal. Hence when we consider nonoptimal procedures, we also want to take into account those situations in which responses ought to be required but in which, in fact, they do not take place.

Approximate Maximizing Procedures

We have already alluded to the notion that standard economic theory does not indicate the procedures necessary to achieve maximizing or optimal results. This may be partly due to the fact that it is practically impossible to state all of the procedures necessary to achieve a maximizing solution without knowing the specific circumstances. One thing seems clear: Any procedural program is likely to involve a fairly long list of items.

Consider how many procedures are involved in trying to carry out a maximizing decision. Here is a list, probably a partial list, for a great many problems: (1) obtain all the correct information up to the point where the additional cost of information is greater than the additional gain; (2) analyze the distinctiveness of the particular choice situation; (3) determine, on the basis of external information, the options available; (4) determine (dredge up), on the basis of "internal information," all of the additional options; (5) work out a preference ordering for all relevant options, or work out the utilities associated with different options; (6) make assessments on the basis of correct logical or mathematical principles; (7) do not avoid details, but do not get unduly caught up in worrying only about details; (8) avoid irrelevant emotions associated with options or with other elements of the choice process; (9) avoid irrelevant considerations, facts, and so on; (10) do not follow others in making choices—consider the uniqueness of your own situation; (11) do not rationalize any particular choice after the fact; (12) delegate tasks to others where delegates can do an acceptable job at equal or lower cost; (13) have an optimum periodic reassessment plan especially for decisions involving different periods of time. Although this is not necessarily a complete, detailed set of procedures, nevertheless one can see that a procedural view of a specific decision suggests that maximizing behavior is far from simple.

Clearly what is involved is a careful search for preferences, options, prices associated with options, constraints, and related types of information. Also, one has to decide where the appropriate calculations are to be made, and how they are being carried out, checked, and evaluated. One has to go through various searches and careful calculation and evaluation of the products of such information searches. For an attempt to specify specific maximizing procedures under various circumstances likely to be faced by the firm, see Alexander Cornell's *The Decision-Maker's Handbook* (1980). It is interesting that, for many categories, the list of procedures involves twenty-five or more specific items.

Once we understand the complexity of the procedures list that approximates optimizing decisions, we can readily see that deviations from such lists imply the existence of nonoptimal procedures. Such nonoptimal procedures, although involving some search and calculations, are likely to be incomplete, or improperly carried out. Thus while imperfect procedures may, in some cases, be superior to context-reactive procedures, they still may not contain enough careful search and calculation to approximate optimization.

Are Noncalculating Procedures Optimal?

All procedures, even those that represent simple routines, could be optimal. Consider a firm-determined standard operating procedure. Assume that the particular procedure in question has been developed quite carefully at some fairly high managerial level. The managers have noted that a certain type of context and demand seems to repeat periodically. Under some circumstances, there appears to be no point in reconsidering, in each instance, what it is that has to be done. But clearly it would make sense for management to consider the option of developing a standardized decision procedure for a situation which is roughly a standardized context requiring this type of decision. In other words, managers might as well make a decision once and for all as long as the context keeps repeating itself with a certain degree of regularity, and has roughly the same characteristics. Here we are considering a repeatable situation in which nothing is gained by going through all the steps of working out a carefully calculated decision each time.

Consider the operation of a fast-food franchise. The franchise company may decide on some standardized way of producing, say, a hamburger, and in each case people are trained to carry out the procedure in a standardized manner. Cooks may also be trained to offer customers a very limited set of options instead of all the possible options. Such a decision may indeed be optimal for that type of enterprise. Similarly, a very high proportion of all other activities in the enterprise may be of this kind. Thus, in an approximately repeatable context, it makes sense to develop a near-optimal set of standardized reactions. This suggests that quite simple (or complex) routines, as well as a variety of noncalculated decisions in particular instances, may be optimal when part of a carefully calculated decision procedure taken at an earlier time.

However, while it is possible for such simple routines to be optimal in the sense just developed, it does not mean that actual routines, or actual context reaction decisions, are in fact optimal. There are various reasons for this. To start with, suppose that the initial decision is made in the manner indicated above. Then, in the course of time, circumstances change. Contexts that once had certain characteristics may gradually lose these characteristics and, as a result, what was optimal in the first period is no longer optimal in the subsequent period. If the decision were to be made anew, a procedure would be developed for the second period that was different from the first one. As a result, if the procedure developed in the earlier period persists into the next, what was once an optimal procedure may no longer be optimal. In other words, those who developed the procedure initially may, indeed, have developed an optimal procedure; but the procedure set may not contain any means of reassessing the procedure from time to time, so that what was originally optimal ceases to be so, and yet persists.

A significant element in the persistence of procedures is that the past frequently sanctifies the initial procedure, even if later some superior procedures are available. Thus the fact that a procedure has been used for some time implies to many in an organization that it should be continued. Even if a superior alternative is readily available, the burden of proof would seem to lie on the alternative, rather than on the past procedure. In other words, "This is the way things are done around here."

Equally important is the fact that most procedures are not developed on an optimal basis to start with. They are not the product of a careful search for alternatives, a careful search for information, or a careful calculation of benefits and costs over time. Hence the initial procedure may not be optimal at all; but if nothing like a crisis is involved, then the initial procedure does not seem to be clearly undesirable, and is quite likely to persist. Indeed, it may persist into a number of periods, even though it may get worse over time, until it goes beyond some inertial threshold, at which point the procedure is reconsidered. (This is discussed at greater length in Chapter 4.)

Now, a procedure may arise in various ways: the processes of careful search, evaluation, and calculation are not the only ones. A procedure may arise at some point as a consequence of very quick decisions made by somebody quite high up in the hierarchy and, as a result, the procedure continues over time. Alternatively, a procedure may arise because some individual employee is given the responsibility for doing something, and the procedure that he or she chooses is the one that becomes gradually sanctified by practice. Also, the procedure may arise as part of a compromise decision of a number of employees involved in carrying out a certain activity or class of activities, and this compromise, which includes elements of individual taste, becomes the informally recognized appropriate procedure. In all such cases, it is likely and possible that there is no careful search, evaluation, calculation of benefits and cost, or provision for revising the procedure. As a result, there is both the possibility and the likelihood that, on the average, many of the procedures used during low-pressure periods are nonoptimal.

The Yerkes-Dodson Law and Decision Procedures

There exists a well-established psychological law, the Yerkes-Dodson Law (1908), that helps us relate optimal to nonoptimal decisions. The essence of this law is the relationship between performance and stress or pressure. Effectiveness is assumed to increase with stress up to some point, possibly flatten out at that point, and then decrease as stress or pressure continues to increase. If we visualize performance on the or-

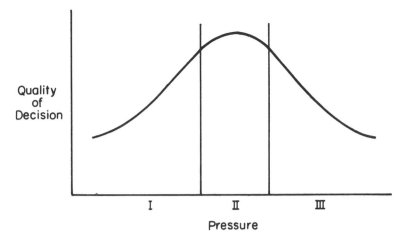

FIGURE 2.1

dinate and pressure on the abscissa, we may perceive the Yerkes-Dodson Law as being represented by a roughly bell-shaped curve. (See figure 2.1.) Since 1908 a large experimental literature has developed, involving both animal and human experiments, that validates the Yerkes-Dodson Law. The law itself seems intuitively extremely plausible. It is clearly the sort of law that is likely to be invented or reinvented periodically. The reason it seems plausible is that it fits, for most people, their sense of everyday experience.[2]

If we view decision making as a form of performance, then we may visualize the effectiveness of decision making (degree of closeness to optimality) to increase in some specified sense with the pressure that exists within the context. There is experimental evidence from psychology that as motivation increases, decision performance comes closer to maximization. This seems to be closely related to the notion that pressure, from whatever source, will result in a movement toward procedures closer to maximization. Of course, beyond some point pressure may be too great for objectively sensible behavior. The emo-

2. The Yerkes-Dodson Law seems to be so well established among psychologists that the citations to the original experiments (Yerkes and Dodson, 1908) are rarely made. See Broadbent (1971), especially pp. 109–112 and 454. For a more general treatment see Atkinson and Birch (1978). There are really two Yerkes-Dodson Laws. The first relates stress to performance. The second states roughly that the more difficult the task the lower the stress at which the optimum performance occurs. In Chapter 2 only the first law is used.

tions related to very high degrees of stress influence the result so that effectiveness declines (Edwards, 1956, p. 177–188; Siegal and Goldstein, 1959, p. 150–155; Broadbent, 1971, p. 453–456).

In general, the argument is that when pressure is low most individuals are likely to behave in a nonoptimal manner, and only when pressure is sufficiently high are they likely to behave optimally. Beyond some point, pressure may be so high that they find it rather difficult to cope. To amplify this idea, let us think of careful calculation as the procedure used in order to make optimal decisions. The argument then suggests that before sufficient pressure exists, individuals will make decisions by means other than careful calculation. As pressure increases they move toward more careful and more calculating methods until at a sufficient pressure range the degree of calculation and related decision behavior approximates maximizing behavior. For the time being we will neglect the part of the curve under which pressure is too great to cope effectively with decision making and under which the individual falls back on less-effective decision procedures. We will focus on pressure area I, in which there is less than adequate pressure to induce the search for and the use of optimal procedures.

An alternative and useful interpretation of connecting the Yerkes-Dodson curve to the quality of decision is that for all individuals there exists a mix of optimal and nonoptimal decisions. The ratio of optimal to nonoptimal is lower when pressure is low and rises as pressure increases until a maximum is reached. Of course, beyond some point the ratio declines as pressure becomes too intense.

The Emotion Spillover Theory of Decision Making

Why do individuals not maximize under low pressure? We could simply start with the Yerkes-Dodson Law interpretation *as a postulate* and proceed from there, that is, draw out the implications of the theory in which this is a postulate and see if it works in practice. However, we can also go beyond the Yerkes-Dodson application and look at more fundamental aspects of behavior.

One reason individuals do not maximize under low pressure is that emotions can affect decision-making behavior. Optimal decision making will usually require some degree of control of one's emotions, or control of the influence of emotions on the quality of one's decisions. Furthermore, varying amounts of external pressure in the decision context are likely to provide varying incentives for control and assessment of one's emotions, apart from inertia.[3]

In ordinary situations one is likely to experience a variety of emotions, and there is likely to be a high degree of variability in one's emotional state for the same or similar decision contexts. Furthermore, the feelings may be unrelated, or only partly related, to the decision contexts faced. This variety arises partly in response to external stimuli, and partly in response to one's personal history, usually relatively recent history. But such emotions interfere with optimal decision making by distracting one's attention or distorting one's assessment of the options.

An optimal decision may require two types of control. The first is emotional organization. Clearly, one has to somehow see the outside world the way it is and not the way one would like it to be, nor the way very temporary emotional states may suggest it is.[4] Thus, one may have to exert some effort to call forth feelings that contribute to inner balance and focus—to achieve a mental state that helps one to feel cool, collected, and organized in judging information so that one's judgment will be as disinterested, and therefore as accurate, as possible.

The second type of control, repression of contaminating emotions, consists of the ability to constrain those more enduring emotions that give a false view of the world, or at least take such influences into account when making a decision. Thus, one may have to control one's emotional response to highly temporary stimuli, and control any more sustained inner state that might contaminate rational decision making.

The basic postulates we make are (1) that the more emotional states are allowed to contaminate decision-making processes the less likely it is that decisions will be optimum; and (2) that, up to a point, as pressure increases emotional states will be increasingly prevented from contaminating decision making, then, beyond some point, emotions will increasingly affect decisions.

The desire to control emotions does not in most instances, occur naturally or spontaneously. One could readily think of observed instances of anger and rage in which emotions seem difficult to control.

3. See the next section, as well as Chapter 4, on the role of inertia. Our discussion here considers emotions apart from inertia, although inertia is also an element that contributes to suboptimal decisions under low pressure. For present purposes we do not have to determine whether human inertia is entirely "emotional" or partly physiological.

4. On this point see the extended discussion in Pears (1986). See also Strongman (1978) for a more extended discussion of theories of emotion.

However, a certain amount of pressure in a context that calls for objective decision making is likely to increase one's motivation to control contaminating emotions. Thus, up to some point, as pressure increases emotional control is likely to increase accordingly. Of course, beyond some point the pressure itself becomes a contaminating emotion, so to speak. Increasing pressure beyond this point then leads to greater and greater degrees of disorganization. The conclusion is that the individual is likely to allow emotional spillovers to influence decision making at low pressure levels and at the highest pressure levels. At intermediate levels such emotional spillovers are likely to be minimized, and as a consequence something approximating optimal decision making can take place.

Inert Areas and Procedural Decisions

An essential concept needed at this point is that of the inert area. This refers to the "area" within which the stimulus-response system is employed. The inert area idea is related to the ordinary notion of inertia, and suggests that within certain bounds, inertial considerations determine the repetition of simple signal-response behavior, or complex signal-response behavior. Beyond the boundaries of the inert area, there is a shift toward considering alternate responses. That is, there are likely to be certain pressure thresholds (or bounds) which, once reached, operate as a stimulus mechanism so that the individual reconsiders whether to perform in a routinized manner. At present we are simply concerned with inertial areas, and the bounds within which routinized decision making takes place. Later we will be concerned with pressure changes sufficient to force individuals to examine the possibilities of changing behavior patterns.

The Employment Contract and Commitment Decisions

An important category of decisions made by firm members is intracontract decisions. Normally the employment contract is incomplete. Usually the wages are specified but many aspects of the work, and work conditions, are left unspecified. Thus, effort is a variable open to some degree of discretionary choice by individual employees. As a result, employees are faced with numerous intracontract decisions about their own effort levels. The employment contract gets partly filled out on the job by adversarial, cooperative, or neutral relations between firm members. These relations are established in the process of work and become part of the contract. (On relational contracts see Macneil, 1974). In an important sense the contract gets filled out by conventions and "commitment decisions." Nevertheless, despite continuing work relations, some gaps or misunderstandings in the contract are likely to persist. We now examine what we mean by commitment decisions, and how they are connected to the effort part of the employment relation.

Commitments are basic decisions that, at least at first, an individual makes to himself. They need not be communicated to anyone else. Thus, each employee may commit himself to carry out the contract in a given way, that is, he may commit himself to achieve a certain effort level. If nothing is said by a superior, or peer, or a relevant outsider (such as a customer), then the commitment may stand. Otherwise, there may be a period of trial and error within which the commitment may shift in response to external influences. However, the individual does not necessarily yield to all external influences.

Each firm member may make a variety of commitments in the course of performing his or her work. While initially they are made to oneself, eventually they may be made to superiors, to peers, to subordinates, to suppliers, and to customers. Some may be explicit, others unvoiced or implicit. The basis for some of them may be emotional, or in response to ethical or normative criteria, while others may be calculated and rational.

Commitments to oneself may turn into commitments to others. Clearly, commitments involving behavior toward others may be made strictly to oneself without informing the other party. However, if one notices signs of reciprocity of some sort, then this may lead to an implicit mutual commitment. An example would be unspoken tit-for-tat behavior that gradually takes the shape of a behavior pattern. A mutual commitment is likely to imply that the two parties hold an unspoken contract. Various interactions between individuals are possible that result in transitions from commitments entirely to oneself, to implicit or explicit mutual commitments between individuals.

The main point is to recognize that commitments involve a special type of decision making. In a sense they are similar to other decision procedures in that some of them are potentially nonmaximizing. More important, some commitments may be mutual, representing "psychological contracts" with others. These types of decisions will be considered more fully later. They play an extremely important role in the analysis of various aspects of hierarchy.

Summary and Conclusions

There are many reasons why nonoptimal procedures may be employed. We have mentioned the possibility of inertia. Procedures that initially were optimal may not change as circumstances change and hence become suboptimal. Habit is a close variant of the same idea. Of special significance is the adoption of conventions; that is, people adopt conventional procedures used by colleagues without raising or considering the question of optimality. (More will be said about conventions later.) Perhaps most important is the influence of emotions. An objective assessment of one's surroundings is not a natural endowment of most human beings. Emotions interfere. Under some circumstances we may struggle against our emotions to make better decisions. Under other circumstances emotions overwhelm us.

Real decisions are usually made on the basis of procedures—mental and physical activities of some sort. Even a simple, everyday optimum decision is likely to imply a number of procedures. One advantage of the procedural approach is that it enables one to distinguish between optimal and nonoptimal procedure sets for particular situations. Through this means it follows readily that nonoptimal procedures are possible, and hence nonoptimal decisions are possible.

Procedures may be person-specific, group-specific, or firm-specific, even industry-specific. How specific or general a procedure may be is not important for present purposes. The generality of procedures will appear more significant when we examine the question of conventions, and decisions made on the basis of conventions. Our main interest here has been to establish the procedural basis of decisions and to distinguish optimal from nonoptimal procedures.

In order to indicate the frequency with which we might expect the use of nonoptimal procedures, we specified a variant of the Yerkes-Dodson Law. As applied to decisions the law implies that a relation exists between pressure and the quality of a decision. Up to a point, the greater the pressure the closer to optimality the decision mix will be. Beyond some point the inability to cope with pressure enters and decision quality declines.

We also introduced the concept of inert areas within which behavior does not change even though some significant independent variables do change. Thus, changes in the environment do not induce, within some range, changes in any decision variable with which we are concerned.

It is worth emphasizing that in standard theory, history does not play a role in decision making. Only the existing circumstances and expectations of the future determine optimal decisions. However, once procedures become the basis for decisions, and since available procedures depend on history, then history clearly plays a role in decision making.

CHAPTER 3

On the Anatomy
of Decisions

In what follows, some of the issues examined in the last chapter are considered from a somewhat more formal and abstract viewpoint. One reason for studying the "anatomy" of decisions is to assess the expectable range of behaviors in a context that calls for a decision. We will develop a description of decision procedures that can be used to classify such procedures. This classification was developed to provide insight into the possibility and the likelihood of optimal decisions and of nonoptimal decisions. By reducing a decision-making procedure to its components, and looking at the range of possible behaviors each component suggests, we will be able to assess the likely range of decision-making behaviors. In particular, we will see that an examination of the components of decision making suggests (1) the possibility of nonoptimal behavior, (2) the likelihood of nonoptimal behavior, and (3) the likelihood of behavior that involves a mixture of maximizing and nonmaximizing decision making.

Decision Triggers and Finalizations

The beginning of the decision procedure will be referred to as the decision trigger. The idea here is simply that something has to determine that a decision has to be made. We will refer to the end of the decision procedure as the finalization—that is, the point at which a decision has to be completed. Finalization will also include cases of default where a decision is made by not completing it. Since not completing a decision will usually have consequences, it is also a type of decision. The book club example, where not completing a decision results in the purchase of a book is one such. In what follows we will focus on the components that are in between the trigger and the finalization, namely, obtaining the options, finding a rule of selection, and processing either the options or the rule of selection or both. Thus, the five components of a decision procedure are: (1) triggers, (2) search procedures, (3) options, (4) rules of selection, and (5) finalization. Each component may have one or more procedures.

Three types of decision-triggering mechanisms come to mind—routine-imposed triggers, externally imposed triggers, and unsatisfactory psychic states.

Our various routines usually require us to carry out certain decisions at routinized junctures, frequently according to some time schedule. For example, mealtimes during workdays will be routinely determined for most people, making it necessary for them to decide the exact things to eat at routinized times. Work routines themselves will usually require decisions to be made at various junctures. Work situations frequently involve deadlines that trigger allocation of effort decisions. School routines require students to make course-choice decisions at certain specific times depending on the deadlines of the academic calendar. Innumerable routine-determined triggers easily come to mind.

A great many decisions are triggered by the requests of others. These involve offers to make exchanges, offers of other kinds, and requests to do certain things. Some of these decisions can be avoided or deferred. In many cases such offers are in the interest of the party making the offer rather than in the interest of the recipient. But in any event, ordinary working experience involves requests (or demands) of certain kinds that trigger decisions.

A third type of trigger may not depend on either routine or the requests of others. Rather, it depends on the psychological state of the decision maker. Under those psychological states that are accepted as the norm, no decision need be required. However, at various junctures an individual may note a growing deviation between what is presumed to be the norm and his or her actual psychic state. The awareness of deviation leads to an awareness that a decision has to be made. For instance, on nonworkdays an individual without a watch has to decide when to eat based on the deviation between his or her normal state of satisfaction and a growing sense of hunger. At some point the deviation will trigger a decision to eat. Similarly with respect to health, deviations between some sense of a norm and the actual state of an individual may also stimulate a decision to see a doctor. In other types of situations, a growing deviation between what is believed to be the normal psychological state and the actual one will trigger the sense that something has to be done. In essence, it will trigger a decision.

Options, Selection Rules, and Search Processes

The essence of decision making in between the trigger and the finalization is the application of a selection rule to a set of options. We shall focus on this aspect of decisions, assuming that appropriate triggers and finalization criteria exist. Visualize a set of selection rules and a set of options. Let us write $\mathcal{R}$ ($\mathcal{O}$) for the set of all selection rules and the set of all options. Thus, a specific selection rule is a member of $\mathcal{R}$ and a specific group of options is a subset of $\mathcal{O}$.

Now consider various categories of selection rules and options. The first one describes conditions necessary to guarantee that a decision will be optimal. Let us write (O^c) for the subset of options that is complete, and hence contains the optimum option (or options). R^r is that selection rule that involves ranking the options. R^i involves ranking options *and* choosing the best one. Note that ranking and option completeness are necessary but not sufficient conditions for an optimal choice. The rule must also contain the requirement that the highest-ranked option is chosen. Thus, R^i (O^c) represents an optimal decision procedure. Now, there are other possible subsets of selection rules and options. Let O be an option set where the options are not complete and let O^- be an incomplete option set in which the optimal option is known to be missing. Also let O^* be an incomplete subset of O which does contain the optimal option. Consider the following three alternatives:

1. R^r (O), where the options are ranked but the options are not complete,
2. R (O^c), where the options are complete but the selection rule does not require ranking, and
3. R (O), where the options are not complete nor does the selection rule require ranking.

It should be clear that where either ranking or completeness do not exist there is the possibility of nonoptimal decisions. In case 1 the option set may not contain the optimal option, and as a consequence the decision will not necessarily be optimal. In case 2 the option set contains the optimal option, but the selection rule does not require ranking, and thus will not necessarily result in the optimum being chosen. In the third case, R (O), where neither completeness nor ranking exists, there is obviously the possibility of nonoptimal decisions. In fact, none of the procedure classes other than R^i (O^c) guarantees that an optimum will be chosen.

Of course, R^f (O^*) would be an optimal decision. However, without completeness, in some sense, of the option set it is difficult to know whether such a subset would contain the optimal option. Nevertheless, there may be cases where an option subset may be easily seen to lack the optimum on the basis of some general characteristic (such as, in a purchasing decision, those options that are too far away geographically to be taken seriously) so that the remaining subsets $O^* = O^c - O^-$ may be known to contain the optimum.

Various possible rule and option combinations are shown in table 3.1. The outcomes are shown in the squares indicating the rule-option combination category. Note that most of the outcomes are nonoptimal. Furthermore, the subset of rules R is not really a single rule but involves a variety of nonranking rules—habits, conventions, other precedent procedures, emulation of others, random procedures. Thus, if it were necessary we could extend the table considerably by substituting particular rules for R, and thus obtain many more nonoptimal outcomes.

TABLE 3.1.

	O^c	O	$O\star$	O^-
R^f	Optimal	?[a]	Optimal	Nonoptimal
R^r	Nonoptimal	Nonoptimal	Nonoptimal	Nonoptimal
R	Nonoptimal	Nonoptimal	Nonoptimal	Nonoptimal

a. $R^r(O)$ is unclear. As O is defined, we do not know if the optimal option is contained in O or not. All we know is that there is no definite knowledge that it is not in O, as is the case for O^-

A word should be said about the completeness of an options subset. It is not strictly necessary that a search procedure examine every option. It would be sufficient if there were a "completeness test" whereby the decision maker could assure himself that the options considered are as complete a set as he wants, given the costs of searching for additional options. In other words, he carries out, at the very least, a mental benefit-cost analysis of searching for additional options given the subset of options he has already obtained. Thus, we can interpret (O^c) as the subset of options that has passed a completeness test. In the case of R (O) we mean that no such test has taken place.

Now, consider the types of selection rules that are possible under R (O). A selection rule may depend on past behavior, or it may not. Examples of past-behavior selection rules would be habits, conventions, or any kind of procedure that has been used in the past and somehow sanctioned by precedence. This is probably the largest subset of selection rules that actually exists in practice. Selection rules that do not depend on past behavior would be those that are purely random, such as tossing a coin or choosing a number out of a hat, or possibly some of those that involve emulation of some sort. What is important is that here we have two types of selection rules that will not guarantee optimal decisions; they are subsets of R and not R^r.

In what follows we shall stress the use of type R (O) decision procedures within organizational contexts, for two reasons. One is that organizations tend to apply a particular selection rule under a wide variety of circumstances instead of tailoring selection rules to fit specific circumstances. This makes it likely that general selection rules will be used, at times, in specific situations in which they are not optimal. Second, and equally important, it is difficult in a hierarchy for those at a higher level to transmit the preference ordering of those at the highest level to those lower down. After all, such preference orderings are internal to the person involved, and it is hard for anyone to imagine all the circumstances that might present options, let alone convey so much information. As a consequence, R^r cannot be completely transmitted to the locus of decision making. Hence, selection rules without complete ranking by higher-ups must be employed by subordinates.

It is difficult to determine what the probability is of making an optimal decision unless we make some very strong assumptions. However, we can speculate. Suppose that R and O are fairly large. That is, suppose there are a fair number of selection rules and a fair number of options to choose from. Then, clearly, if the selection rule were chosen at random there would be a low probability of making an optimal decision. The larger the sets R and O are, the smaller the probability of an optimal decision. In addition, if there is inertia in the system, then both the selection rules used and options taken will be biased in favor of what they were in the past. Then, as the environment changes and additions occur to the options and selection subsets, the probability that a decision based on past choices will be optimal becomes further reduced.

How people make decisions under a variety of circumstances, where they choose from both selection and options subsets, can be subject to experiment. It would be interesting to discover what experiments would reveal about the nature of such choices.

We could add to this picture by adding a search component to the selection rule and options subsets. There are a variety of procedures for searching for selection rules, and of finding additions to the options set, not all of which are equally good. In other words, both optimal and nonoptimal search procedures exist. Visualize three sets, $\mathcal{S}$, $\mathcal{R}$, and $\mathcal{O}$ (for search, rules, and options). The overall decision procedure is presumed to take place through the choice of noncontradictory subsets of $\mathcal{S}$, $\mathcal{R}$, and $\mathcal{O}$, the first two of which contain procedures themselves. Usually, only one selection rule will be used. It should be apparent at this point that if $\mathcal{S}$, $\mathcal{R}$, and $\mathcal{O}$ are each of reasonable size (say five items or more) then the number of combinations of subsets is very large, and any decision procedure selected in a fairly random way is likely to result in a nonoptimal choice.

It would be reasonable to presume that, on average, nonoptimal search procedures would lead to the selection of nonoptimal selection rules, as well as nonoptimal option subsets. Of course, individuals are unlikely to make such choices on a completely random basis. Some decision-procedure components, although possible, will not be selected under any circumstances because they would be recognized *prima facie* as ineffective or silly. Nevertheless, even if the clearly ineffective components are eliminated, the possibilities that remain will still be reasonably large so that choosing from them in a way that approximates randomness is not out of the question.[1] It takes effort to determine which procedures are effective. When pressure is relatively low such effort is not likely to be exerted.

Note that the more complex a decision procedure is the less likely it is to be optimal. That is, the larger the number of decision-procedure components the greater the likelihood that an optimal decision procedure will not be chosen when ranking and completeness of options are not the case. Suppose we break up the search technique set into internal and external search techniques. By internal search techniques we have in mind looking into ourselves in order to determine what selection rules we want to use in making a decision. In external search we are concerned with the external environment. This would add an additional component subset to choose from in selecting an overall de-

1. It may be argued that individuals would never, or almost never, choose a selection rule randomly. However, no matter what the basis of choice, the circumstances (environment) surrounding the option will determine whether maximization or some degree of deviation from the maximum occurs. These circumstances are likely to vary randomly, and in such cases the approximate randomness argument would hold even if the choice of the rule of selection was nonrandom.

cision procedure. In other words, we would include an internal search technique, an external search technique, a selection rule, and an options subset in our description of the decision procedure. Similarly, if we expanded the components to include possible triggering mechanisms to respond to, and possible completion signals, this would expand the number of decision procedures available.

This discussion suggests two things. (1) The procedure or procedures required in order to pursue maximization can be quite complex. (2) In situations where we do not have an option set that we know contains an optimal option, and the selection rule requires ranking, then it seems unlikely that the procedure chosen will lead to an optimal decision.

Notes on Procedures and Procedure Sets

A procedure may be defined as a commitment to do things in a certain way. This commitment may be self-imposed, in the case of habits, or it may be imposed by some agent outside of the individual. The latter can be very clearly seen in medium- and large-sized organizations where there are accepted procedures for a large variety of purposes and activities, which are imposed on employees by a hierarchy.

It is usually possible to aim for a specific purpose, or to carry out a specific class of activities in many different ways. However, the essence of following a procedure is that it restricts the way of doing things to a predetermined way. Other possibilities are eliminated. In the extreme case all possibilities but one are eliminated. In other cases there may be more than one procedure to follow for a given "activity class." Nevertheless, if the procedural subset is meaningful, it eliminates a number of possible behaviors for those people who follow procedure.

An important consequence of creating procedures is that it frequently results in procedure sets that have gaps. Certain activities will not be carried out because an appropriate procedure does not exist. A particular organization may have procedures for setting wages, but no procedure for addressing less-obvious aspects of employee motivation. There is no rule guaranteeing that a procedure will exist for addressing every problem, every opportunity, every contingency. This does not mean that an activity that lacks a defined procedure will never be carried out; there may be ways of getting around a procedural gap. However, it is most likely that a procedural gap will hinder certain activities from taking place. It will deter some individuals from attempting to carry out activities because of a reluctance to disturb the status quo. It may also promote a failure to recognize, or foster complacency about, problems and opportunities for which no procedures exist. Thus, procedural gaps may lead to activities not being carried out.

An additional possibility is that developing procedures may create obstacles to carrying out certain activities. For instance, the procedure of filling out a form may require certain information that is not available, and yet the procedure cannot be fulfilled unless this information is somehow noted on the form. In other words, a "Catch-22" type of situation may arise because document A has to be obtained before obtaining document B, but document B has to be obtained before obtaining document A. Thus, for some activities the requisite procedures may involve inconsistent or contradictory requirements.

What should be evident from this is that the procedures that exist at any particular time will not necessarily be the most efficient procedures for the purpose at hand. There is no reason for existing procedures to be the best way of doing things. Existing procedures may be the best for some circumstances, but not for others. Thus, non-maximum decisions may occur because inefficient procedures are required in order to make these decisions.

Another consequence that follows from the definition of a procedure as a commitment to do things a certain way and the fact that a procedure eliminates other potential behaviors is the likelihood of inflexibilities. The set of procedures established in an organization is likely to reduce the flexibility of the organization's responses to market conditions and opportunities. In other words, a certain degree of variation in some economic variables (such as price or quantity) may not take place because gaps exist in the procedure set, or because obstacles exist that cannot be overcome. For example, a strict cost-plus-markup procedure may make it difficult or impossible for employees to lower prices, es pecially in the short run, even when market conditions call for lower prices. Similarly, following strict inventory rules that depend on existing stocks of inputs may make it impossible for employees to take advantage of temporary price reductions for such inputs. In the long run all procedures that create excessive problems can be changed. Nevertheless, the shorter-run consequences resulting from inflexibilities have to be taken into account.

Conclusions

Any particular decision may require a complex procedure R^r (O^c) to achieve the optimal outcome. The more options, selection rules, and search procedures available to the decision maker, the more likely it is that the outcome will not be the optimal one if the option and selection rule are chosen somewhat randomly. Under low pressure it is unlikely that decision makers will exert the full effort needed to determine the optimal procedure. Inertia will bias the choice of options and selection rules in favor of those used in the past. As conditions change, procedures based on precedence are likely to become increasingly suboptimal.

The *R (O)* type of decision procedure is likely to be common in organizations because of using selection rules generally rather than tailoring them to particular circumstances, and the inability or difficulty of the upper levels of the hierarchy to transmit their desired ranking of options for every decision their employees face. Such decisions, based on an incomplete subset of options, or selection rules without ranking, are unlikely to lead to the optimal outcome.

By definition, instituting a procedure restricts the possible ways of doing things. This can lead to suboptimal outcomes in several ways. A procedure set with gaps may hinder certain activities from occurring, through discouragement or complacency. Certain procedures may create obstacles through inconsistent or contradictory requirements. A set of procedures may reduce the short-run flexibility of the organization's response to market conditions and opportunities.

Thus, the anatomy of decision making suggests (but does not determine) that there are a great many ways of making decisions, very few of which imply an optimal choice as the outcome. Of course, our anatomical analysis by itself will not tell us how people will actually behave; in addition we need to know something about motivation. In Chapter 2 we argued that rational considerations are not the only factors motivating behavior. Emotional forces and inertia also play a role, and can lead to nonoptimal choices. Hence, if we add the possibility of emotional forces to the possibilities of the analysis above, then we come out with an argument that favors a mixed maximization-nonmaximization theory of decision making.

CHAPTER 4

Economics of Inertia

Inertia is a ubiquitous human and social phenomenon. Behavior within an inertial framework will play a role in most of the phenomena that we will consider.[1] The concept of inert areas, and the broader idea of inertia can be applied to almost all aspects of economic life, and to a great many aspects of economic analysis. Personal habits, social conventions, and inaction are the categories of inert behavior that will concern us. Many economic variables are subject to such inertial forces. Since various interpretations of inertia are possible, we will set forth in this chapter the particular interpretation we will employ.

One can think of inertia in two senses: not doing anything, and doing something within a well-recognized pattern. Both are examples of invariant behavior. Not doing anything can lead to decisions by default. For instance, the book club and record club examples mentioned earlier usually employ a system which, if you do not send them a "don't want" card by a certain date, the book or record will automatically be sent to you. You have made the decision to buy simply by not making the decision not to buy.

Most forms of inertial behavior involve doing something more or less repetitive within a recognized pattern. Most of our institutionalized and quasi-institutionalized arrangements are of this type, such as mealtimes, normal working hours, nature of meals, and sleeping times. A good deal of what we will consider here will involve invariant behavior within certain bounds.

It is because of inertia that we are able, to a considerable degree, to make predictions about other people's behavior, and about the world in general. In a general sense, we care more about the inertial behavior of other human beings than whether such behavior is or is not optimal. If various modes of public transportation keep the same schedules for

---

1. By the inertial framework I have in mind the set of elements that influence the inertial behavior of a specific dependent variable. This is explained in greater detail in the next section.

long periods, we may view this as an *imposed* inertial phenomenon. It is such schedules that enable us to make our plans and to meet obligations with relative ease. We count on such predictability and behave accordingly. We force our own behavior into certain inertial frameworks in order to mesh with the activities of other people. Thus, we establish patterns for our sleeping and waking hours, for our meals, times at work, and frequently, times at play.

By following the inertial patterns of others, and by forcing our own behavior into such inertial patterns, we help to maintain the inertial system and the partial predictability of such a system. In other words, each person makes plans and behaves, to some degree, in accordance with the patterns of behavior of others. But by each and every person doing so their own patterns become predictable. This is not to say that all economic behavior is predictable. That is far from being the case. But the less predictable part of our behavior is enmeshed in a subsystem that *is* largely predictable.[2] This subsystem is largely based on habits and social conventions. For example, investment rates may not be predictable, but hours of work, periods during which business is transacted, and a host of other arrangements are predictable.

Inertia is also a common type of psychological experience. We not only observe inert behavior in others, but we ourselves feel a desire to resist activity or changes in routines. There are times when we feel we just want to lie around and do nothing, or do something that appears to be almost completely mindless. Sometimes we almost unconsciously want to carry out routinized and almost nonthinking activities. At other times we want to do what we have always done. We want to have the *comfort* of our usual bath, our usual breakfast, our usual departure for work, and so on. While at times we may seek more novel activities, this is in contrast to our experience of inertia. We even experience inertial ways of thinking and not thinking. There are, perhaps, certain difficult decisions that we do not want to face just now. Not facing things is an inertial activity. Clearly, we can divide our thinking into inertial and noninertial types of thinking. As we consider inertial feelings, we distinguish such feelings from inertial behavior, but of course, these two elements are closely connected. It is the experience of inertial feelings that supports observed inertial behavior.

2. By the inertial subsystem I have in mind all those elements of an individual's or a group's behavior that behave according to inertia and hence are predictable within certain limits. Other elements of behavior not subject to inertia, and not part of the same subsystem, are not predictable in the same sense.

Inertia is also related to pressure. As pressure builds we expect that at some point, enough pressure will jolt an individual out of his inertial behavior. Thus, small deviations between what we believe to be a normal price and the actual price will go almost unnoticed. However, a large deviation will, in a sense, pressure us to consider an alternative form of behavior.

Modeling Inertial Frames

There are several ways in which we could model behavior which has inertial characteristics. We will present a particular way of doing so which will fit the dependent variables in the system to be considered in this book. However, the scheme presented below is not the only possibility.

To start with, consider a two-variable system where the activities an individual performs are a function of working conditions, including the wage rate. Thus, we set

$$A = f(W)$$

where A is the activity and W is the cost of providing the working conditions for the individual. If A is subject to inertia, then the amount of activity will continue at the level at which it was at some initial time even if the working conditions change. A simple example would be a step function under which A is constant for one subset of values of W, and then at some critical value of W, A rises and stays constant for another segment, and so on. This is illustrated in figure 4.1.

This view of inertia is not likely to be intuitively convincing. We do not expect the dependent variable to depend on this independent variable alone. It is too simple a situation to capture the basic idea of inertia. However, it does capture the basic aspect, that is, that there will be stable values of the dependent variable for changing values of the independent variable within certain bounds.

What is missing is that inertia is likely to depend on time. That is to say, the strength of inertia depends on how much repetition or experience has occurred over time. Thus, in the simple case, the intensity of the activity A depends on how long it has been carried out. If it has been carried out for weeks or months at a rate of, say, 20 units per hour, then we would expect it to be closer to a stable pace than if it had only been going on for fifteen minutes. In other words, we expect inertia to reflect that some behavioral patterns become set over a period

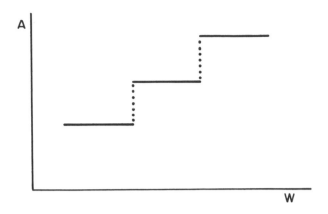

FIGURE 4.1

of time. Thus, we should set up the equation so that the activity A depends on both W and T (time), and beyond certain critical values of T the inertial system is established. Also, the critical bounds surrounding the independent variable depend on T. Thus, if any value of A, say A^*, proceeds for some time associated with a certain value of W, say W^*, then there will be critical bounds of $\overline{W}$ and $\underline{W}$ (upper and lower bounds) which will determine the thresholds of the inert area. Within these bounds the inertial value of A will persist.

To take the impact of past experience into account it may be best to restate the relation as follows:

$$A = f(W_t, W^*, A^*, T_{A^*})$$

where W_t is the current level of working conditions, A^* is the past continuing level of A, W^* is the "equilibrium" level of working conditions related to A^*, and T_{A^*} is the time that A^* has been in force. W^*, A^*, T_{A^*} are given by past experience. Thus, even if W_t is different (but not too different) from W^*, and A^* has been going on long enough, then W_t will be within the inert area bounds, $\overline{W}$ and $\underline{W}$, and the value of A will not change from what it was during the period $t-1$; that is, $A = A^* = A_{t-1}$. Beyond the lower or upper bounds, A is no longer stable but changes to a new value.

An example based on consumption may help to indicate what we have in mind. Suppose a housewife purchases a certain amount of breakfast food for her family. Within limits she will continue to purchase the same quantity Q of breakfast food although its price changes. Beyond some point the price gets so high that this creates a "shock," as it were, and she reconsiders her decision. Thus, we have the following simple system:

$$Q = f(P_t, P^*, Q^*, T_{Q^*}).$$

The boundaries of the inert area will depend on how long this behavior pattern has persisted. Thus, the upper and lower threshold prices will depend on T. This basically describes the inertial system as far as we care about inertia as such. In other words, we define the inert area of the independent variable, in this case the price, by certain upper and lower bounds. Beyond some values of T these will be the maximum upper and lower bounds. If the actual price goes beyond, say, the upper bound, then the housewife will reconsider her behavior. In other words, this phenomenon triggers a search procedure so that there is a movement to a more sensible quantity of the breakfast food, given the high price.

Figure 4.2 shows the usual demand curve where the quantity bought depends on the price, and the function is negatively inclined. But for a specific P we show the inert area with its upper and lower limits. We now have to interpret the meaning of the demand curve given the inert

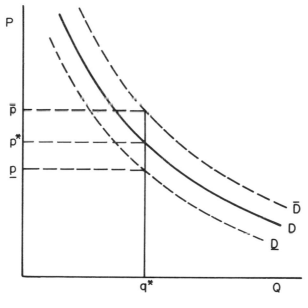

FIGURE 4.2

areas shown in the figure by line segments. Essentially, the point on the demand curve is the optimal quantity purchased at that price. However, inertia leads to the decision to purchase nonoptimal quantities of the breakfast food within the inert area. After all, the basic idea is that inertia involves nonchanges in behavior whereas careful calculation at every juncture would result in a change in the dependent variable for any change in the independent variable. As suggested in Chapter 2, inertia helps to explain the persistent use of nonoptimal procedures.[3]

In figure 4.2, D is the usual demand function. D is surrounded by $\overline{D}$ and $\underline{D}$, which are the upper and lower bounds of the inert area. As T gets larger, $\overline{D}$ and $\underline{D}$ become wider until some maximum is reached. If T is small then the inert area is narrow; that is, $\overline{D}$ and $\underline{D}$ are very close to D. We see from figure 4.2 that q^* will continue to be the rule as long as p is within the bounds $\overline{p}$ and $\underline{p}$.

Note that the inertial frame is made up of two components. One is the inert area part of the system, and the other is the adjustment between inert areas. At present we are primarily concerned with inertial behavior, and hence with the inert area part of the system. Adjustment is set in motion after the independent variable breaks through the inert area bounds. Adjustment is likely to be a dynamic procedure in which people search, partly through trial and error, and partly on some other basis, for a new value of the independent variable. Adjustments may depend on the history within the previous inert area, that is, on how long the individual agent was in the inertial mode, and to what extent P fluctuated during the inert area period. The adjustment procedure may differ for different aspects of behavior.

The picture can be complicated by adding independent variables, but in principle this does not change the basic nature of the analysis. Thus, the item purchased may depend not only on price but also on income, or any additional variables. Inertial behavior would still operate in the same way. The housewife could still purchase the same amount of the breakfast food if both price and income changed simultaneously to some degree. We would then be operating with many variable thresholds for

3. I no longer hold the position on inertia found in *Beyond Economic Man*, which gave the impression that individuals in inert areas do not move because they have taken into account the cost versus the advantage of moving and concluded that it is preferable not to move. In my current view it is only necessary to postulate that economic agents in inert areas do not move, within certain bounds. There is no special need to explain why. Rather, my view is that some degree of inertia is a basic psychological and physiological condition. It usually does not depend on any conscious calculation of the cost of moving versus its advantages.

the inert area. Once these inert area boundaries are pierced, the decision maker faces the option of a new mode of behavior, namely choosing a new quantity to be purchased. The elements that enter the adjustment path might be somewhat more complicated than in the single independent variable case, but the idea of an inert area to express invariant behavior within certain bounds remains the same.

Some Consequences of Inertia

The basic consequence of using the concept of inertia is that it permits nonoptimal behavior and indicates the circumstances of shifts away from such behavior, possibly toward optimal behavior. Thus, the use of inert areas permits both optimal and nonoptimal decisions within the same model. In other words, it allows for the reasonable proposition that most people's behavior will in some instances be nonoptimal, while in other situations will approximate optimality.

The inert area idea allows us to surround certain critical variables in our theory with inertial frames. The inertial frame connects one day's behavior and the next. It says that, unless the environment changes quite a bit, people will behave today the way they behaved yesterday. Thus, it helps to explain fairly long-lasting relationships as well as long-standing behavior patterns. Among the important variables to be surrounded or contained within inert area bounds are employment, effort, perception of the environment, discretion, hierarchical relations, peer relations, certain motivational forces, and so on.

A very important aspect of inertia is that it increases the predictability of the behavior of others more than otherwise would be the case. Certain norms of behavior and conventions are categories of inertial behavior that contribute to predictability.

We will argue later that certain basic relations in firms are of a Prisoner's Dilemma type, but that the Prisoner's Dilemma solution is avoided by the adoption of effort conventions and wage conventions. It is inertial forces that allow such conventions to arise and persist in the first place.

One interesting aspect is the role that inertia plays in assessing the implicit rate of discount, or what is the same thing, the trade-off between present satisfaction and long-run consequences. Consider the case of smoking. Suppose the individual involved knows that there is a certain probability of smoking being injurious to his health in the long run. He takes this knowledge seriously enough so that if he had not already been smoking he would not start. Furthermore, if he could project his life a number of years into the future and experience the ultimate health consequences of smoking, he would stop. But at the time we observe him, he has been smoking and no consequences have shown up on a day-to-day basis. One can argue that it is inertia that keeps him smoking. The point is that the trade-off between the pleasure of smoking and the long-run hurt is such that he would stop were it not for the inertial influences. Thus, inertia can distort the rate of discount between the present and future. Such interferences with trade-offs may exist in a great many other situations. Hence, one has to be careful in calculating implicit discount rates simply by observing current behavior and knowing the differences between the current payoff and the long-run payoff.

The patterning of many aspects of behavior supported by inertial forces allows for a great many implicit contracts where such contracts would be too complicated to develop in detail. This is of considerable importance. It permits the inclusion of fairly wide-ranging components in contracts so that a great many types of exchange are facilitated, without being bogged down in excessive detail.

CHAPTER 5

Productivity:
The Hidden Prisoner's
Dilemma Analysis

How should we think about productivity problems within firms? How do practices such as those in the Japanese system of management fit into such thinking? The approach used here is that an intellectual framework is needed to aid in seeing how management policies result in low productivity even where management (and owners) desire high productivity. We will attempt to provide a set of intellectual lenses, so to speak, through which we will look at management-employee relations, and examine how these relations impinge on productivity.

Productivity outcomes result from the simultaneous interactions of policies chosen by management, *and* the options employees choose. We will see that employees may face managerial policies that are not in the best interest of employees and simultaneously not in the best interest of management either. This assertion may appear strange, but makes sense once we look at both managerial and employee options in the context of the Prisoner's Dilemma framework.

Some recent management literature appears to suggest that if management would only adopt theory A, B, Y, or Z all would be well, the implication being that if a set of slogans becomes part of management philosophy all management problems would be solved. Our analytical approach is quite different. It suggests that no specific gimmick will work. The reason is simply and easily stated in terms of a medical analogy. If someone proposed a specific medicine as a cure for all illnesses he would be read out of his profession as a snake-oil salesman. Diagnosis of each particular medical problem is required, yet behind the diagnostic procedure there are usually some general principles. Similarly, in order to diagnose low-productivity problems, an underlying general framework or philosophy of the problem area is required.

We will explore two central themes: the application of the Prisoner's

Dilemma framework to productivity analysis, and the notion that this problem may be fully or partially hidden from management's view for a variety of reasons. Briefly put, Prisoner's Dilemma problems usually involve circumstances in which, when people try to do the best for themselves, things turn out badly for all concerned. We will also argue that while Prisoner's Dilemma "solutions" are having their effects there may also be a lack of awareness of the difficulties present because ongoing practices mask the fact that pressing problems exist. The operative word is *pressing*. In a great many cases performance has become more or less routinized, despite the fact that the "solution" is far from optimal.

Self-Interest and Trust: The Prisoner's Dilemma Example

We have already seen that not all contracts can be fully specified. In fact, most employment contracts are rarely specified in any detail. Trust is of paramount importance in such relationships; it saves on negotiation costs and transaction costs, and decreases or eliminates detailed monitoring. The need for trust exists because of discretionary behavioral possibilities, and the lack of trust is frequently an important aspect of Prisoner's Dilemma problems.

An interesting case of the significance of trust is contained in Anatol Rapoport's (1962) example of the Prisoner's Dilemma, based on the libretto of the opera, *Tosca*. We will see that this example (reworked slightly) highlights certain aspects useful for our purposes.

The main protagonists are Tosca, a beautiful singer, and Scarpia, chief of police in Rome during the Napoleonic occupation. At the point relevant to our purposes, Scarpia has captured Tosca's lover, who has been sentenced to be shot. Scarpia makes Tosca an offer she cannot refuse. If she will sleep with him, he will substitute fake bullets for the real ones. She accepts. On the way to the rendezvous, Tosca discovers a dagger which she can use to kill Scarpia, if she so chooses. Let us now stop the story in its tracks, so to speak, to consider the options. Scarpia can (1) stick to the agreement and order blank bullets used, or (2) he can leave the real bullets in and get rid of his rival for Tosca's affections. Tosca now has two options: she can honor the agreement and sleep with Scarpia, or she can use the dagger on Scarpia, and maintain her honor. Table 5.1 shows the payoffs in terms of utilities.

In cell I Tosca sleeps with Scarpia and Scarpia uses the blanks. This has a relatively low but positive payoff for both. While Tosca saves

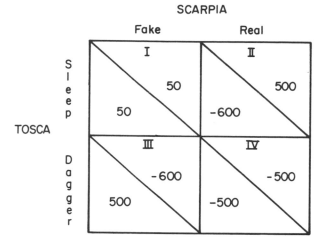

TABLE 5.1

her lover, she yields to the hated Scarpia. Similarly Scarpia enjoys Tosca, but he does not get rid of his rival. Cell II is the best for Scarpia since he enjoys Tosca and gets rid of his rival. This has a high payoff for Scarpia (+500 utils), and the lowest possible payoff for Tosca since she loses her loved one and yields to Scarpia. Cell III is the reverse of cell II. Here Tosca is best off since she gets rid of the hated Scarpia and saves her lover. Cell IV is clearly inferior to cell I for both. For Scarpia it is worse since he gets killed. For Tosca it is worse since her lover is killed.

How will they choose? If each tries to choose independently we can see that the Prisoner's Dilemma outcome (cell IV) occurs. Consider Scarpia's logic: if Tosca will succumb he might as well get rid of his rival and not substitute the blank bullets. If he thinks Tosca will refuse or might kill him then he certainly has no reason to substitute the blanks. Hence he opts for the real bullets. Tosca's logic is similar. If Scarpia sticks to his bargain and has given the order to substitute the blanks then there is no point in yielding to him. She might as well use the dagger. If Scarpia has not given the order, then of course, she will kill him for revenge, rather than submit. Obviously, this type of thinking on both their parts results in the Prisoner's Dilemma outcome. Since the opera is a tragedy, it follows the logic of the situation. In the end, all the main characters go to their doom. The final scene has Tosca throwing herself off the rampart of the Castel Sant' Angelo after killing Scarpia, and upon learning of the death of her loved one.

For economics, the *Tosca* example of the Prisoner's Dilemma is more fundamental than the original Prisoner's Dilemma story. In the original, the fact that the two prisoners did not *communicate* was of the essence. In *Tosca* distrust is of the essence. In *Tosca,* the contending parties could, and did, communicate. In fact, they had worked out a satisfactory contract. What they did not have was mutual trust, and the *mutual incentives* to keep the contract. Present self-interest based on distrust made both parties worse off than would have been the case under the contract. Thus, the *Tosca* story is a member of a class of Prisoner's Dilemmas, which is essentially a mutual distrust dilemma.

What is the relationship between self-interest and trust? Should one be trusted in a situation where self-interest is involved, and should the other party trust if there is a lack of certainty that trust is warranted? Since we cannot read other people's minds, there is always a lack of certainty. Self-interest that negates a commitment is frequently present in situations where it is to the benefit of the individual (or the firm he or she represents) to take advantage of the other party who continues to show trust. But frequently these are precisely the circumstances where *mutual* trust is mutually beneficial because of the possibility of a Prisoner's Dilemma solution. In other words, where self-interest is involved there is, at the very least, a tension between acting according to the trust of the other party, and taking advantage of the situation. Note especially that in completely ahistorical situations there would be no basis for trust and hence no reason to offer trust where it is not clearly advantageous to do so by each individual considering his benefit independently.

In summary, we note that only an overriding moral commitment to abide by a contract can overcome a tendency toward the Prisoner's Dilemma solution, since there is no mutual incentive to keep the contract and since each side has an incentive to take advantage of the other party's demonstrating trust. While questions of trust are a very important aspect of some strategic games they are not the only aspect.

A general element of Prisoner's Dilemma as well as non–Prisoner's Dilemma games, is that no player or protagonist controls the outcome. Each may choose on the basis of whatever assumption he or she pleases, but it is the combination of *both* choices that determines the outcome. This is the essence of all strategic games. Thus, a basic assumption of our theory is that management faces, in part, *strategic* and not dictatorial choices. In addition, in Prisoner's Dilemma situations, if each tries to do as well as he or she possibly can, then an inferior outcome results.

A slightly different way of looking at the matter is to think of games as containing both cooperative and adversarial components. In the Tosca-Scarpia game a cooperative strategy for both is possible (cell I). This strategy choice results in the best both can achieve simultaneously. An alternative strategy available to either player is for one to try to take advantage of the other who behaves cooperatively. This results in one doing very much better than the other and better than when both cooperated. Thus, if each assumes cooperation on the part of the other, it pays for each to use an "adversarial" strategy. In other words, the attempt to obtain either II upper or III lower as payoffs involves strategies of partial noncooperation, but when both adopt such strategies simultaneously the result is disaster for both. We will argue that management-employee relations are of this kind, especially the intrafirm productivity problem, although such relations are sometimes hidden from the players.

It is also worth while to look at the Tosca-Scarpia problem in "moral" terms. If both Tosca and Scarpia had had a strong sense of what might be referred to as "bourgeois morality," and believed that "a contract is a contract," they both would have been better off. Scarpia would have honored his side of the contract and used false bullets and Tosca would have slept with Scarpia—a long life might have been had by all. Instead they exhibited a type of "heroic" morality (perhaps appropriate for opera and individual maximizers) that led to disaster all around. The point is not to argue for one type of morality over another, but to stress that the existence of a certain moral or ethical stance toward keeping contracts is important in Prisoner's Dilemma situations in order to avoid disaster all around.

It would be useful to explain here the original Prisoner's Dilemma example that gave rise to the title of this kind of problem. Two prisoners who have committed a crime jointly are urged, separately, to squeal on each other. The one who turns state's evidence gets a light sentence, while the other receives a harsh sentence. If both squeal they each receive harsh sentences, and if neither squeals they receive intermediate sentences. If each tries to do the best for himself then, of course, both will squeal and both will receive harsh sentences. Once again this is only a problem if each tries to do as well as he possibly can at the expense of the other. No such problem exists if they have a strict moral code against squealing. Thus, for example, this would never be a problem to strict adherents of the Mafia code of *omerta*.

The Productivity Problem in the Prisoner's Dilemma Framework

We now shift our concern away from opera, crime, and morality to a direct treatment of the productivity problem. We shall see, however, that some of the general principles developed above are completely applicable to productivity. To lay the groundwork for seeing productivity as a Prisoner's Dilemma problem, we must specify three basic (and reasonable) postulates about behavior. (I have used these postulates elsewhere in the development of X-efficiency theory.) The postulates are as follows: (1) some effort discretion is open to all firm members; (2) the amount of effort put forth by a firm member will depend on the matrix of motivations within which he works; and (3) everyone is subject to some degree of inertia within certain bounds. The distance between these bounds are known as inert areas.

We now turn to the basic Prisoner's Dilemma interpretation of the productivity problem. Productivity depends, on the one hand, on how much effort workers put forth, and on the other hand, on the incentives and other motivations that management policies provide. We must keep in mind that managers are also employees (in fact, they play a dual role) and hence they do not necessarily do, in all cases, as well as they possibly can for the enterprise. In the example that follows we consider three options available to employees and three symmetrical options open to management.

Consider the employees' options, which we will refer to as the golden-rule standard, the peer-effort standard, and the parametric-maximization standard. (1) Under the golden-rule standard, employees work as well as they possibly can on behalf of the firm's interests, to the extent that they understand these interests. Thus, they try to choose a set of *activities,* the *pace* and *quality* levels of work for each activity, that are the best they can muster. In other words, under the golden-rule standard they perform as cooperatively as possible with management, given their capacities. (2) By the peer-effort standard we have in mind that each employee is aware that all other employees perform in accordance with some average effort level. Each tries to perform according to that level but neither very much above nor very much below. We assume that the peer-effort standard is definitely below the golden-rule standard. (3) Under the parametric-maximization standard, each individual pursues his own interests using his effort discretion as much as he can, just short of causing him to be discharged. Here too, we assume for the sake of simplicity that this standard involves a relatively low effort level, certainly lower than the peer-effort standard.

The three options available to management have similar names but somewhat different interpretations. (1) Under the golden-rule standard, managers try to treat their employees as well as they possibly can given the firm's resources. They provide the best working conditions, salary, and fringe benefits possible. Thus, this involves maximum cooperation with and on behalf of employees. (2) Under the peer-effort standard, management pays according to the size of the average peer-effort level but does not try to go above or below it. Thus the wage and benefits level in this case would be lower than under the golden rule. (3) Under the parametric-maximization standard, managers try to behave in a way such that the firm pays as little as possible (and provides the least additional benefits), and gets as much as possible out of employees. Thus, under this scheme, the payoffs are lower than under the other two options irrespective of how well employees perform.

It seems best to approach the problem in easy stages. Let us first look at the situation in terms of the extreme options available to each side. The payoffs are illustrated in table 5.2. If we compare table 5.2 and table 5.1, we can readily see that the situation faced in this management-worker relations problem is very similar to that faced by the protagonists in the *Tosca* example.

Suppose all employees make the same effort choice, but they have two options: a golden-rule effort option, and a maximizing-private-satisfaction option. The firm has two similar options: golden-rule or

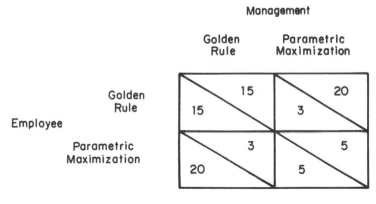

TABLE 5.2

parametric-maximizing behavior. As illustrated in the payoff table (table 5.2), the symmetrical choices give higher values for the *mutual golden-rule* choice than to the individual maximizing choice.

Given the numbers in table 5.2 we can readily see that this is a Prisoner's Dilemma situation. First, consider the choice problem from the firm's viewpoint. If employees operate according to the golden rule, then it certainly pays for the firm to choose maximization. Similarly, if the firm assumes that employees are private maximizers, it also makes sense for the firm to choose maximization. A very similar argument can be made for employees. They also choose maximization under both cases of the firm's choices. As a consequence, the joint choice will end up being maximization. But this joint choice is clearly inferior to the cooperative choice of the dual golden rule. Thus, if each side attempts to behave "rationally" and maximizes given the other's behavior, then the result is the Prisoner's Dilemma outcome.

The more complicated case of three options for each group and the payoffs associated with combinations of options are shown in table 5.3. Given the payoffs we can readily see that this is a Prisoner's Dilemma situation. For each choice made by employees the employer is best off on the basis of parametric maximization. This is especially the case where the employees operate according to the golden-rule standard. The same situation holds for employees. They are best off where management operates according to golden-rule standards and they perform according to parametric maximization. If each tries to do as well as each possibly can the outcome will be W_1E_1 (see table 5.3). This is the worst outcome for both sides simultaneously.

We will now examine the situation illustrated in table 5.3 in greater detail. To begin with we must state two simplifying assumptions of our model. The first is that choices made by both management and employees are made simultaneously and involve long-term commitments. The second is that higher productivity is associated with higher profits. We will see later, however, that these restrictive assumptions are not really critical to the logic of the argument.

Now let us look at what each side has to offer the other under each option. Employees essentially offer a level of productivity. Under parametric maximization, where each employee does as little as possible, it is clear that the effort level valued by management is at its lowest, resulting in the least productivity. Similarly, under the golden rule employees work ideally from management's viewpoint and, hence, what they offer is the highest level of productivity. Peer-group effort levels

Employee Options		Management Options Golden Rule W_3	Peer Group Standard W_2	Parametric Maximization W_1
Golden Rule	E_3	7 / 7	8 / 4	9 / 1
Peer Group Standard	E_2	4 / 8	5 / 5	6 / 2
Parametric Maximization	E_1	1 / 9	2 / 6	3 / 3

TABLE 5.3

are somewhere in between, and represent intermediate productivity levels. We indicate the three productivity levels by E_1, E_2, and E_3, where E_3 is associated with the golden-rule option, E_2 with the peer-effort level, and E_1 with parametric maximization. Of course E_3 is greater than E_2 which is greater than E_1.

Management, in each of its options, provides a package composed of wages plus working conditions for employees. Under the golden rule it offers the highest wages *and* the best working conditions, denoted by W_3. Under parametric maximization it offers the lowest wages and least-cost working conditions (that is, W_1). Under the peer-effort standard we have a situation that is in between, that is, (W_2). We denote these options as W_1, W_2, and W_3. W_3 is greater than W_2, which is greater than W_1. The payoffs to management involve the value of the productivity less the wages and costs of working conditions. While it is possible for a higher set of working conditions to cost so much more than the lower set that the increased productivity does not make up for it, we will assume, to start with, that this is not the case. (Later we can relax this assumption.) The numbers in table 5.3 reflect payoffs generally consistent with the assumptions we have made and arranged in such a way that we have a Prisoner's Dilemma situation. However, we use the Prisoner's Dilemma idea only to show the nature of the situation. We will not argue that the Prisoner's Dilemma logical *outcome* necessarily takes place. Indeed, we argue that people generally do not necessarily behave according to the type of logic that inevitably forces them into a Prisoner's Dilemma outcome. We will see that this is a very important aspect of our view of the productivity problem. Nevertheless there is some force to the Prisoner's Dilemma outcome. It is as if the Prisoner's Dilemma outcome, W_1E_1, has a kind of gravitational attraction for players; the gravitational pull, however, is not so strong that it cannot be overcome.

Of course, if everyone operates according to a type of individualistic, greedy logic, the outcome must be the worst possible for everyone concerned. Managers will, under this logic, pay as little as possible, and employees will do as little as they can get away with. The result will be the lowest productivity-profit level for both. No matter how one side behaves, it pays for the other to be a maximizer. We can go through each option separately and see that this is true. How, then, can the players escape this outcome? We shall see that the basic way is to adopt a *convention* or *code of behavior* permitting each side to behave according to that convention and *not* according to maximization. Since conventions are critical to our analysis we shall look at them in greater detail in Chapter 6.

Peer-Group and Golden-Rule Standards

Now return to the Prisoner's Dilemma problem illustrated in table 5.3. One way of avoiding the worst joint outcome is for management and employees to decide on a peer-group standard. This is likely to evolve out of the history of the enterprise, or out of the crafts and professions employed within the enterprise. New employees frequently bring with them a sense of the effort standards acquired elsewhere under roughly similar circumstances. However, they are likely to be willing to adjust, at least partially, to the local average standard of behavior. Those without previous experience will tend to look to the current effort level for guidance. Of course, personal characteristics will play a role. More ambitious and independent-minded individuals may produce at a higher standard, while others with different characteristics may perform at a standard lower than the average. Most employees are likely to stick to a standard *within certain bounds*, determined by some mix of vertical approval and disapproval, and peer-group approval and disapproval. In a similar spirit management may choose the peer-group standard as roughly appropriate for employees and as a basis for the wage scale.

The question that immediately comes to mind is, Why cannot either side cheat on the peer-group standard? The answer, of course, is that they can, and furthermore if they do the peer-group standard disintegrates and the Prisoner's Dilemma solution (that is, the worst joint solution) results. The point is that many conventions are strong enough to overcome such temptations to cheat. A sense of proper behavior and fairness matters to most people. We may all have our price, but the price at which we are willing to cheat may be quite high compared to the gains to be derived from cheating. Ordinary social intercourse, some aspects of the law, and normal relations with fellow human beings, support conventions. The emulation of behavior in some firms of those in other firms will usually help to support the peer-group standard. Furthermore, each side may sense that all-out attempts to take advantage of the other side can be mutually disastrous. Hence each side may, in fact, be looking for a reasonable standard to focus on as agreeable. A peer-group standard usually presents itself as a "natural" solution.

Note that there is a multiplicity of possible peer-group standards. Hence there is more than one effort-productivity level that can fit the requirement. If the current standard is very low our analysis shows that it can be higher. However, there may be other peer-group standards such that very much lower ones are not only possible but likely.

Of course, within the framework of our example there is something vastly superior to the peer-group standard, namely the double golden rule: each side chooses to behave in accordance with golden-rule standards. This is likely to be effective *if* golden-rule behavior is an established convention. Alas, this is very rarely the case. Neither management nor employees see themselves under obligation to perform according to the golden rule. Each side usually is aware of its options apart from the other side's reactions. Thus management is likely to emphasize cutting costs, while employees use their discretionary options so as to skew their efforts toward their own interests and away from the interests of the firm.

Western culture does not emphasize altruistically cooperative behavior for its own sake. Most of our sports, significant aspects of the legal profession, and many other elements of everyday life are basically adversarial in nature. We expect winners and losers. It appears more natural to try to be a big winner by performing according to a win/lose strategy rather than by adhering to an extremely cooperative convention. We no longer have sociocultural or strongly religious motivations for golden-rule behavior on a day-to-day basis.

If the double golden rule is so vastly superior, why then could not both sides *negotiate* such a standard? To begin with, both parties to the negotiations must be aware of the possibility of such a behavior standard before it can even be considered. Both parties also must be able to see productivity in a Prisoner's Dilemma framework before the *need* to negotiate this type of mutual behavior would occur to them. At present intrafirm relations are usually viewed as hierarchically authoritarian in nature. That is, the people above tell those below what to do. This is thought to be true even when higher-level decisions are determined by committees rather than individuals. This accepted way of thinking about intrafirm relations militates against the golden-rule approach.[1] Furthermore, it is likely that even if agreements on double golden-rule behavior were reached, neither side would trust the other not to cheat—to completely carry out the agreement. Yet, in order to derive and sustain gains from the mutual adoption of a golden-rule standard it is necessary for each side to behave according to it even if the other side lapses from such behavior.

The problem of maintaining golden-rule behavior lies partially in the fact that individuals cannot artificially impose changes in their feelings about cooperation. If they have not been raised and nurtured in a culture that stresses cooperation in day-to-day activities, a golden-rule standard does not come naturally. In the United States there are no horizontal supports for such behavior, nor are there many firms with completely cooperative internal relations to emulate. In essence the problem exists because both sides are aware of conflicting motivations. On the one hand there are the gains to be gotten through cooperation, and on the other hand there appear to be the greater gains, at least in the short run, to be obtained through behavior that is at the expense of the other party.

It may be helpful to see this problem in terms of a continuous set of options. We picture it as being similar to the illustration in table 5.3, but not limited to three options. In fact, there is an infinity of possible options. We may think of these options as containing an infinity of peer-group standards between the golden rule and parametric maximization. Thus, in figure 5.1 both managers and employees have choices similar to those in table 5.3.[2] However, managers can now offer

1. This approach is probably closest to the parametric maximization strategy in table 5.3.

2. The direction of improvements, which in tables 5.1 to 5.3 was along the northwest diagonal, now shifts to conform to conventional use in economic diagrams. The mutual gains line now goes along the northeast diagonal, so the P.D. solution is now in the (0,0) corner and the mutual golden-rule situation is now in the northeast corner.

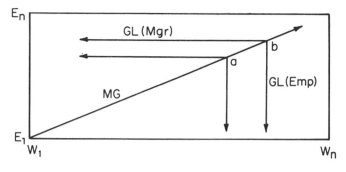

FIGURE 5.1

a variety of wage–working condition bundles shown in the diagram by the choices, $W_1, W_2, \ldots, W_n$, where $W_1 < W_2 < \ldots < W_n$. The larger the subscript the higher the cost for wages and working conditions. Similarly employees can offer lower versus higher effort levels and hence lower or higher productivity levels. The latter are shown as the essential options going from $E_1, E_2, \ldots, E_n$, where $E_1 < E_2 < \ldots < E_n$. In the figure the diagonal line is marked *MG* (mutual gain). This represents a set of options in which movement in the direction of the diagonal arrow results in a gain for both parties. In other words, movements in the direction of or parallel to the arrow involve simultaneously higher wages and higher productivity. Consider two points on the mutual gain line, *a* and *b,* and a move from *a* to *b*. In this case employees produce more at *b*, and the increased production more than pays for the increased wages. In other words, the mutual gain path is drawn in a way such that every small increase in output can be distributed between employees and management so that there is both an increase in wages and an increase in profits.

However, observe at the same time the arrows in the horizontal and vertical direction marked *GL*. Either of these represents "gain-loss movements" in the direction of the arrow. The horizontal one, *GL*(Mgr), represents a gain-loss movement in favor of management and against employees, while the vertical one, *GL*(Emp), represents a gain-loss movement that is to the advantage of employees but against the interest of the firm.

We should note that Prisoner's Dilemma situations are such that gain-loss movements for each side involve greater gains for one side than would be the case when compared to the appropriate point on the mutual-gain diagonal. In other words, for every position on the mutual-gain diagonal there exists a horizontal gain-loss movement to the advantage of management and a simultaneous gain-loss movement to the advantage of employees. Clearly, if each side tries to do as well as it possibly can in terms of its gain-loss movements, both obtain the simultaneous worst outcome.

We can look at this dilemma in terms of two strongly opposing motivations. On the one hand only cooperative behavior would result in a fairly good outcome, but each side is aware that partially adversarial behavior would result in an even better outcome for itself. The Prisoner's Dilemma results from the fact that there is a stronger pull toward the adversarial behavior than toward the mutually cooperative behavior.

The dilemma is usually hidden because only one side of the problem is seen by each group. Thus management assumes that employees cannot do much more and hence focuses on the horizontal *GL* direction. Management concentrates on cutting costs to such an extent that it loses sight of the strategic nature of the employment relation, and does not see the net gains in productivity that are possible from moves along *MG*. Employees do not expect management to do any more for them so they focus on the vertical *GL* direction. Neither side readily sees the mutual-gain diagonal which requires each side to behave in terms of a high degree of trustworthiness, and the incentives to cooperate.

The Scientific Management movement of the 1920s, developed by Taylor, the Gilbreths, and associated workers, was faulty, in part, because they saw only half the picture. Their measurements indicated very clearly that employees in manufacturing industries could certainly produce very much more than they did. In other words, they established the vast difference between existing effort levels and optimum effort levels. What they missed entirely was that optimum effort levels could not be achieved if the motivation was not there. They essentially missed both the motivation and the Prisoner's Dilemma component of the problem. Without strong high-effort-level conventions the adversarial nature of the work situation led to mistrust because of the existence of mixed motivations. Employees perceived that there were risks in raising the effort level since this created a motivation for management to lower piece rates. Nothing they did could change this perception or its basic accuracy (On Taylorism see Nadworny, 1955; Aitken, 1960; Litterer, 1961; Nelson, 1974; Kelly, 1982).

In looking at the continuous options case it is evident that even if a choice is made along the cooperative diagonal, the vast majority of choices will be inferior to the mutual golden-rule choice. We may locate the mutual golden rule as the one associated with the extreme position, W_nE_n, shown at the northeast corner of the diagram. A specific peer-group standard may be located somewhere around the middle of the diagonal. Of course there is an infinity of possible peer-group standards between the two extremes of the mutual golden rule and the Prisoner's Dilemma solution. Which particular standard will emerge will be considered in Chapter 6.

The Twofold Prisoner's Dilemma Problem

There is at least a twofold Prisoner's Dilemma game involved here. In fact, there is a multifold game, but it is best to consider it one stage at a time. For simplicity, only two sides, management and employees, have been considered. We have argued *as if* the two sides behave as two individuals would behave, or *as if* there was a representative individual making decisions for each of the opposing sides. This makes sense not only in terms of simplifying the problem, but also because, in fact, when latent problems surface they frequently emerge as two-sided problems.

However, it is important to note the additional complications which, in essence, involve free riding by members of each group. Each side, management and employees, contains a large number of individuals, and each individual has conflicting interests vis-à-vis his peers. Thus, it may be desirable for each employee to want employees as a group to be sufficiently productive so that the firm can continue as a successful, viable entity, but each individual employee may correctly feel that his contribution is too small to make a great deal of difference.

Thus, *within* each group there are free-rider incentives. That is, every employee may wish to work as little as possible in the interests of the firm, and deflect effort toward his own interests, even though, if he gave it some thought, he might desire all others to work effectively so the enterprise flourishes and his job and internal opportunities continue. These are clear-cut free-rider incentives, and they are likely to exist at every level in the enterprise. Thus, even if through the use of some exceptionally wise tactics the adversarial feelings between employees and management were eliminated, the free-rider incentives and free-rider options would still exist, and would be employed.

Free riding within a group by itself involves a Prisoner's Dilemma solution. Each individual wants to free ride, but each wants to do so in the absence of others free riding. However, everyone feels the same way. Thus, when all members of the group free ride everyone is worse off, that is, the Prisoner's Dilemma solution results. (Hereafter, "Prisoner's Dilemma" will sometimes be abbreviated as P.D.)

Although it is somewhat less obvious, members of the management group are also subject to free-riding incentives. Managers may not wish to impose monitoring or other disciplinary measures on others. In addition, like all employees who are maximizers, they may wish to divert their energies to their own uses. Thus, managers may want to free ride on the same basis as anyone else, and if they all do so the outcome that results is the P.D. solution.

It follows directly from this that if free riding leads to low effort and also to a low application of management skills then clearly we have a P.D. solution for the enterprise as a whole. The reader should not presume that this is the solution that occurs in practice. The nature of actual solutions will be explained in Chapter 6.

Summary and Conclusions

One of the great difficulties that frequently face management is its inability to break away from an authority-subservience hierarchical system of operations. Such systems, and their related conventions, are sanctioned by too much past history to be readily altered. Furthermore, it is felt that breaking existing conventions probably risks worse outcomes. Nevertheless, it is only such a breaking away that can result in both management and employees being made very much better off. But this requires leaps of imagination on both sides toward a set of motivations that vaguely resemble a double golden-rule system. In other words, such a change in conventions would result in a scheme under which much more is offered by management and much more is expected from employees—one under which the elements of cooperation and mutuality are emphasized.

What has been presented here is a way of looking at the productivity problem. We see the problem as one in which low productivity exists because both management and employees have chosen wage–working condition packages (and their *related* productivity implications) which, while they are very much better than the "logical" Prisoner's Dilemma solution, are nevertheless much lower than they need be. Furthermore, given that effort discretion exists, we expect that up to some point there will be some gradual deterioration from average peer-group effort standards to somewhat lower averages—an entropylike effect. Countering the consequences of such behavior are the introduction, by management, of mechanical aids to human effort. However, the introduction of such aids does not alter the fact that existing effort levels are very much less than optimal.

There is no easy solution to the problem of low productivity since the Prisoner's Dilemma aspect of the problem is usually not seen. Each side is likely to be too much involved with its own position to be clearly aware that vastly different options are possible. Also when things go reasonably well for a time, the intense adherence to existing practices on both sides gives such practices a basic stability, but at the same time hides the possibilities for improvement.

Hindering the adoption of something that comes closer to the double golden-rule standard is the fact that basic aspects of Western culture emphasize competition and adversarial relationships. Therefore, in order to break the vicious circle of suspicion, reduced effort, and diminished gains for all parties which results from everyone doing only what is best for himself, and which makes up the problem of low productivity, a conscious and concerted effort must be made by everyone concerned to recognize the Prisoner's Dilemma aspects of the problem, and at least to contemplate a local "cultural change."

CHAPTER 6

Conventions, Coordination, and Decisions

For present purposes we will separate norms, conventions, and institutions in terms of generality. By a norm we mean some sort of a standard, without considering the extent to which others adhere to this standard, or whether different individuals expect others to adhere to it. By a convention we mean a regularity of behavior that has a high degree of adherence *locally,* and a high degree of expectation that others will adhere to it. Thus, some norms may not be conventions, although conventions include norms. By an institution we mean a *nonlocal* convention. For example, in some cities normal hours of work may be an institution, but the time of the morning coffee break at company Alpha may be merely a convention.

Many customs operate by convention or institution. Mealtimes are usually a matter of convention, which implies having one's meals at socially prescribed times. The two most ubiquitous institutions, which dominate our lives, are the calendar we observe and the language we speak.

In some respects conventional behavior is similar to habitual behavior. We define habits as repetitive forms of behavior *that do not involve others in an essential way.* Whether we put our right sock on before our left sock, or vice versa, does not depend on anybody else's behavior, nor is it of any consequence to anybody else. If we do it the same way every time we put on our socks, then it's a habit. It may be useful to view conventions as social habits. Thus, by way of contrast, shaking hands is a convention. If we shake hands, or fail to shake hands, when we meet someone, that does involve others in an essential way.

Shaking hands and putting one sock on before another are decisions. Behaving routinely in these ways would seem to most of us not to involve any decision at all. They are things we do so automatically that we don't even notice them. What we *are* likely to notice is the absence of a conventional practice. We are likely to notice what may appear as a refusal to shake hands. (This would frequently be viewed as a conscious decision.) Nevertheless, acting according to a habit or a convention are ways of making decisions. I will argue that in a great many cases following some convention is the decision procedure taken.

It would be simple to show by innumerable examples that a great many economic decisions are based on conventions. For example, many exchanges involve recognized weights and measures, which are conventions. Individuals following conventions as a means of making decisions represents a significant class of intrafirm behavior. Moreover, conventions can play a crucial role in other significant types of decision making where more than one decision maker is involved in an essential way in determining an outcome. In particular, conventions are related to (1) coordination problems, (2) strategic decision problems, and (3) possible conflict situations.

A very important aspect of the analysis to follow is that there is an important sense in which conventions serve as "solutions" (but not necessarily the only solutions) to those difficult situations involving latent Prisoner's Dilemma and latent conflict tendencies of the type described in Chapter 5. These types of problems are ubiquitous in a large group of decision-making situations, especially within organizations. Their analysis requires an understanding of the relation of conventions to various types of decision contexts.

In the sections that follow we will briefly trace the development of the modern theory of conventions, especially as it has been developed on the basis of the theory of games. Conventions are the basic components of institutions, but not all conventions are institutions. A separation of these two concepts, and their relation to each other, has to be worked out. We will try to show the connection between conventions and coordination problems, especially those situations that could be coordinated in a multitude of ways.

Here and in Chapter 7 we will show the role that conventions often play in latent Prisoner's Dilemma situations, and that the standard Prisoner's Dilemma outcome need not occur. We have already argued that many organizational problems, including the effort problem, are latent Prisoner's Dilemma situations. Conventions can provide superior solutions to such problems, but a solution so obtained will not necessarily be the optimal one.

While conventions may solve many internal problems, they do not necessarily solve all of them. An essential feature of the analysis will be to show how nonoptimal decisions, based on conventions, are superior to other options such as uncoordinated solutions, and to show how these ideas are related to basic intraorganizational decision problems.

The Theory of Conventions

We may view microeconomics as the study of a coordination problem. This is already evident in the writings of Adam Smith (1776, chapter 2), and more recently it has been clarified by Hayek (1945). The wide distribution of resources in any country and the various demands by people for the fruits of these resources immediately suggest that somehow these resources and demands all have to be coordinated in some manner. In other words, economic activity requires a *coordinated* allocation of resources so that it meets the demand for transformed resources (goods). For economists with neoclassical training, it seems natural to view the market as one of the greatest coordinating mechanisms ever discovered. This idea becomes most evident in the 1920s and 1930s debate on the organization of a socialist economy. In that debate it was socialists with strong neoclassical training who recommended what was essentially a market solution to the economy's organization problem (Lerner, 1934; Lange and Taylor, 1948).

Nowadays we would see at least one deficiency in the market solution: no connection is made between the ownership of the resources and the motivations that would result. In other words, the coordination problem is divorced from the motivation problem.

But another question that arises is whether markets are sufficient to solve all necessary coordination problems. Some reflection on the fact that activities internal to the firm are not handled by market coordinating mechanisms (because of transaction costs, or for other reasons) should suggest that some coordination mechanisms other than markets are necessary. This raises the question of whether something like conventions or institutions are required *inside* the firm to substitute for the sort of things that markets do outside the firm.

There is another sense in which markets may not be sufficient: the operation of markets themselves may depend on various complementary conventions and institutions. The suggestion here is that the market exists as a powerful coordinating mechanism, *but only when supported by other coordinating mechanisms of a nonmarket character*. Probably the simplest example is the system of weights and measures. Without a set of conventional weights and measures it would be extremely difficult to carry out exchanges. The sense of quantity of the commodities being exchanged must be understood and agreed upon if effective mutually desired exchanges are to take place. Furthermore the idea of price, and calculations that depend on price, require a conventional unit of the commodity. One can easily imagine how much more difficult it would be to carry out trade if such conventional units did not exist.

The current work on conventions, coordination, and institutions may be said to begin with some brief remarks contained in von Neumann and Morgenstern's theory of games. In their book they speak of games having multiple solutions, and of the particular solution chosen being determined by "standards of behavior" (von Neumann and Morgenstern, 1947, p. 44). This remark is much better understood now than it was at the time it was written.

Much of the recent work emanates from Thomas Schelling's concern with coordination games. In his words,

> The coordination game probably lies behind the stability of institutions and traditions and perhaps the phenomenon of leadership itself. Among the possible sets of rules that might govern a conflict, tradition points to the particular set that everyone can expect everyone else to be conscious of as a conspicuous candidate for adoption; it wins by default over those that cannot readily be identified by tacit consent. The force of many rules of etiquette and social restraint, including some (like the rule against ending a sentence with a preposition) that have been divested of their relevance or authority, seems to depend on their having become "solutions" to a coordination game; everyone expects everyone else to expect observance, so that nonobservance carries the pain of conspicuousness. (Schelling, 1960, p. 91)

While the essentials are contained in Schelling's remarks, it was the philosopher David Lewis (1969) who worked out some of the details and developed a formalization of the concept of convention. Note that we refer to *a* formalization rather than *the* formalization, since more than one formalization is possible.

A significant distinction that Lewis makes is between unique and nonunique solutions to coordination problems. If it is obvious that there is only one way of coordinating the activities of two individuals, then there is not much of a problem. There is no need for a "convention." But where more than one solution exists, a choice has to be made between "solutions." This becomes evident when we consider the problem as to whether automobiles should be driven on the left or the right side of the road. Clearly, everyone driving on the right or everyone driving on the left are equilibrium solutions. But a choice has to be made between left or right for *all* drivers. Hence there is the need for a "convention." It is critically important that all people agree to drive on the right or on the left; however, it is not very important whether it is the right or the left.

Consider the payoff matrix in table 6.1. The payoff in blocks I and IV is in two parts. The first part represents the intrinsic value of choosing the same side of the road, and the second part represents obtaining the approval, or avoiding the disapproval, of other individuals. If both A and B choose to drive on the right they gain 20 units of utility each. The same is true if both drive on the left. In both cases they each gain from others another 5 units for "good citizenship." They avoid the disapproval of others by both driving on the same side. This helps us see the point that conventions will frequently be followed even if in some particular instance it does not pay to do so. Thus, some individuals will not go the wrong way up a one-way street if a bystander is observing them, even though they are certain that there are no other cars going in the opposite direction, because they would lose utility from a bystander's disapproval. In some cases the convention will have become internalized into an ethic, and the individual will not go the wrong way on a one-way street even if no one else is there.

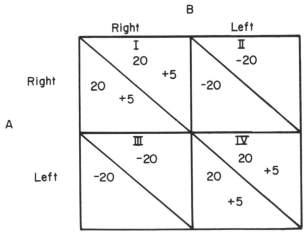

TABLE 6.1

Another example is jaywalking. In cities where antijaywalking ordinances are strongly enforced, city residents will not jaywalk when no one else is around, although strangers will frequently do so.

In table 6.2 we consider another example: should a group of people choose a queuing convention while waiting for a bus? As the utilities are indicated, it makes sense for individuals to choose a queue rather than always attempting to reach the bus or counter without one. The utilities in box I are listed with a plus sign between them. The first number indicates the intrinsic utility attributed to queuing. The second number indicates that each receives 5 utils from the approval, or lack of disapproval, of others. This implies that even in situations where queuing does not make sense, and hence the intrinsic value of queuing (10 utils in box I) drops to zero, the individual may still abide by the convention if others are around. This suggests that conventions may persist after their intrinsic usefulness disappears. In the table it is also assumed that an individual suffers a utility loss from group disapproval if he breaks the queue while others do not. Some important characteristics of this example will be taken up later.

Another thing to keep in mind about conventions is that in some cases the convention is followed even though unpleasant aspects are associated with it. Consider the case of choosing a place to meet. Suppose A does not like Joe's Bar but he knows that B frequents Joe's Bar. Rather than not meet with B at all, A goes to Joe's Bar. It is even

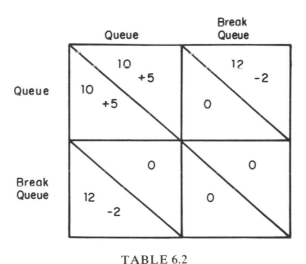

TABLE 6.2

possible that members of a group may meet in a place that a majority
of them in fact do not like.

Conventions as a Formalism

To Lewis (1969) a convention is the choice of an equilibrium solution
when there are a multiplicity of such solutions. We may best see what
is involved if we consider Lewis' "rough" definition: "A regularity R
in the behavior of members of a population P when they are agents in
a recurrent situation S is a *convention* if and only if, in any instance
of S among members of P, (1) everyone conforms to R; (2) everyone
expects everyone else to conform to R; (3) everyone prefers to conform
to R on condition that the others do, since S is a coordination problem
and uniform conformity to R is a coordination equilibrium in S." (p.
42) Note that Lewis retains the idea that the equilibrium solutions are
in fact the consequences of maximizing behavior.

Edna Ullman-Margalit's work (1977) is of interest since she explicitly
introduces the concept of "social norms" as solutions to coordination
problems and Prisoner's Dilemma problems.[1]

It is important to note that the theory of conventions and institutions
to be presented is concerned only with the role of *existing* conventions
and does not include a theory as to how conventions are, in fact, developed or determined. How conventions get started and how they are
finally determined is a much more complex problem, beyond the scope
of this book. But the evolution of conventions will be considered briefly.

The variety of possibilities as to how a convention gets started is
numerous indeed. The initial choice may be purely accidental; or it
may depend on the choice of some strong personality; or some historical
incident may determine the choice; or some individuals or groups may
attempt to impose rules on the behavior of others, which eventually
become conventions. Of course, this is not an exhaustive list. It is likely
that in most cases the emulation of the behavior of some people by
others will be the most important, or one of the most important forces
involved.

Let us speculate a bit further on the possible development of conventions. We usually become aware of a convention when it is fully
functioning and give little thought to its origins. As a result the origins

1. "Social norms" appears to be European usage for what in the United States are
referred to as conventions.

get lost. Since there are no recorded histories of how most conventions got started, all we can do is try to imagine certain possibilities, and to present some conjectures. We develop such conjectures only for illustrative purposes.)

Consider the custom of shaking hands with the right hand as a form of greeting. This custom undoubtedly arose in Europe. It may have started, as is frequently conjectured, when weapons were held in the right hand. Thus, offering an empty right hand indicated peaceful intent. Shaking hands thus became an instance of mutual peaceful intent. Perhaps someone observed some accidental instances of handshaking and it was gradually copied and spread. This would seem to fit usage within Semitic languages such as Arabic and Hebrew in which the word for peace is the common greeting.

Hours of work in an urban setting are usually subject to a general convention. They usually do not follow agricultural working hours which are determined by the hours of light and dark, time of year, and climatic conditions. Urban hours are more regular, frequently the same in a given area in both winter and summer. Hence it is possible such hours were determined when some powerful individual set certain hours for his employees and these were followed by others. One can envision a period when different establishments initially adopted different hours, but that eventually some degree of uniformity was established as weaker firms copied stronger enterprises.

Copying the conventions of others is probably a very common form of establishing a convention. This is clear in the case of written languages. Perhaps the clearest case is that of the Japanese copying the Chinese written language system. As it turned out, given that Japanese and Chinese have very different language structures, the Japanese had to introduce some additional symbols for their own grammatical purposes. It is noteworthy that at some point the Japanese developed a syllabary of fifty symbols which was easy to learn and functioned very well as a means of written communication. In fact one of the great Japanese classics, *The Tale of Genji,* was written in this syllabary (Waley, 1935). Despite this the convention of using Chinese characters as the basic system of Japanese writing continues to this day.

The clearest cases in which we can trace the beginnings of a convention are connected with historical incidents that established some legal convention. The meeting of King John of England with his barons at Runnymede in 1215 and the contract that was drawn up between them, the Magna Carta, established due process of law from which the principle of habeas corpus, among other things, has been derived. Habeas corpus became part of the British legal tradition and part of the legal systems (the Common Law) wherever the British Empire held sway.

There are probably many cases where the founder of an enterprise initially establishes certain internal procedural rules. These rules become the conventions of the enterprise and frequently continue in operation long after the founder ceases to have any connection with the company.

Determining when to use a convention may require a fairly subtle interpretation of the circumstances involved. Conventions are frequently quite complex in their usage. In such cases, particular historical instances will set precedents for similar situations that occur later, determining when the convention is applicable and when it is not, under what may appear to be almost the same circumstances.

Clearly, a particular history is usually the major factor in the determination and development of a convention. Furthermore, the particulars of the historical circumstances are likely to be significant in determining various aspects of the convention in question. Thus, the early period in the life of an organization may turn out to be extremely important in determining how efficient its operations are, since it is in the early period that some critical procedures will be established.

What is of special interest, in my view, is the relationship between the development of a "new" convention and the existing set of norms, conventions, and institutions within the culture. What is missing is the simple and obvious conjecture that organizations will frequently copy conventions already in practice elsewhere.

The basic ideas can be most readily discussed in terms of specific examples. A great many conventions deal with problems of time. The times associated with work, meals, holidays, and so forth, are frequently conventions and sometimes institutions. Consider the question of a starting time of work. Since time is infinitely divisible, there are infinitely many possibilities. For illustrative purposes, consider only half-hour divisions from 6:30 to 9:00 in the morning. There are two general options. One is for each individual to make a separate contract with the firm. The other is to simply accept a starting-time convention.

In the tables that follow we consider along the NW to SE diagonal all of the times in which the individual's start-up time is coordinated with everyone else's. We assume that the payoff to coordinated time is very much greater than the payoff to uncoordinated time. In table 6.3a the coordinated payoffs are all equally good; in table 6.3b they

O

A \ O	6:30	7:00	7:30	8:00	8:30	9:00
6:30	10 / 10	3 / 3	2 / 2	1 / 1	1 / 1	1 / 1
7:00	3 / 3	10 / 10	3 / 3	2 / 2	1 / 1	1 /
7:30	2 / 2	3 / 3	10 / 10	3 / 3	2 / 2	1 / 1
8:00	1 / 1	2 / 2	3 / 3	10 / 10	3 / 3	2 / 2
8:30	1 / 1	1 / 1	2 / 2	3 / 3	10 / 10	3 / 3
9:00	1 / 1	1 / 1	1 / 1	2 / 2	3 / 3	10 / 10

(A = Person A, O = Others)

TABLE 6.3A

are all different, but all of the coordinated values are much superior to the uncoordinated ones. (For the time being, we will discuss only table 6.3a.) A convention is desirable since there are so many means of arranging hours of work. In this case there are six solutions where A and O start work at the same time. Coordination requires that one out of the six be chosen.

The fact that a coordinated solution may have greater value than an uncoordinated one is the basis for the economic value of a convention or institution. If a convention is superior for all participants, it is likely to be maintained. If it is optimal for all participants, it is likely to be self-enforcing by maximizing individuals. Clearly, having an institution may be superior to not having one, and the relative superiority may be significant. Here we are not concerned with the question as to how the convention is chosen. What is important is that it exists. Since a great many conventions already exist at any one time, it is important to consider the value of existing conventions or institutions.

The ubiquitous example of a convention is a language. There are many possible combinations of sounds and meanings. Many combinations are equally good. What is necessary is that the members of a group agree on the relation between sounds and meanings. In other words, the same sound/meaning connections have to be coordinated among members of the group. The group has to have at least one common language, and this is basically a coordination problem.

Now, we can use the example of language to summarize many of the ideas expressed so far. (1) First, a coordination problem exists. (2) More than one coordination solution is possible. This is obvious in the case of languages, since there are many languages that succeed as vehicles for communication, although not all are equally well suited for all purposes. (3) A clear-cut optimum solution may or may not be chosen. (4) Coordination may be achieved by ways other than by a convention. For instance, it may be achieved by someone giving directions to others so that they behave in a coordinated manner. However, conventions are an important way of achieving coordination. (5) Finally, the convention need not be completely universal in order to work.

A convention is a fairly complicated entity. Perhaps the main characteristic is mutual perception by all of those subject to the convention of (1) the applicable contexts within which the convention can be followed, (2) agreed-upon variations of the applicable contexts, (3) the appropriate behavior that indicates that the person is following the convention, (4) agreed-upon variations of the convention, and (5) a sufficiently high degree of adherence so that others believe the convention is being followed.

A convention is basically an agreed-upon regularity of behavior appropriate within a certain set of contexts. It is quite immaterial how this agreement has been achieved. All that matters is that as a result of history such agreement exists. Similarly, in the course of history the appropriate contexts that call forth the conventional behavior will also be agreed upon. Of course, many conventions may be in a state of flux. The degree of adherence may be changing, or variations in behavior or contexts may be changing. Nevertheless, at any one time the convention may be seen to exist. The case emphasized here is the one in which the contexts are changed but the appropriate convention remains the same.

We will make no attempt to determine the appropriate degree of adherence to a convention. Whether it is adhered to in 99 percent of instances, or in 95 percent, does not make any difference as far as the principle is concerned. What matters is that behavior for the adhering group continues to be fairly automatic. It is conceivable that below some critical value of adherence, behavior becomes strategic. At that point the value of the "convention" ceases. What we need to maintain a convention is simply a high enough value of adherence so that all those who adhere do not question whether or not they should do so.

How do conventions change? As a general rule they are very stable and there is no formula for changing them. Because they are so stable it usually takes new and unusual circumstances (a shock to the system) to make a change. Under what are deemed as "revolutionary" circumstances, *some* conventions may be changed. For example, in his attempt to modernize Turkey, Kemal Ataturk introduced the Roman alphabet for use in written Turkish. On the other hand, the French revolutionaries, after 1789, attempted to introduce a ten-day week, but this never succeeded.

Some conventions, especially complicated ones, appear to be flexible at the *margins,* but others are not. Thus languages change at the edges over decades but the core of a language remains the same over many centuries. Some conventions which have been codified as part of an established legal system may be changed by changes in the appropriate law, but others cannot be so readily changed. Furthermore, it is frequently difficult to know how to organize a change even if it would be useful to do so. For example, George Bernard Shaw's will left a reward for the simplification and standardization of English spelling, but no one has been able to achieve such a change, and very few have tried. People *do* want a high degree of behavioral stability, especially on the part of others. As a result conventions are valued almost unconsciously for what they are. It is very useful to know "how things are done around here," and to be able to follow "established procedures." Apart from a crisis or shock, where everyone has some discretionary power in determining his behavior, a convention is likely to be very difficult to change.

Does a Convention Have to Be Optimal?

Let us consider some other possibilities. Does a convention have to be optimal? Here it may be useful to recall the discussion on decisions in Chapters 2 and 3, and to connect conventions and decisions. Because following conventions is a type of noncalculated decision procedure it is likely that many conventional behaviors are suboptimal. Many conventions are probably established without careful calculation of their optimality. Furthermore, some of the considerations that enter into the "creation" of a convention are noneconomic. Once established, conventions have an inertial tendency to persist that discourages individual adaptations to changing circumstances, which again makes suboptimality likely.

Consider the situation in table 6.3b. Not all of the coordinated choices (on the diagonal) are optimal. Keep in mind a basic assumption: there is considerable Pareto superiority of the nonoptimal coordinated option over *any* uncoordinated option. If a nonoptimal convention already exists, then there would seem to be no reason for individuals not to adhere to it. If an individual does not adhere, then of course he is clearly worse off since the optimal convention is not really an option. Keep in mind that an individual cannot choose between one convention and another possible convention. Only one convention exists. Thus the only choice is between the existing convention and an uncoordinated option.

Do nonoptimal conventions have the necessary properties of a convention? By going through the set of properties it becomes readily apparent that this is indeed the case. Clearly, we can visualize a regularity of behavior in response to perceived repeatable contexts as existing without having to be optimal. Similarly, there may be mutual agreement

O

		6:30	7:00	7:30	8:00	8:30	9:00
	6:30	7 / 7	3 / 3	2 / 2	1 / 1	1 / 1	1 / 1
	7:00	3 / 3	8 / 8	3 / 3	2 / 2	1 / 1	1 / 1
A	7:30	2 / 2	3 / 3	9 / 9	3 / 3	2 / 2	1 / 1
	8:00	1 / 1	2 / 2	3 / 3	10 / 10	3 / 3	2 / 2
	8:30	1 / 1	1 / 1	2 / 2	3 / 3	9 / 9	3 / 3
	9:00	1 / 1	1 / 1	1 / 1	2 / 2	3 / 3	8 / 8

(A = Person A, O = Others)

TABLE 6.3B

on the variations of these regularities, and mutual recognition of the signaling contexts without the resulting behavior being optimal. In addition, there may exist a high degree of adherence to the convention. Thus, in general a convention may exist, having the necessary properties, without anyone having any idea whether it is or is not optimal.

Another question is whether a nonoptimal convention will be stable. Here, the concept of inert areas is useful. The basic idea is that there exists a set of bounds, say, upper and lower bounds, within which any decision maker will follow the convention. A shock or crisis is necessary to destabilize the convention or institution. This clearly describes a common type of inertial behavior.

A suboptimal convention may be stable simply because it may not pay anyone to try to arrange a shift to an optimal convention. The gain for any individual in shifting is likely to be less than the cost of attempting to persuade everyone to move away from the current convention and adopt a new one. Hence, existing nonoptimal conventions can persist.

Assume for a moment that an alternative, superior convention exists and that its nature is known to all adherents to the suboptimal convention. If we can show that in this case continued adherence to the suboptimal convention is a possibility, then surely it would also be a possibility in weaker cases. The main point is that no individual will necessarily move to the superior option, since it is not a superior option unless everyone else also moves. There is no incentive for anyone moving unless everyone else moves simultaneously. But others will not move unless each one can be persuaded that everyone else will move simultaneously. As long as people feel that the difficulties of persuading others are relatively great, there is reason for individuals to believe that others will not move. Hence, one can readily imagine situations in which the convention in place, although inferior to some alternative, is nevertheless the convention that persists.

Applying the theory of inert areas, it is possible for everyone to be in his inert area with respect to the inferior convention. The larger the group, the larger the cost (effort, psychological, and financial) of getting everyone to change. It may not pay for anyone to risk that cost because there is always the chance that not everybody would be persuaded, and hence no one would move. In addition, various uncertainties are apt to increase the degree of stability. For example, people may believe that it is *extremely* difficult to persuade others to move, even when it may only be *somewhat* difficult to do so. Furthermore, people may have fears that whatever new convention arises will make them worse off than the convention they know. In other words, the process of generating change, without being certain of the end point, may generate fears that favor the status quo. Note that we are not arguing that all nonoptimal conventions are stable, but only that it is possible and likely that many will be.

Another interesting case is one in which no clear-cut optimal solution exists. Thus, it is possible that as we move from one coordinated option to another, some are made better off and others are made worse off. Consider the case where some people are "naturally" early risers and others are late risers. Setting the starting time early benefits the early risers, but is against the interests of the late risers, and vice versa. Nevertheless, a coordinated option so that everyone comes to work simultaneously may be superior to any uncoordinated option. Here the distinction between a convention and an institution may be significant. If the convention exists for each firm separately, then some firms may choose early hours that appeal to early risers, while others choose late hours. There is a choice since these conventions are restricted to individual firms. However, if the hours are an institution, say, the same hours for an entire city, the hours that are best for some will not be best for others. Still, even though a convention, in this instance, may be superior to an institution, both may be superior to an uncoordinated option.

One of the interesting properties of conventions and institutions is that they are frequently self-enforcing. Thus, a convention may not require much monitoring, whereas the same rule may require considerable monitoring when imposed by an authority. A question worth considering is whether sanctions are necessary for a convention to be self-enforcing. According to Schotter, following Lewis, ordinary coordination conventions are by themselves self-enforcing without sanctions, but Prisoner's Dilemma conventions do require sanctions (Schotter, 1981). Consider a coordination convention. If the convention is, as defined by Lewis, one that has many *optimal* solutions, then an argument could be made that sanctions are not necessary. If everyone gains by the convention, and if the convention is indeed optimal, then there would seem to be no need for sanctions. However, this would not necessarily imply that sanctions do not exist. One possibility is that those involved in adherence to the convention may not know that everyone gains. Furthermore, a convention may hold for a variety of circumstances, and under some circumstances some individuals may wish to be free riders. Thus, even though the convention is to everyone's benefit on some sort of an average basis, or in the "long run," there may nevertheless be particular instances where some would not adhere to the convention. This may call forth sanctions from others.

The argument in the Prisoner's Dilemma case is fairly straightforward. If sanctions are not applied, then everyone involved would have an incentive not to abide by the convention, and as a consequence sanctions would be necessary in order to enforce the convention. Consider the case in which there is a convention for stores that have certain closing hours. Some shopkeepers may gain by keeping their stores open slightly later. Unless other shopkeepers are able to impose sanctions the convention may not be maintained. This is a Prisoner's Dilemma situation in the sense that if the convention and related sanctions did not exist, everyone would keep open all the time. The demand for their products might nevertheless be constant, and as a consequence, shopkeepers would simply be working longer hours without any additional reward.

Summary and Conclusions

Conventions are social habits, or socially agreed-upon regularities of behavior in certain contexts. Conventions are characterized by mutual perception of (1) the applicable contexts, (2) variations of applicable contexts, (3) appropriate signals for conventional behavior, (4) permitted variations of the convention, and (5) a sufficiently high degree of adherence.

For our purposes, conventions should be seen as decision procedures. Furthermore, they are procedures that frequently turn out to be suboptimal solutions. Even though suboptimal, they are usually superior to uncoordinated solutions.

Conventions may provide solutions in situations where markets do not exist—especially in intrafirm group decisions such as (1) multiple-solution coordination problems, (2) strategic decisions (Prisoner's Dilemma situations), and (3) latent conflict situations (such as those described in Chapter 5).

Coordination conventions may be self-enforcing because of the superiority of the utilities obtained compared to those of uncoordinated solutions. The same solution imposed by an authority might require considerable enforcing. Even so, in some situations sanctions might arise in support of a coordination convention. Prisoner's Dilemma situations require sanctions to enforce a convention because each individual sees gains from acting independently, which can break down the convention.

Conventions need not be the only solution available, nor does a convention need to be universally adhered to in order to function effectively. Conventional behavior may persist even when intrinsically suboptimal for the individual because of utility gains from approval of others (or utility losses from disapproval). Conventions which are suboptimal overall for the group may persist because they are clearly superior to uncoordinated solutions, and/or because of the high cost and uncertainty associated with moving to a different convention. Like other inert behaviors, it may require a shock or crisis to motivate people to change their conventions.

CHAPTER 7

Conventions as a Solution to the Intrafirm Prisoner's Dilemma Problem

Since the possibility of suboptimal outcomes for intrafirm production problems is one of our major concerns, let us consider how such outcomes may arise. To do so it will help to restate the Prisoner's Dilemma interpretation of the intrafirm production problem.

Intrafirm interactions have both cooperative and competitive (or adversarial) aspects. The existence of discretionary effort, and wages and working conditions, controlled by a number of decision makers separately and simultaneously, means that no one controls all the variables. Hence the decision problem is a game theoretic one. The basic argument is that there are (1) conflicting interests between *representative* individuals in different hierarchically ordered groups, and (2) simultaneous, free-rider effort options for peer-group members. Both incentives tend toward a *latent* Prisoner's Dilemma (P.D.) solution. However, we will see in this chapter that the P.D. outcome is avoided by the existence of effort conventions and working-condition conventions, which are usually suboptimal.

The particular discretionary areas available to economic actors that we focus on here are the *pace* and *quality* of effort of employees, and the wages and working conditions provided by management. We assume that within a given range employees can vary effort, and management can vary wages and working conditions.

With the aid of figure 7.1, consider adversarial behavior between two levels in a hierarchy, say employees and managers. Employees have some degree of effort discretion *(E)* while managers have discretion with respect to wages and working conditions *(W)*.[1] Employees' effort

---

1. This postulate is relaxed later. Wages can be determined by negotiation and the essence of the analysis can still be retained.

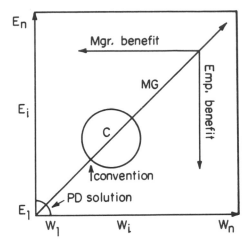

FIGURE 7.1

options are ordered as follows: $E_1 < E_2 < \ldots < E_n$; that is, E_n is the greatest effort level. Managers have wage and working condition options whose costs and value to employees are as follows: $W_1 < W_2 < \ldots < W_n$. The less W costs for any effort level, the higher the profits. Now, for any given effort level, the firm (managers) would want to move toward W_1, which involves the lowest cost per employee. The representative employee usually has the incentive to put forth more effort toward his personal interests and less in the firm's interest (up to a point, say the point E_1). For any given level of W, employees want to move toward E_1. Thus, the incentives in the system lead to a latent Prisoner's Dilemma result if both sides attempt to operate as individual "maximizers," that is, to do as well as they can irrespective of what the other side does.

Simultaneously, *within* each hierarchical group there are free-rider incentives; that is, every employee may wish to work as little as possible even though he may desire that others work reasonably effectively so that the enterprise and his job continue. These free-rider incentives exist at every level. Even if some exceptionally wise management eliminated the adversarial feelings of employees toward management, employees' free-rider options would still provide incentives toward a latent P.D. outcome.

However, the latent P.D. outcome does not normally occur. Usually, conventions exist that determine the effort level and solve not only the adversarial problem between two *groups,* but simultaneously solve the free-rider incentive problem of individual members of each group. The latter will certainly turn out to be the case if managers accept the effort convention and pay accordingly, that is, according to a wage-and-working-condition package that *roughly* approximates the value of effort, on average. (More on this later.) In figure 7.1, C is the effort convention. The circle suggests the inert area bounds around the convention. As illustrated, the effort convention is superior to the latent P.D. outcome but not as good as the optimal outcome $W_n E_n$. Points along a mutual gain line *MG* show Pareto improvements as one moves in the direction of the arrow.

Since higher points on *MG* involve more effort, more productivity, and hence a higher gross revenue to the firm, it is possible to have a distribution that would both benefit employees through higher wages and yield higher profits. There are many other "diagonals" roughly parallel to *MG* that would also involve Pareto-improvement loci. Note that once the effort convention exists, only the convention is observable and management is not necessarily aware of the latent P.D. problem.

The emphasis here is on conventions that "solve" Prisoner's Dilemma problems because the employment relation is seen as intrinsically involving such a latent conflict. An important distinction has to be made between latent and open conflicts. We will see presently that effort conventions and working-condition conventions allow people to *avoid* the conflict inherent in the underlying Prisoner's Dilemma situation.

There are also likely to be conventions that provide people with procedures for solving conflicts once one erupts into the open. For instance, in some industrial relations situations there may be the convention of appealing to an arbitrator once a strike begins or appears likely to begin. In various athletic games there is usually an appeal to a referee if there are conflicts about the rules, and in some instances there may be an appeal to a higher authority (an umpire) if there is disagreement with the referee. Nonetheless, in normal economic situations conflict-avoidance conventions are likely to be more prevalent than conflict-resolving conventions in day-to-day behavior.

The Effort Convention

We shall now consider, separately, the establishment of an effort convention, and the establishment of wage-and-working-condition conventions. Of course, these processes do not take place in any particular sequence; they are conventions that exist simultaneously. But for expository purposes it is best to examine them separately. To begin with, assume that the effort convention is determined entirely on an intrafirm basis; that is, it is determined on the basis of considerations and events that occur entirely inside the firm. For the time being, assume that W (the wage-and-working-condition convention) is determined by *inter*firm considerations such as competition and emulation. Later we shall consider interactions between E and W.

Now, assume that some degree of effort discretion exists for all employees. The employee's decision is to determine at what point in the discretionary range his or her effort level will lie. This assumption about the existence of discretion is in no way arbitrary. In general it seems to fit what goes on in reality. In almost all cases it is impossible to define the effort aspect of the contract completely and explicitly. Hence, discretion will exist for those who carry out effort. In many cases some discretion will be exercised by employees, even if management did not intend this to happen. Some discretion is bound to exist because of knowledge differences. There is little point in a superior trying to learn all aspects of every subordinate's job. The subordinate may have detailed information that enables him to tailor the job in a much better way than the superior could possibly do. This is especially true where high levels of professional knowledge are involved. In any event, discretion is a significant element in our analysis.

Now let us turn to the components or dimensions of effort. The simplest approach is to look upon effort as being made up of three interrelated components: the activity, its pace, and its quality.[2] In actually carrying out effort these are all part of the same process. What a person does includes the nature of the activity (or activities), and simultaneously the pace at which the activity is carried out, as well as its quality level. The activity as such is determined by the person's interpretation of his job. However, both pace and quality are components that are independently variable; the person can carry out an activity at various pace levels—slow, intermediate, or fast. Similarly, it is possible to visualize the activity being carried out at low, intermediate, or high quality levels. Since pace is probably the easier component to measure, we shall carry on our discussion as if our metric is pace, or in some sense

2. For some purposes it may be useful to break down "the activity" in a job interpretation into a *set of activities*. In that case the *sequence* of the component activities can become an important characteristic in addition to pace and quality. However, for our purposes the simpler set of components described in the text is sufficient.

proportional to pace, and assume that the activity and its quality level are given. Later we will consider variations in the quality of the activity and the nature of the activity separately. The complexity of the metric of effort does not affect the argument.

We shall examine the evolution and maintenance of an effort convention first from an individual's viewpoint, and then from a group viewpoint. Three questions come to mind: (1) How does the convention get started? (2) Once started, how does it "congeal" to become a convention? and (3) Once it is a convention, how does it persist over time? The last is the easiest, hence we shall start with that.

Suppose an effort convention exists in a department of an enterprise in which quite a few individuals work (say, more than twenty). Over time some people leave the department and others enter; that is, replacements are hired for those who leave or retire. How does the new entrant know what to do? Various possibilities come to mind. To start with we assume that others in the department are doing the same or similar jobs. In part a new entrant may be told what to do by someone in authority, or he may inquire from others similarly placed, or he may observe what others are doing and try to emulate them. Any one of these methods, or some combination, will lead to experimentation with various interpretations of his job. These experiments will simultaneously involve the activity, its pace, and its quality.

By watching others he may determine what he notices is an acceptable pace. Two types of interactions with others are likely to refine his effort. He may receive approval or disapproval about the way he is doing things from peers and make adjustments accordingly. Some peers may observe that he is working too slowly and as a result he will pick up his pace, or if it is hinted that he is working too fast then he will slacken it. In addition he may receive approval or disapproval from his superior and adjust accordingly. In the unusual case in which he receives conflicting signals from peers and superiors he may have to find a solution to the uncomfortable task of choosing whom to please. If the peer group is relatively large, it is likely that the peers will win.

In any event, through these various means he will learn what to do so that, on average, he handles his job in approximately the same fashion as his predecessor did. One can readily see in such a situation that there will frequently be strong pressures for conformity. The greater the pressure for conformity, the greater the chance that the convention will be strictly transmitted, and the effort of the entrant will be close to that of the person he has replaced.

How is an effort convention likely to start? This is a much more arbitrary process than the transmission process and will probably involve a greater degree of experimentation. Once again there are a number of possibilities. The originator may be the first employee in the department who interprets in some way what he thinks his boss wants him to do. He then transmits this interpretation to the second employee, and to the third, and so on. Or, alternatively, the originator may drop his teaching role and others will take it up as additional employees are added to the group. Or someone on a higher level may suggest a way of carrying out the activity which one or more employees attempt to interpret and follow. There will frequently be a period of trial and error in determining how something should be done, but gradually the effort aspects of the job become stabilized and people cease their attempts to work out or influence new interpretations.

The most difficult question to answer is how new interpretations congeal within a group so that they turn into a convention. Assuming that some initial interpretation exists, a competing interpretation may develop within a peer group and there may be some jockeying for position as to which interpretation will prevail. But it is likely that at some point people will see that there is some advantage to being close to some standard level of performance.

In addition, there is an accountability motive. Any person who feels he may have to account for his performance will have a clear incentive to try to do as much work as the average in order to avoid being singled out for sanctions by his superiors. In some cases employees may work out a compromise between opposing pressures from superiors and peers. Peers may press for a lower pace level while superiors press in the opposite direction, but both will accept a peer-group standard that turns out to be a compromise between the two.

The accountability argument is not the only reason to expect a potential convention to congeal. Other possibilities come to mind. To start with, there is no reason for people in general to want to behave differently with respect to what are perceived to be "normal" work activities. Indeed, casual observation indicates that most people want to behave similarly to others under most circumstances; it is safer to do so if accountability is a concern. In addition, most people do not wish to appear to "stick out" in their behavior. Frequently there are sanctions against those who do stick out in various ways, and hence this will operate as a deterrent. Sameness and ordinary working behavior challenge neither peers nor superiors. Hence, people are likely to be reluctant to present such implicit challenges without a good reason to do so. Thus we should expect a movement toward gradual sameness in working behavior—this is what we mean by the convention congealing. The degree of pressure toward behaving similarly to others is likely to depend both on the number of other individuals involved and on the time duration in the situation. The greater the number of peers in the working group, the greater the chance that each additional individual will behave similarly. This would seem to follow from the notion that the greater the number of peers the greater the penalty of conspicuousness. In addition, the longer a latent convention appears to go unchallenged, the more habitual and entrenched this type of behavior will appear to be, and the more conspicuous any deviations will seem. Thus, with enough time and accretions to the group the convention gradually congeals so that at some point a reasonable and consistent answer can be given to the question, "How is this done around here?" Once such an answer exists we have an effort convention.

It may help to get at the essence of the effort convention if we formalize the relations, to some degree, in order to show the connection between individual adherence to the effort convention and group behavior. Recall that there are two aspects to conventions: (1) a convention is a regularity of behavior out of a set that includes two or more possibilities, but only one such regularity can exist at any one time; and, (2) sanctions supporting a convention are frequently applied when deviant behavior goes beyond certain bounds. It is assumed that the *effort* convention is based on history, sanctions, and the observation of the average effort norm set by others. Thus each person will choose an effort level depending on what he learns about the way things have been done or are being done, signs of approval or disapproval (especially from peers), and his estimate of the observed effort norm.

Once a convention exists people do not normally reappraise it; rather behavior becomes part of a stimulus-response mechanism. When the context (the stimulus) for the use of a convention arises, people employ the convention automatically. Thus, people who know many languages will normally speak in the language of the community once they determine that it is appropriate for the context.

In the same spirit we can think of an effort convention as determined by a peer-group standard. Entrants to the firm observe the average effort level, and set their own effort approximately at, or fairly close to, the observed average. If the observed level were higher, many would simply shift their own level upward, and similarly if it were somewhat

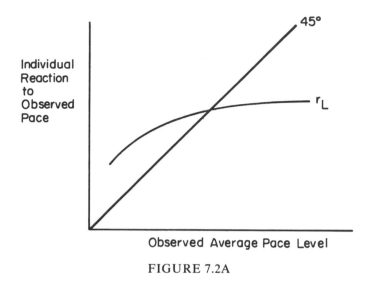

FIGURE 7.2A

lower. The individual reaction curve r_L for person L is shown in figure 7.2a. We can add all the individual reactions, for every observed pace level, and divide by the number of individuals in order to obtain an average reaction function.

An equilibrium effort level is established (point C in figure 7.2b) when

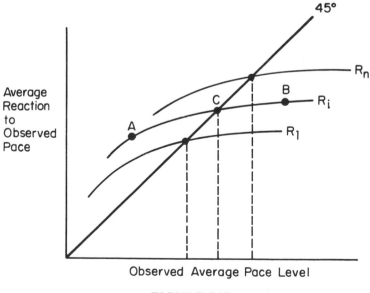

FIGURE 7.2B

people react to the observed average level of effort by choosing the observed level, that is, when there is no incentive to move away from the observed level to a higher or lower effort level. At points *A* and *B* in figure 7.2b we can see two cases of disequilibrium. At point *A*, person *L* will react to the observed level by choosing a higher effort level; at *B*, person *L* will react by choosing a lower effort level.

Figure 7.2b illustrates the general notion. The abscissa indicates alternative average pace levels. The ordinate indicates the average of individual reactions to each alternative. The reaction curve indicates the average reaction of individuals to various observed rates and is denoted by the letter R_i. Now, there is a large set of possible reactions to a given observed rate; and hence, each reaction curve depends on some initial (or historical) response to an observed rate, so that the reaction curves range from R_1 to R_n. It is especially important to note that different histories yield different reaction curves. The 45-degree line indicates the set of possible equilibria between observed rates and reactions to them. The distance between R_1 and R_n on the 45-degree line indicates all the possible equilibrium effort levels. Clearly, if the convention is R_1, it need not be an optimal solution, but once chosen it will continue to be the solution. In the illustration we chose "pace" to signify effort. However, other components of effort, such as the quality levels of the activities carried out are implicit in the example. The main point is that individual reactions to the observed *components* of effort determine the equilibrium effort *convention*.

An effort convention need not depend only on a peer-group standard. It is also possible that some type of work ethic, or the Japanese consensus system, could create conventions that are superior to some, or all possible, peer-group standards. Thus, there may exist a wide range of alternative latent solutions along the cooperative diagonal (see figure 7.1).

Many effort conventions do not have to be adhered to in every detail—they can be strict or loose. An example of a strict convention is driving on the left or right side of the street. We cannot choose to drive up the middle. When a loose convention is operating, people attempt only to follow the convention approximately, rather than exactly in the same manner on each occasion. The idea of such loose conventions may be captured in our graphical interpretation by the use of a fat reaction curve (see figure 7.2c). Here there is an equilibrium range of values, rather than a specific value, that fits our interpretation of a loose convention (shown by the area *AB* in the figure).

It is worth noting that an effort convention within the production

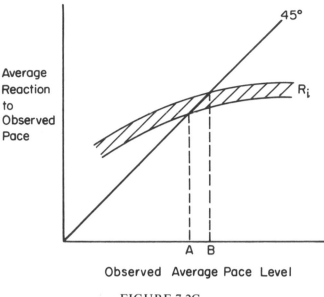

FIGURE 7.2C

setup may be viewed as playing the role that price does in competitive markets. The price becomes a *parameter* under competition that solves a coordination problem. Similarly, the convention serves as a parameter with respect to the coordination of effort since it permits different individuals to "rally around" the convention and to use it as a basis for their individual effort decisions. In other words, conventions solve game theoretic problems by "parameterizing" the environment for individual decision makers.

Working Conditions and Wages

We now treat working conditions in the same manner that we treated effort. The main aim is to show that the analysis of working conditions is essentially symmetrical to the analysis of the effort convention. However, a greater number and variety of components are involved in working conditions.

Most elements of working conditions are not negotiated for by most employers. They are usually not part of the contract agenda, whether the employment contract is oral or written. For simplicity we assume at the outset that all working conditions are based on convention. (Later we will treat wages and other possible negotiated conditions separately.)

Among the components of working conditions are: the exact place of work, the physical structure within which work takes place, the environment of the work setting, time of work, hours of work, degree of job security, the career possibilities or openings available to a person in that particular job, various fringe benefits such as health insurance and retirement contributions, the number of holidays, and the power of various people in the hierarchy to punish deviations from explicit or implicit contracts or conventions. Of course this is not a complete list. The length of the list is determined by the nature of the occupation and the nature of the organization. What is clear is that, given the potential complexity working conditions, it simplifies the employment relation to have most of these elements determined by conventions.

A basic consideration is that most of the elements of working conditions are likely to cost money. A profit maximizing management would, other things being equal, prefer to spend less rather than more on working conditions. The nature of the elements and the extent of their provision are all variable within certain ranges. Thus, if management, in representing the owners, behave as individualistic maximizers, they will try to reduce working conditions and working condition costs to the minimal level possible. Thus, working conditions, given the discretionary power held by management, can be part of the strategic moves made by management vis-à-vis employees. In this sense it is similar to the effort variable, given the discretionary power on the part of employees. Combining the adversarial incentives available to management and employees we have the latent P.D. problem.

The way the working-condition convention gets started is likely to be similar to the way an effort convention gets started. Some manager may have originated certain conditions. After all, some working-condition decisions must, of necessity, be made at the outset of a firm's existence. Successive managers are unlikely to change the conditions unless there are strong reasons to do so; for example, as a consequence of employee complaints, or extremely different conditions in competing firms. Once certain working conditions are established they gradually become taken for granted. They become the stable environment under which work is done. From time to time some specific condition may be adjusted by management in order to avoid deviations from neighboring firms. To some degree, emulation between firms and competitive pressures play a role. But it is unlikely that such pressures will be completely determining factors so as to eliminate all differences between firms. In any event, both *intra*firm emulation and *inter*firm emulation will result in a gradual congealing of working-condition conventions.

The transmission of the working-condition convention over time is easily seen at the individual level. An entrant to the firm will usually accept the working conditions provided without much question. In most cases it is likely to be a nonthinking, passive decision. An active decision is likely to be made only if there is a large deviation between the working conditions found by the entrant and his experience elsewhere. For a new manager joining the firm the process is probably similar. He accepts what exists or what he is told is the appropriate management behavior. That is, he learns the conventional management behavior in the area involved. In this way the working conditions become part of the effort equilibrium of the managers.

Working-condition conventions fall into two categories. Let us call them A and B. Type A includes those conventions that handle a coordination problem, but do not involve any significant variations in costs. Type B includes those that can involve significant costs when the variable involved in the convention is changed. Examples suggest what we have in mind.

Those that fit type A might be: hours of work, mealtimes, normal days off within a week, and so on. Consider starting and leaving times. Whether the normal day is 8 to 4, or 9 to 5, or 10 to 6, is of no special significance. What matters is that employees start and stop simultaneously so that their necessary interactions are facilitated. If the total number of hours each person works in a week are not changed, then starting and stopping times involve only a coordination problem without involving any variation in costs. The convention, if there is one, solves the coordination problem.

Type B conventions include such elements as health insurance, safety costs, retirement contributions, job security, and number of holidays. Management could offer more or less of each of these. Consider the matter of safety equipment in somewhat hazardous work. What will each manager want to provide for subordinates? If he feels he is in some sense completely independent of subordinates then he may want to provide the minimum possible. (See the line marked *MIN* in figure 7.3a.) However, this is unlikely if he feels responsible to a degree for the output and welfare of those under him. In that case, two opposing considerations are involved. On the one hand, he may want better safety conditions for subordinates, but on the other hand he is aware of the costs of more safety equipment, which may be held against him by his superiors. Thus, his reaction curve may be as illustrated in figure 7.3a by the line r_L. The reaction function will also depend on history, since this will give him some sense of the appropriate or fair amount of safety equipment. In figure 7.3b, the average of the aggregate reaction functions is indicated by R_i and the equilibrium is determined by the interaction of the average reaction function and the 45-degree line. The function R_1 illustrates the average reaction curve for a different history under which there is a different sense of the appropriate safety equipment level. As before, the equilibrium is at the point where the reaction is equal to the observed average level of the provision of safety equipment. At that point there is no overall incentive to provide more or less safety equipment. A similar analysis can be carried out for any of the other type B working conditions.

In discussing the determination of effort we argued that the effort convention solves both the adversarial and the free-rider problems simultaneously. The same holds for the working-condition conventions. The free-rider problem is somewhat more subtle and complicated than in the case of effort, although the essential logic is similar. Any specific manager would want the other managers to do their work carefully so that the others contribute to the welfare of the enterprise, with the result that the enterprise remains a viable entity. However, there is no special incentive for any *individual* manager to work as hard as possible. Instead, a specific manager has the incentive to pursue his individual interests rather than the company's interests. This holds for all managers.

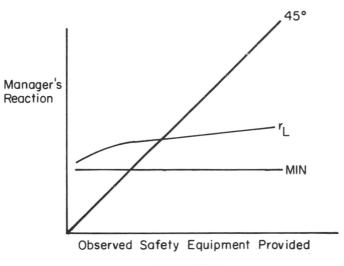

FIGURE 7.3A

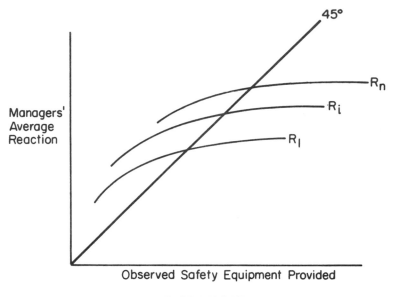

FIGURE 7.3B

How this works out in terms of productivity, and especially in the provision of worse rather than better working conditions for subordinates, is somewhat more complex. In the employee effort case it was reasonable to presume that individuals had a free-riding incentive to pursue less rather than more effort, and it was also reasonable to presume that this implied lower output derived from effort. Since managers frequently have a variety of areas of discretion, many of which influence working conditions for subordinates, the relation between the pursuit of personal interest and the provision of desirable working conditions is more complicated but the logic remains the same. An example will indicate at least one area where the relation is clear-cut. In some military organizations certain officers are responsible for the acquisition and provision of food for the men under them. However, there are cases where officers divert some funds for food to their own concerns and interests. Clearly it is possible to imagine parallel situations in business in which general free-rider incentives result in managers neglecting the interests of their subordinates so that less rather than more desirable working conditions result. The existence of working-condition conventions solves the free-rider problem.

Wages: Convention or Negotiation?

Casual observation suggests that wages are usually negotiated rather than depending on convention. Nevertheless, convention plays a significant role in wage determination. At least part of the wage bargain is likely to be embedded in a matrix of conventions, whether bargaining is implicit or explicit. In this section we consider various alternatives to wage determination and examine how they influence the general approach considered here, especially how they determine the extent to which the employment contract is suboptimal. We consider two alternatives: wages determined by conventions, and wages determined by negotiation.

Wages may be determined by convention even in cases in which they appear to be subject to negotiation. Much depends on whether or not the employer is in the position of being a wage maker, and the employee a wage taker. In a great many instances, especially in large firms, the firm sets the wage and the employee who fits into the category has only the choice of accepting the wage or going elsewhere. Hence the answer to our question depends on how the employer sets the wage. One possibility is for wage setting to depend on some procedure that is itself a conventional procedure. Thus the wage may be set by standards of the industry, that is, what workers in an equivalent class receive elsewhere. For example, policemen and firemen are frequently seen as being in the same general category, and it is customary for policemen and firemen to be paid at the same rates without considering the relative productivity of policemen versus firemen. Another possibility is for the wage-setting procedure to depend on some rule, such as an assessment of various categories contained in some personnel manual or system. There may also be the possibility of some calculation rule that follows such assessments.

Some significant conventions surround wages in most relatively large-scale organizations. Extremely important is the implicit convention that says that the money wage rate cannot fall; that is, the existing money wage sets a lower bound. Thus, employees will expect that in the course of their employment their wages will rise but that they will not fall. There is always an aspect of this convention that is obscure, and that is whether the no-wage-reduction convention is in nominal money terms or in real terms. This is one reason inflation is frequently found to be very disturbing in the sense that it questions the validity of this convention in real terms. Nonetheless, this convention clearly involves important inflexibilities in wage setting. A frequently observed convention is that usually a wage increase is expected merely for length of service, whether or not length of service is related to increases in the value of output. Another, usually implicit, convention is the one that suggests that individuals in the same category receive the same pay. This is likely to hold despite the fact that it is frequently recognized that different productivities exist for individuals within the same category. Thus we frequently find the operation of a number of conventions that by their very nature cause deviations between the wage rate and productivity. In any event, it can generally be seen that in many instances conventions play a role in determining a specific wage determination even if market forces also play some role.

Consider the case in which the wage is determined entirely by convention. Here we may refer to our initial diagram (figure 7.1) where it was assumed that all of the wage-and-working-condition costs are determined by convention. These may then be compared with the effort level determined by convention, and we can then examine whether or not both the effort level and the wage-and-working-condition level are optimal. Since there are a great many levels at which they are both suboptimal, it seems probable that a suboptimal EW solution will result, and only rarely will an optimal solution occur.

It must be evident that the productivity of the effort convention and wage-and-working-condition costs must have at least a rough relation to each other. If the value of the output is considerably below the wage then the firm will either be in the long run forced into bankruptcy, or forced to continuously subsidize a small segment of the enterprise that is operating at a loss. Clearly beyond some level of operating loss a value of product below wages would not be sustained because the managers of the enterprise would be induced to make changes.

A wage that is very much below the value of output would also generate forces to reduce the large differential. Under such circumstances (other things being equal) profits would be exceptionally high and other enterprises would be induced to compete in terms of price with the firm in question. Alternatively, the high profitability in the situation is likely to induce entrepreneurs to set up competing firms. In addition, employees might seek to renegotiate the wage level either through unionization or other means.

The upshot is that there are bounds to the magnitude of the difference that can exist between a value of product and wages (that is, the inert area bounds), beyond which there would be pressures and incentives for the economic actors to make changes. In other words, within certain bounds an equilibrium can be said to exist, but beyond these bounds one would expect changes to take place.

An especially interesting case is the one under which the wage would be equal to the value of the marginal product of effort. This meets one, but only one, of the equilibrium conditions for an optimal solution. It would still yield a suboptimal solution in the cases under which a suboptimal effort convention rules. The reason for this is that under these circumstances it is possible to conceive of a higher effort level, and a higher value of output, out of which there could be a distribution that yields both higher wages and higher profits.

It may be helpful to connect some of these ideas about the suboptimality of conventions with our previous graphical analysis. Figure 7.4 involves the same variables considered in figure 7.1. Start with the Prisoner's Dilemma solution indicated by the point A. Then draw two boundary lines indicated by A_e and A_m which contain, inside the bound-

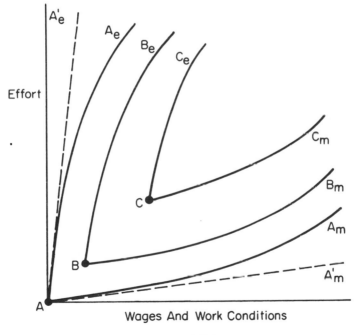

FIGURE 7.4

aries, all the points that are Pareto superior to the P.D. solution. Thus the boundary A_e is the indifference curve for employees. It is the locus of points under which the representative employee is no better off than the point A, the P.D. solution. These are points at which the utility of the increase in wages and working conditions just rewards employees for their additional effort, but no more.

The employee indifference curve A_e is shown as a curved line on the assumption that there are diminishing marginal returns to wages. If the marginal disutility of effort $U'(E)$ were to increase proportionately with the marginal utility of wages $U'(W)$, then the employee indifference curve would be a straight line as shown by A'_e. This follows from

$$\text{Net } U'(E) = U'(W) - U'(E).$$

Symmetrically, the boundary A_m is the indifference curve for management. It is the locus of points at which management is no better off than the point A. That is, these are the points at which the employer uses the value of the additional effort exclusively to pay for better wages and working conditions so that profits are the same as under the P.D. solution.

The term A_m represents the indifference curve for the firm where profits (Prf) equal the value of effort minus wages:

$$\text{Prf} = V(E) - W.$$

We assume in figure 7.4 that $V(E)$ decreases marginally with increases in wages so that A_m has a curved shape. In other words, we assume diminishing marginal returns to effort (due to either a decrease in the productivity of effort or a fall in prices, since $V(E) = P(E) \cdot \text{Prices}$, where $P(E)$ is the productivity of effort). If $V(E)$ were to increase proportionally as effort increased, then the firm's indifference curve would be a straight line like A'_m.

All points within (but not on) the boundaries $A_e A_m$ are then Pareto superior points to A in that both employees and management gain by such solutions compared to the P.D. solution. We could also visualize a set of boundaries $B_e B_m$ for any point B inside (but not on) $A_e A_m$ which then contains all points superior to point B. The point involving maximum effort and maximum wage and working conditions $W_n E_n$ is the optimal point. With this graph we can then consider the superiority or inferiority of any two points determined by effort level and wage-and-working-condition level. For instance, as the graph is drawn, B is Pareto superior to A, but C is Pareto superior to B.

It is evident that if the effort level is not optimal, and wages are set so that in some way they are connected to the value of effort, then the combined *WE* solution will also be suboptimal. This includes the interesting case in which wages are determined by competitive conditions, but effort is determined by convention, and the effort convention is nonoptimal, so that the overall outcome will also be nonoptimal.

The situation can readily be generalized. If any convention, whether it involves wages, effort, or working conditions, is of a suboptimal nature then the outcome, of which the convention is a part, must also be suboptimal. Clearly if we add a suboptimal component to an aggregate then the aggregate is suboptimal. Earlier we may have appeared to have quite arbitrarily separated aspects that we *assumed* to be determined by convention, and other aspects that we assumed to be determined by negotiation. But while these assumptions were made arbitrarily in the interest of simplifying and more readily illustrating the argument, it is important to note that the seeming arbitrariness has no impact whatsoever on the general result. Note especially that whatever the mix of the conventional and negotiated aspects, as long as there are some conventional components that are nonoptimal, then the outcome results, in general, in a nonoptimal solution. Thus, the analysis and conclusions hold for a variety of particular situations within which there are different mixes of negotiated elements and elements determined by convention. Of course it follows that this includes those cases where negotiation occurs under competitive conditions, but under which suboptimal conventions exist.

On the Stability of Conventions

Conventions are essentially stable because no individual is likely to be in a position to undertake the difficult task of convincing everybody in a large group to change their behavior. This would necessitate such activities as contacting every individual, determining how he feels about his behavior, determining how flexible he is about changes, allaying various fears with respect to change, determining a new course of behavior that everybody will agree to, and overcoming the bias against busybodies and those who interfere with existing arrangements.

Even if there is a residual desire to sacrifice to some degree for the good of the group, it is unlikely that this will be sufficient to overcome all the disutilities involved in the activities that have to be undertaken, as well as to overcome the sense that it is unlikely to work. As a result, it is possible to conceive of all individuals being in a position in which they do not believe that they could successfully overcome the obstacles involved.

Especially important is the fact that the incentive to share in the gains of the group as a consequence of a convention change is usually absent. An individual in his normal work cannot claim that he succeeded in changing a convention and therefore has a right to share in its profits. In other words, he cannot set himself up as a residual claimant or partial residual claimant. Only particularly placed individuals are by contract or convention residual claimants in the firm. These are usually owners, manager-owners, or exceptionally placed executives who share directly or indirectly in profits in a significant sense. There are normally strong conventions against anyone other than a contractually placed individual setting himself up as a residual claimant. In fact, achieving success in such attempts may involve "proving" to others that the individual has no financial stake in the outcome to allay their suspicions of his efforts.

Summary and Conclusions

The underlying assumption on which our discussion of conventions has been based is that both employees' efforts, and managers' provision of wages and working conditions are discretionary. This postulate is not arbitrary; it was chosen deliberately to take account of what is commonly seen in real firms. The aim has been to show how conventions limit and constrain the discretionary areas available to employees and managers.

Both effort conventions and wage-and-working-condition conventions arise idiosyncratically, may involve modifications before congealing, and tend to persist due to various peer, managerial, emulative, or competitive pressures on people to conform. Different conventions may be more or less strictly adhered to; that is, they may be tight or relatively loose. The difficulties of convincing a group of people to change their behavior, even if it is in their joint interest to do so, is what stabilizes any particular convention. An individual usually faces such difficulties without the incentive of being able to claim any significant part of the benefits accruing to the group from the change.

An effort convention serves as a parameter for coordinating the effort levels of individuals. An effort convention will reach an equilibrium once individuals react *on average* to the observed average effort level by choosing that level. Although conventions are usually suboptimal effort levels, they are superior to the P.D. effort levels that result when each side behaves in terms of individual maximization. Note especially that relaxing the maximization postulate allows us to recognize that people adopt and stick to conventions even when it does not pay for them to do so. This is probably the main reason why conventions can overcome free-rider incentives.

Wage-and-working-condition conventions are symmetrical to effort conventions, but involve more elements; hence, they are likely to appear more complex, but the basic logic of the argument is the same. We divided wage-and-working-condition conventions into two types: those involving simply a coordination problem, and those that also affect the costs of the firm. The latter type raise cost-cutting incentives in management. Considering wages and working conditions based on convention alone, we examined the conflicting incentives managers can face in their dual roles as employees and managers. Working conditions of other employees are part of managers' effort equilibria.

Wages that appear to be determined by negotiation may really be determined by convention if the firm is a wage maker. Even when wages are negotiated they are embedded in a matrix of conventions that are not negotiated. Among the important conventions of this type are: that wages will not fall, that wages will increase for length of service, and that wages will be the same in the same job category. The embedded conventions contradict payment according to the productivity of individuals. However, incentives and economic forces exist that tend to keep the productivity of the effort convention, averaged over groups of employees, from diverging too far from wages—on average.

When wages and working conditions are determined by a mix of negotiations and conventions the overall outcome will be suboptimal if the conventions entailed are suboptimal. This applies when an effort convention is suboptimal even if wages are equal to the marginal product of effort.

Most important, the pressures on employees and managers to conform to conventions will help *to counter* manifest or latent incentives that tend toward a P.D. outcome. However, the behaviors established as conventions are very likely to be suboptimal from the viewpoint of the individual and the group, and to yield suboptimal output levels for the firm.

CHAPTER 8

Intrafirm Effort Decisions: Monitoring and Sanctions

Alfred Chandler and Herman Daems (1980, p. 1) have pointed out that large firms in the United States and Europe have at least a six-level hierarchy. Here we shall look at a very limited aspect of hierarchy, the power of hierarchies to elicit effort through sanctions, how this relates to nonoptimal effort decisions, and the relation between peer sanctions and effort conventions.[1]

Although employment contracts are incomplete or ambiguous, they usually permit the firm to apply many types of sanctions. Individuals can be fired, laid off, refused pay increases, refused promotions, not given sufficient status, forced to accept salary reductions, demoted, and generally, have various privileges withheld. But despite its latent power, the hierarchy frequently does not succeed in eliciting as much effort, or as high a quality of effort, as one might expect.

Most decision makers are only vaguely aware of the sanctions that can impinge on their decisions, since they make their decisions in a way such that they rarely bump into the sanctions that could be applied. We shall be especially concerned with the various systems of latent hierarchical and peer-group sanctions that can surround individual effort decision making.

---

1. The role of hierarchies in economics is a large and growing subject. Williamson's *Markets and Hierarchies* (1975) is probably the most important book in recent years. Some works worth mentioning are Beckmann (1977), Calvo and Wellisz (1978), Chandler (1977), Chandler and Daems (1980), and Hess (1983). Nevertheless, the penetration of hierarchy concepts into microeconomics is slight. Needless to say, we do not consider hierarchies generally or formally here.

The Voluntarily Motivated Effort Hypothesis

Consider the following basic proposition: an individual could perform *voluntarily* at a significantly higher effort level than he would under monitoring with the threat of sanctions for failure. In other words, there are effort levels beyond those attained by monitoring that are significant and *could* be achieved when effort is voluntarily motivated. Notice: "could," not "would." Factors such as morale and team spirit exemplify the potential significance of voluntary motivation. While general experience supports this proposition, it is frequently not recognized. Voluntary motivation is especially likely to be important to the quality of effort.

Of course, this hypothesis is hardly new. In one form or another it has probably been rediscovered frequently. For instance, in 1858 Henry Varnum Poor wrote about "the grave difficulties of adapting human capabilities and current business practices and institutions to the severe requirements demanded by the efficient operation of such large administrative units." He further worried about the problems resulting from "regarding man as a mere machine, out of which all the qualities necessary to be a good servant can be enforced by mere payment of wages. But duties cannot always be prescribed and the most valuable are often voluntary ones." (See Hayes, 1979). It is important to keep in mind that this hypothesis is not consistent with the idea of a production function or with the idea of the firm as primarily a monitoring entity vis-à-vis production (Alchian and Demsetz, 1972).

Not only are there limits to the quality and type of effort that monitoring can extract; there are also monitoring costs that will reduce the net gain from monitoring. These include the cost of supervision, the cost of reducing employee enthusiasm for effort, and the cost of shifting effort away from unobserved toward observed activities.

There are obviously some monitored levels sufficiently low so that some voluntary effort levels would be higher. The obviousness of this proposition is simply that whatever the monitored level is, there is a voluntary response that is at least equal to it. The interesting question is, Is there a voluntary level of effort that cannot be equaled by the net return of a monitored level?

Consider the highest monitored level. We want to show that the overall outcome is superior if the same level is achieved on a voluntary basis. Namely, the situation is better and cheaper if it is *not* monitored, or is monitored only loosely. To start with, there is the supervision cost of monitoring. Clearly, the overall output level is higher if the cost of monitoring is lower; manpower used for monitoring could be used for other productive purposes. In addition, monitoring may reduce employee enthusiasm for effort in several ways. First, there is the utility of work to those performing on a voluntary basis. In other words, we assume that there is some negative utility associated with being monitored, and hence there is a positive utility if one achieves what there is to be achieved on a voluntary basis. Any motivation from this positive utility is then lost under monitoring.

Second, and probably more important, is the emotional reaction to the distrust perceived from monitoring. Inevitably, beyond some point monitoring sends a message that the employee is not completely trusted. Lack of trust operates in many ways. The way it is most likely to operate is a sense by the individual that exemplary effort, or even effort beyond a minimum, will not be rewarded. This is likely to dampen employee enthusiasm for effort. Such distrust of being rewarded for effort could be compounded if the group within which an individual sees himself as a peer-group member is quite large relative to those, say in the personnel department, who are in a position to arrange rewards. In such a situation of distrust, enthusiasm could be further dampened if subordinates believed that additional effort, once shown, would be expected by superiors to persist. The flexibility that an individual may believe he has at low effort levels would seem to disappear or be compromised if a fairly high effort level were revealed as a possibility. All of these elements are, of course, augmented by group feelings. If the group as such shows a lack of trust that greater efforts will be rewarded, then this is likely to set up resistance to attempts by the hierarchy to induce, in one way or another, greater effort levels by those below.

Many arrangements that initially assume mutual trust are likely to be delicate ones. Suppose that somehow an arrangement is offered under which employees promise to do their best while managers promise to arrange for the highest payment possible, given the employee's effort. Suppose middle-level managers have to check with superiors. There is no sure way for the parties involved to assess the quid pro quo in this particular situation. If the employee increases his effort in stages, he will expect the manager to increase remuneration in an amount that the employee feels is fair and proper. To meet the employee's expectations the manager has to give what the employee feels is appropriate. But if the manager pays more than *he* feels is appropriate, he will expect still greater effort from the employee in order to make up for it. Clearly any disagreement in such a set of sequences is likely to sever the bond of trust that was the basis of the original arrangement.

A fairly pervasive bureaucratic bias for accountability is likely to interfere with any kind of sensible wage and effort arrangement. As a consequence, the middle-level manager is really hampered in any attempt to deliver on a quid pro quo arrangement. Once the inability to deliver becomes clear to basic employees, then the effort incentive, initially based on trust of fair rewards, disappears since it is impossible for the employees to judge how relatively unknown and faceless members of the bureaucracy will react.

In addition to the costs of monitoring reducing its effectiveness, certain characteristics of effort cannot be achieved on a monitored basis. For instance, it is usually impossible to monitor some aspects of quality, especially the extent of caring about the quality of one's workmanship so that a high-quality output results. The extent of caring about the quality of one's effort has value for productivity even if the particular quality of the product can itself be monitored. In other words, there are reject costs, or "doing over" costs because of sloppy work. In addition, in the course of many jobs (perhaps all) the individual meets unexpected circumstances. While monitoring can usually handle repeatable situations, it can seldom handle special problems.

An element that usually cannot be monitored is information known only at lower levels. This could arise in a variety of circumstances. Visualize the hierarchy as a pyramidal chain. Those higher up have more power, responsibility, and provide more abstract information to those below. The most detailed information is at the lowest level where employees work directly on the product or service. As one goes up the chain information becomes more abstract or more summary. A basic asymmetry is that those higher up have greater power to obtain detailed information from those below, while those below have less power to obtain abstract information from those above. Thus, in principle, someone at the top has *access* to all the detailed information available at the bottom. However, while such an individual may have the power to obtain detailed information on which he explicitly focuses, he does not have the time or capacity to obtain all the detailed information.

The basic employee is likely to gain certain information about the details of the production process that may be of value to the hierarchy. He or she will invariably have the discretion to communicate this information or not. The hierarchy has no way of monitoring whether information it does not know about has been communicated. For instance, this may arise in circumstances where there is learning by doing. As a consequence of experience, information that is usable by others may be gathered but not communicated. This may involve knowledge about the possibilities of superior effort or improvements in quality. Such information is not only a determinant of effort of the particular employee involved, but it may also have value in improving the effort levels of all similarly placed employees.

Another difficulty, frequently inherent in hierarchies, that cannot be improved by monitoring is the lack of participatory enthusiasm on the part of those in specific posts presumed to carry out the firm's objectives. The nature of hierarchical attachments, whether they are specific to a particular superior, or abstract, can determine the degree of an individual's enthusiasm for his tasks. This, in part, involves enthusiasm to discover what his task is, or ought to be, in terms of the interests of the principal. One can think of loyalty and motivation to serve a specific individual, but it is quite different if the person being served happens to be in a particular *post,* and the individuals change but the post does not.

Finally, the imperfect transfer of information from one level of the hierarchy to another reduces the effectiveness of monitoring. There is likely to be a dilution of purpose, especially in its intensity, as one travels down the hierarchy toward those carrying out basic activities. (See Williamson, 1967, on this point.) Once one gets to the basic activities level, the message from the top is extremely diluted. In part, this is because those at the top are not aware of the extent of the exact transmission of their desires, and at each level firm members have considerable discretion in carrying out their activities. Two consequences result: a skewing of direction away from the original purposes, and the possible increase of discretion toward subordinates and away from principals. Of course, the real principals (stockholders) are usually not in a position to state their specific interests, however imperfectly.

Hierarchical Sanctions

We now examine the power of the hierarchy over employees and whether the use of sanctions is likely to elicit high levels of effort. To start with, we consider the situation of a representative *basic* employee who works on some aspect of the product. We then consider the situation as faced by a member of the hierarchy at various levels in the hierarchy.

Start with the isolated employee. From his viewpoint the hierarchy will appear to be extremely strong, given the availability of possible sanctions against him. But the employee will appear relatively weak if and only if he considers his position in isolation from others in the enterprise. Thus the possibility of being fired, not having one's salary increased, or having some types of privileges withheld appears to provide overwhelming sanctions to the hierarchy. However, if the individual considers himself in relation to his peers, the situation appears somewhat different. What power does the hierarchy have against *all* of the peers simultaneously, or under equal treatment of all peers?

Clearly, the costs to the hierarchy of sanctions against an individual are likely to be quite small. Also, the costs of sanctions against *all* individuals in a given group are likely to be high. In each instance the cost is against a single individual, but the sanctions have to be applied equally to all individuals if management is not to be perceived as unfair. If the individual in question is representative, he can count on the belief that sanctions will not be taken against him when it is not possible for the firm to take sanctions against all others similarly placed. From that viewpoint, the hierarchy appears rather weak. So the hierarchy could develop reasonably acceptable sanctions with respect to "abnormal behavior," but not for what is viewed as normal or conventional behavior.

Thus, the representative individual who takes into account the power of the hierarchy under equal treatment is aware of sanction limitations. He or she chooses an effort level in relation to what appears to be normal for the group. In fact, he may perceive a range and may consider going to the lower bounds of that range. Here it becomes clear that history is important. The ideas of normal and abnormal performance will depend on what has been normal in the more recent past and in the distant past. The reasonableness of the sanctions of the hierarchy will depend on the history of performance.

In general, we might conclude that (1) the hierarchy is relatively weak in imposing sanctions in view of the "voluntary-enthusiasm" proposition. (2) The hierarchy is weak if it has to move against all peers in the group equally. (3) The hierarchy is likely to be weak if it has to consider power and informational divisions within the hierarchy.

This last deserves elaboration. It is one thing for a given "boss" to impose sanctions when that manager is in complete command. But this is not the case in a four- or five-level hierarchy. No member of the hierarchy, even if that individual has considerable responsibility for the monitoring of performance, is likely to be in a position to carry out sanctions according to his own personal whims, or according to what he believes is appropriate. He must take into account the reaction of others at different levels in the hierarchy. Here a basic asymmetry is likely to be significant. Those highest in the hierarchy are likely to have the most power to carry out sanctions. They are also likely to have the least information about the basic employees against whom such sanctions might be carried out. Those closest to the activities of basic employees are likely to have the most information about possible deficiencies in performance, but they are in a position of least power compared to the others in the hierarchy. Thus lower-level managers or supervisors can apply sanctions only in accordance with some well-established rules. Such rules will usually have to take into account what has been historically determined as normal versus abnormal, or conventional versus unconventional performance.

Finally, it is important to consider that there exists a set of effort/wage-cost combinations that imply the same profit level. Clearly the firm seeking to maximize profits would be quite happy with a lower, rather than higher, effort/wage-cost combination, so as to avoid some of the resistance to high effort levels obtained by monitoring and sanctions. In other words, at very high effort levels there is a disutility to the hierarchy to obtaining that effort, and it is easier to live with a lower effort/wage-cost combination. This is a comparative statement: we are not referring to a *move* from a high-effort/high-wage level to a low-effort/low-wage level, but rather to comparative static equilibria.

Figure 8.1 summarizes some of the ideas. The abscissa indicates the degree of hierarchical sanctions. These may run from mild rebukes, to lesser promotions, to nonpromotions, to employees being fired (the point *F*). The curve *S* is the supply of sanctions for alternative effort levels provided by the hierarchy. For ease of exposition it is shown as a continuous function, but it could be a step function. The curve *SE* is the supply of effort, on average, under *monitoring* for each level of sanctions.

Sanctions that induce effort are likely to be interpreted as applicable within boundaries. That is, they are not continuous for every level of effort. Hence, we have a step function *(SE)* and we should expect that employees will have a tendency to place themselves at the lower end of effort for each step. In an effective system these curves (*S* and *SE*) will cross before sanction level *F*. If the hierarchy sets the sanction curve too low, it will be ineffectual. If it is set too high, then the firm is in a foolish and costly position since it will either opt not to take any

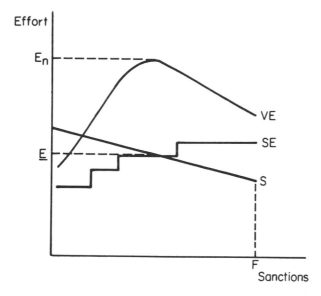

FIGURE 8.1

action, or have to fire all its employees if it operates in accordance with its sanction scheme. Clearly setting the curve somewhere in between is the likely level.

The curve marked *VE* represents the maximum voluntary effort level provided by employees for each level of sanctions. This assumes the provision of the best *positive* motivating forces. *VE* represents how people would behave in the absence of monitoring, but with a sense that sanctions would occur if they were found to fall short of certain standards. Up to some point the sanctions may have a positive influence on voluntary effort, but beyond some point they are shown to have a depressing influence—that is, they lessen voluntary enthusiasm. The arguments presented, and briefly summarized below, suggest that there exist a number of points on *VE* (or on nonoptimal voluntary effort curves below *VE*) that are significantly above the equilibrium point $\underline{E}$.

It may be useful to connect the conclusion of the ideas summarized in figure 8.1 with figure 7.1. Thus in figure 8.2 we show the mutual choice between effort and wages-working-conditions as applicable to the area $\underline{E}E_n$. $\underline{E}$ represents the effort level where effort just meets the requirements of avoiding sanctions, without any extra effort being given. The higher effort levels possible with voluntary motivation, $\underline{E}E_n$, are shown in figure 8.2 with concomitant wage-working-condition levels.

Figure 8.2 shows that there are Pareto superior possibilities for both management and workers above the point WE that results from sanctions. That is, we can visualize a monitored level of effort up to the point WE, at which point the discretionary, voluntary provision of effort takes over. Thus, there is some monitored level of effort that represents the Prisoner's Dilemma point, but beyond which possibilities for higher levels and higher value of effort can be said to exist.

We have considered various arguments in support of the idea that a monitored/sanctioned effort level will be lower than a voluntary one. Among the important elements that motivate suboptimal efforts under monitoring are: a negative utility associated with the monitoring experience, a lower effort in intrinsically unmonitorable activities, suboptimal unmonitorable information transfer, the shift of effort to observed and away from unobserved activities, the costs of monitoring, and the costs involved in finding replacements for those who are fired, or for those who leave because of the monitoring atmosphere.

We noted that the hierarchy is likely to be relatively weak in attempts

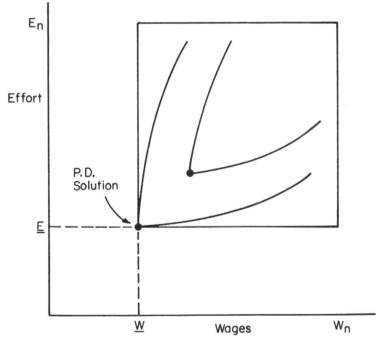

FIGURE 8.2

to extract very high effort levels through sanctions, although its power may be strong against isolated individuals but not against all peers. In addition, the hierarchy does not speak with one voice, or with the same degree of power, or with the same amount of detailed information, at all levels. Hence the hierarchy is weaker than would otherwise appear to be the case once we consider internal divisions. At the same time, remember that at relatively low monitored levels employees are likely to see sanctions as fair, whereas at high levels they would be viewed as undesirable attempts to extract additional effort.

Peer Sanctions and Sanction Levels

How people behave will also depend on the nature of peer-group sanctions, in particular, the degree to which people show their displeasure of nonconventional behavior, and the nature of allowed behavior. In this section, sanctions are classified in various ways and we consider how particular sanctions influence behavior. How peer-group sanctions influence the outcome will depend on whether they are sanctions that (1) *cooperate* with the hierarchy, (2) are *neutral,* or (3) are essentially *adversarial.* Clearly, cooperative sanctions, which frequently exist in the Japanese enterprise, are likely to lead to relatively high effort conventions compared to neutral or adversarial sanctions.

No Group Sanctions
Consider the state of affairs where essentially no peer sanctions exist. Firm members feel that there are no sanctions from peers for any chosen behavior. In this case people may emulate the behavior of others, where it appears to be comfortable to do so, simply to avoid standing out. The implicit sanction is conspicuousness. Of course, some personalities may not be concerned about being conspicuous; others will want to avoid it. This general point has been made by Schelling in which he argues that nonobservance of an institutionalized behavior pattern carries "the pain of conspicuousness" (1960, p. 91). The idea is that even though no specific effort level is institutionalized, the average effort level will have some influence on individuals' behavior.

Under these circumstances, anybody who wants to be an effort free rider would feel free to do so. Hence, we expect certain personalities to approximate free-riding behavior, to divert effort to their own interests and away from firm interests (up to the point that appropriate hierarchical sanctions permit). This is illustrated in figure 8.3a by two curves. The curve marked *FR* indicates complete free-riding behavior and reflects the minimal effort level desired by the individual. Curve *MFR* involves some degree of modified free riding in which an individual attempts to avoid conspicuousness, and hence the curve has a slightly upward slope reflecting the avoidance of conspicuousness. Figure 8.3b shows the reaction curve for all individuals. The intersection of the

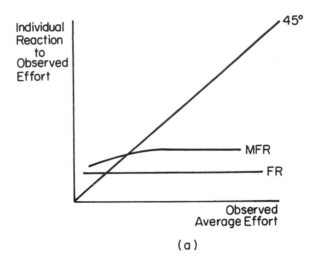

(a)

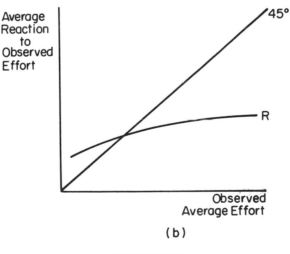

(b)

FIGURE 8.3

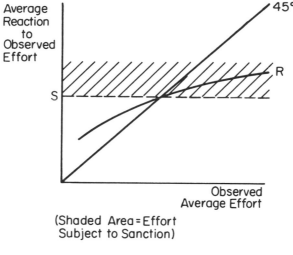

FIGURE 8.4

reaction curve and the 45-degree line represents the equilibrium effort level under which no one will have a desire to change his effort. Of course, around the equilibrium that shows only the average reaction, there is a distribution of individual effort levels. In this particular case, any explicit sanctions are imposed by the hierarchy.

Upper-Bound Sanctions
Under an upper-bound sanction the group indicates that it does not care how low the effort level is, but does not want people to put forth too high an effort level. In figure 8.4 the reaction curve starts out above the 45 degree line which would reflect boredom at very low levels, and rises as the efforts of other individuals rise. The lower bound of the sanction level is shown by the point marked *S* on the ordinate, the equilibrium effort level. Clearly, in this case, there is strong pressure for any individual's effort level not to be above the sanctioned level, and if the sanctioned level is low, then this would constrain individuals to put in less effort than their desires would dictate under individualistic behavior.[2]

This particular type of sanction may be viewed as the standard defense by peers against attempts by the hierarchy to elicit relatively high effort levels. It is symptomatic of industrial relations in the United

2. The curve *R* in Figure 8.3 (and in other figures) is an ex ante relation that shows the alternative effort levels before the equilibrium effort convention is established.

Kingdom and also frequently visible in the United States. Whether or not labor is organized is not important. There is a long history of informal sanctions existing in enterprises without unions.

Lower-Bound Sanction

A lower-bound sanction represents the opposite of the type just considered. Here others want everybody else to make at least a minimal contribution to effort, although how much of a contribution above the minimum is left to the individual. The reaction curve is shown in figure 8.5. If the sanction level is quite low, then voluntary behavior will determine the actual level. Clearly at the tail of the distribution, those who would normally produce at low levels are forced to produce at a higher level, and hence the average is higher than otherwise. The higher the sanctioned level, the higher the average reaction curve. Also, the reaction curve flattens out. Thus, in this particular case, the lower the sanctioned level, the steeper the reaction curve, and vice versa.

This particular case is likely to be one that is, on the whole, supportive to hierarchical interests whether or not the hierarchy has an additional set of sanctions. It has been asserted that such cases are found in efficient German firms where there is considerable respect for the hierarchy and the system of hierarchy. There is no way of determining whether or not this is a general case.

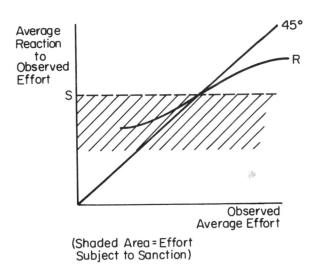

(Shaded Area = Effort
Subject to Sanction)

FIGURE 8.5

Competitive Contribution Sanctions

A competitive contribution sanction comes closer to what one finds in the *successful* large Japanese firms. The group or faction that each individual belongs to not only requires a minimal contribution, but creates an atmosphere in which the minimum rises as others perform. Thus, whatever the performance level of others, it is viewed as the appropriate contributing level. The upper limit is determined by the maximum capacity of the average individual. Those who have greater capacities need not be concerned about producing more, but those with lower capacities will always feel that they have not made an appropriate contribution, and will attempt to find ways of doing so through longer hours or efforts that could only be maintained in the short run. Clearly in this case the equilibrium effort level will be high, as shown in figure 8.6. However, it is important to note that the result need not be the maximum. Those who compete easily, say, those who do not find it difficult to make a slightly above-average contribution, may feel or behave in such a way that they do not put forth their maximum effort, even if their actual effort is an observably high one. Since the maximum contributions are frequently unobservable, there is no reason for the average outcome of the group to be maximum.

It is important to note that under this version one is likely to have a situation under which both the hierarchy and the peers support the sanction. The hierarchy supports it since they are able to obtain highly satisfactory results from the lower-level group by offering some sense

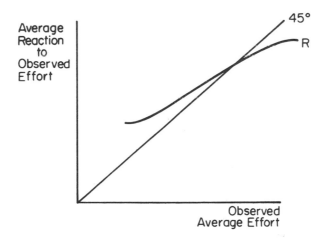

FIGURE 8.6

of shared interests between the individual contribution and the interests of the firm. In the Japanese system such interests are augmented by a relatively *large* bonus system (20 to 35 percent of annual income), which supports the incentives and sanctions that exist (see Clark, 1979).

The competitive contribution sanction is likely to have two components. The group operates as a team. As a consequence, individuals compete, at least to some degree, in their contribution toward team effort in the belief that others will care about everybody else's contribution, and to some extent show disapproval of "low" contributions. But these motivational circumstances are unlikely to persist if there is no reward for higher *team* performance. Thus, this is a system that has to be supported and augmented by the hierarchy. As suggested earlier, the hierarchy has to recognize differences in team performance and has to be in a position to deliver appropriate rewards for increased team performance. Clearly, the type of Japanese bonus system, since it is fairly large, will operate in this manner. But it is the persistence of the subgroup as a clearly identifiable group within the organization, with its own small hierarchy, that is an essential part of the system.

This type of sanction can lead to anxiety and neurosis as a result of individuals attempting to achieve unrealistic effort levels under competitive incentives. It has been argued that this is sometimes the case in Japanese firms. However, some simultaneous concerns for the welfare of one's peers is likely to lead to a realistic upper-level standard at which the competitive contribution stops. Most likely, this situation is not consistent with utility maximization on the job.

Adversarial Sanctions
Where the feelings are adversarial, the outcome is likely to be not very much different in general than that under free riding, except that the effort levels are likely to be lower. Here there are two possibilities. In the first, the adversarial feelings are individual, but are not additionally supported by group sanctions. In the second, there are group sanctions and group support for adversarial attitudes. In general, we should expect that in the group-supported case the effort level would be even lower than the one under the individual adversarial situation.

Fear of Victimization
In some cases there may be group sanctions whose reason for existence is to avoid possible victimization by management. This is reported to be the case in U.K. labor relations in more extreme instances. Usually

there are a variety of work rules, and attitudes associated with work rules, that exhibit unusual sensitivity to attempts on the part of management to increase effort. Under such circumstances, there are likely to be extreme sanctions against almost anyone exceeding the upper-bound level. The net result is that the average performance will be below those situations in which only an upper-bound focus sanction exists. It is the extreme sensitivity to going beyond the boundary that is the essential element here.

The Shape of the Reaction Curve
We have generally drawn the reaction curve so that at low observed levels the reaction is above the observed level, and at high observed levels the reaction is below. What does the slope of the reaction curve represent? It would appear to represent the degree of deviation from uniform behavior between individuals and the group. If sanctions against any deviation are exceptionally strong, then the reaction curve would always be along the 45-degree line until the maximum effort is reached. At the maximum the curve contains a segment parallel to the abscissa (see the dotted line in figure 8.7). However, this is unlikely to represent any realistic behavioral circumstances. People may, to some extent, be pressured toward conformity. They are rarely pressured toward complete conformity. Hence at low levels they are likely to exceed the conformity requirements, and at higher levels they are likely to follow that requirement. The extent of the deviation from the 45-degree line

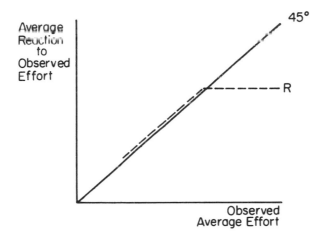

FIGURE 8.7

will depend on the extent to which the sanctions press toward complete conformity.

The equilibrium point will, of course, depend on the nature of the sanction itself. It is very important to note that all such sanction systems are likely to depend on history. Since at various points firm members leave and others enter, those who enter are likely, at least initially, to determine their effort levels on the basis of information about how "things are generally done" in the organization. Thus, firms with different histories are likely to have different reaction curves, different equilibrium effort levels, and different sanctions.

Sanctions and Nonmaximizing Behavior

Allowing for nonmaximizing behavior makes it easier to accept the idea that effort conventions (and related sanctions) will avoid or prevent the P.D. solution. Since imposing sanctions is likely to be unpleasant and entail some effort, the possibility of nonmaximizing behavior enables us to see why people fairly consistently support sanctions. If individuals are not individualistic maximizers and follow some ethic, we can readily see why they would apply sanctions against others by following a desire to do what they believe is "right." Alternatively, individualistic utility maximizers would avoid unpleasantness and not apply sanctions. For example, if a person saw someone else stealing something in a store, he might feel compelled by his sense of what is right to report the incident, even if it took some effort and trouble, and even if it was unpleasant to do so. A maximizer would avoid reporting the situation if it entailed effort, was unpleasant to do, or might involve him in a situation with uncertain repercussions.

Decision making is frequently constrained by conventions and sanctions to a stimulus-response mechanism. Such a mechanism makes it easier for each person to feel confident that others will behave predictably, thus reinforcing trust that people will behave in accordance with a commitment to peer-group behavior patterns rather than strictly following individual maximizing. A stimulus-response mechanism thus makes it easier to believe that people will not flout the convention, even if there is a calculated advantage to doing so. Behavior according to conventions and sanctions is easier to accept if we see such behavior arising out of emotional forces consistent with possible nonmaximizing behavior, rather than from coolly calculated considerations.

Concluding Remarks

Effort decisions are made within certain boundaries. These boundaries are likely to be determined in part both by hierarchical sanctions and peer-group sanctions. Some peer-group sanctions serve as basic defenses against overly ambitious, or against the possibility of overly ambitious, hierarchical sanctions.

The basic conclusion is that sanctions developed by the hierarchy are most likely to leave a relatively wide area of behavioral possibilities beyond which voluntaristic incentives are likely to be stronger than the sanctions. In addition, we have considered a variety of peer-group sanctions that support various effort conventions. Individual support for such sanctions is frequently onerous. If everyone was an individualistic maximizer, everyone would free ride the "duty" of imposing sanctions. But, we can readily account for sanction-imposing behavior under our max/nonmax postulate that allows for nonmaximizing decision occurrences. Some sanctions induce effort below an upper bound, others induce effort above a lower bound, and still others induce greater conformity toward some average effort level. Furthermore, some peer sanctions operate toward greater cooperation with the hierarchy, some are neutral, and some support an adversarial stance between peers and their superiors.

CHAPTER 9

Equilibrium, Entrepreneurship, and Inertia

External pressure is a basic variable in our analysis. For convenience we frequently assumed, explicitly or implicitly, that the pressure was constant. Sometimes environmental circumstances do persist unchanged, such as when entrepreneurship is in short supply. But often pressures from the economic environment on firms will change, either because of the shelter-seeking activities of the firms involved, or because entrepreneurs set up new enterprises. There is clearly a connection between entrepreneurial activities, changing degrees of imperfect competition in an industry, and the extent of external pressure.

Do any of the ideas developed so far have a bearing on our understanding of the nature of entrepreneurship? Although there is a long history of entrepreneurial theorizing and entrepreneurial research, the collective analysis thus far has been inconclusive. Most important, entrepreneurship is not part of standard economic theory. In this chapter we consider how entrepreneurship can be integrated into the type of analysis developed here.

It is interesting to note that while economists have paid considerable attention to entrepreneurship, somehow they have not integrated it into standard economic theory.[1] There are two general reasons why: one is a problem with the concept and the other is a problem with the theory. The entrepreneur has been glorified to such an extent as to become a mystical entity, making it hard for the concept to accommodate mundane activities like buying and selling, work, the use of equipment, and especially the copying of techniques that others may be using. The difficulty with the theory is that it focuses on *tight* equilibria where it

---

1. Schumpeter's view of entrepreneurship was integrated into his view of microeconomic theory, but that did not become the standard view (Schumpeter, 1951).

seems difficult to introduce change. The concept of a *loose* equilibrium developed below will facilitate the integration of the concept of entrepreneurship into our general framework.

Equilibrium and Quasi-Equilibrium

Before going further it is desirable to define the equilibrium state of the individual, the firm, and of a group of firms. This is not a digression, although it may appear as such. We use these concepts again towards the end of this chapter. We will also discuss a state of affairs to be called quasi-equilibrium. This is not quite the same as pure equilibrium, but it possesses enough stability so that statements about such a state of affairs are of interest. The reason for being concerned with equilibrium is that statements about inefficiency within firms assume greater importance if the inefficiency is not a short-run transitory state of affairs. It is especially important in the case of stable equilibrium conditions since this implies that unless some exogenous changes take place the inefficiencies will persist.

Usually equilibrium is viewed as the consequence of a balance of forces; therefore, there is no tendency for change as long as the balance of forces persists. Whatever it is that is taking place during the balance of forces continues to exist within the equilibrium state. However, given the significance of the concept of inert areas in our analysis, we shall focus on the "no tendency to change" aspect as our definition of equilibrium. The idea of an inert area, as developed earlier, implies that inert behavior may occur even where an exact balance of forces does not exist. Indeed, the basic focus is that individuals will ignore the net force in one direction or another, and persist in their behavior. Thus, we shall be primarily concerned with those states of affairs under which individuals, groups of individuals, firms, or groups of firms show no tendency to change their behavior.

The individual will be said to be in equilibrium as long as he or she is operating within his inert area, whatever the relevant dependent variables may happen to be. Of course, we consider only those aspects of an individual's behavior that are pertinent to the questions being studied. In the case where we are concerned with behavior within firms, it is only the individual's work behavior, and not his behavior outside of work that concerns us. For the most part, we ignore the influence of nonwork behavior on work behavior, or vice versa.

We can think of a group of individuals being in equilibrium in the same sense that a particular individual is in equilibrium. Thus, if all members of the group are in their inert area then the group may be said to be in equilibrium. It follows readily that we can extend this concept to the firm as a whole. If all individuals in the firm are in their inert areas, then the firm may be said to be in equilibrium. It is important to note that the definitions of group equilibrium and firm equilibrium presume that the interaction of individuals with each other does not cause any of them to behave in a way that goes beyond their inert area bounds. Clearly this is a significant qualification whenever we speak of equilibrium where more than one person is involved.

We now introduce a type of equilibrium in which all members of the enterprise are *not* in their inert areas. We shall refer to this type of equilibrium as quasi-equilibrium. Consider the case where all members of the firm but one are in their inert areas. The odd man out, so to speak, searches for a new effort position. Let us suppose that he leaves the firm and is replaced by someone whose effort position is roughly the same as someone in a similar position and who is himself in his own inert area bounds. Thus the actions of the odd man out do not really affect anybody else in the firm. We consider such a firm to be in quasi-equilibrium.

The same would hold true if a relatively small proportion of firm members were outside their inert areas, but their activities toward new effort positions for themselves did not cause anybody else in the firm to be forced out of their inert areas. Thus the majority of the firm members would be behaving inertly and, on average, the firm appears to be behaving in a stable manner. We will also refer to such circumstances as a state of quasi-equilibrium. In other words, some people in the firm change their jobs and others leave and are replaced by newcomers, but this activity does not change average firm behavior significantly as long as those making the changes are a small proportion of the whole.

Another way of looking at this is that even though specific individuals move from post to post, and even if some people leave and new people enter specific posts, the average behavior of those who are the post fillers will remain the same. In this sense the quasi-equilibrium is not really all that different from the complete equilibrium except that the names of the post fillers have changed.

What Do Entrepreneurs Do?

Entrepreneurs should be viewed as ordinary individuals with some special business skills and motivational capacities. Consider what entrepreneurs do. The following is a short list based in part on my earlier work (Leibenstein, 1978). (1) The entrepreneur finds and fills opportunities between markets. He may have to purchase inputs in one set of markets, transform inputs into produced goods, and sell the outputs in other markets. (2) These markets, especially the input markets, are likely to be imperfect in various ways. Thus, the entrepreneur has to overcome obstacles in the market and fill gaps. (3) The entrepreneur has to be an input completer. That is, it is not sufficient to overcome some obstacles and fill some gaps, but all of them have to be handled in order to produce outputs for sale. (4) Given the obstacles and gaps that exist, entrepreneurship requires a sufficiently strong commitment to carry out all of the above. Thus, motivation (commitment, perseverance, and the like) is a critical quality of the entrepreneur, and is critical in determining the stock of entrepreneurial talent.

Entrepreneurs may be said to take advantage of economic opportunities. They are opportunity fillers. Each available opportunity can be viewed as an alternative. The maximization postulate used in standard theory suggests that the economic agent will always take the best opportunities and will take advantage of all costless opportunities. It assumes that every chance for gain will be taken. This view leaves out the fact that economic opportunities are not always obvious—they may be partially hidden and difficult to interpret. To take advantage of them, a number of personal qualities may be required. One has to recognize opportunities and possibly search for them. One can search with varying degrees of effort and persistence.

The standard view also leaves out frictions and resistances that interfere with taking advantage of opportunities (such as the effort necessary to overcome bureaucratic resistance to issuing a license). It assumes there is no problem of decisions in the face of frictions and resistances. If all efficient opportunities are filled there is not much to be said about entrepreneurs as opportunity fillers. They are presumed to be fully motivated, leaving only the question of how *the economic system* creates opportunities.

In contrast, the view taken here is that people will not necessarily take advantage of opportunities that exist. We have to have individuals with the requisite personal characteristics and capacities for economic opportunities to be fulfilled. Thus, we have to be concerned about the supply of entrepreneurs. If a sufficient portion of the population is not properly motivated, whatever their capacities, then there may be a scarcity of entrepreneurs.

The Supply of Entrepreneurs and *n* Achievement Theory

That entrepreneurs should be viewed as ordinary individuals with some special motivational capacities and business skills is supported by the work of McClelland and his followers on the *n* Achievement theory (McClelland, 1961; McClelland and Winter, 1969; and Miron and McClelland, 1979). A main characteristic of people who are high in *n* Achievement is that they are likely to take a stronger than average interest in revenue-cost relationships when they consider economic opportunities. In addition, they are likely to have realistic and reasonably achievable goals, and to search for practical detailed steps toward those goals. Thus, a vague desire to be better off, which is not likely to be helpful in reaching specific goals, is not characteristic of those with a high need for achievement. Rather it is the willingness to search for and carry out the detailed procedures necessary to reach a goal that is likely to be characteristic of those high in *n* Achievement.

Research associated with *n* Achievement theory indicates the possibility of the selection of potential entrepreneurs according to their relative motivational characteristics, and the possibility of increasing entrepreneurial motivation through training. It suggests that we can select individuals who are capable of carrying out entrepreneurial activities in a way superior to others, and furthermore that we can teach people the skills and induce the motivations for them to behave in this manner. The people trained in this way in the past have not been exceptional or unusual. Therefore, this work suggests a means of increasing the supply of entrepreneurs.

Unquestionably there are entrepreneurs of unusual talents whose modes of operation cannot be captured, described, and taught to others. But, in my view, such people are at one end of the talent distribution found among entrepreneurs, which ranges from ordinary capacities, to the ability to slightly modify an existing firm, to the borderline of the great entrepreneurial innovators such as Henry Ford.[2] Setting up a new firm is an entrepreneurial act even if the new firm is very similar to an existing one, or just slightly better on cost containment, or product design, or quality control. To be mildly innovative in a technical sense, that is, to introduce a slight change in the ratio of inputs, is technically and actually an entrepreneurial activity. Of course, there is a continuum

2. For a view of entrepreneurs who are highly innovative see the interesting paper by Joshua Ronen (1983).

of novelty in entrepreneurial activities. Here we have stressed the less novel (as opposed to the spectacularly novel) because the less novel is likely to occur most frequently and therefore to have the most impact on changing the structure of the industry and on changing the degree of external pressure on the firm.

The work of McClelland and his followers has not had much impact on the thinking of economists. Some of their later work simply has not gotten into the purview of economists, especially the work on the selection of trainees for entrepreneurial skills, and the motivational training of entrepreneurs (McClelland and Winter, 1969; Miron and McClelland, 1979). The volume by McClelland and Winter, *Motivating Economic Achievement,* was not reviewed in the economics literature and is almost completely unknown by economists. Certainly, their work after 1967 continues to be unknown.

It is interesting that this work is really of a narrow micro nature; it is extremely specific. It suggests that there are techniques available to select individuals in such a way so that we can determine in advance whether, *on average,* the selectees will do better or worse than a control group, or the population at large, if given entrepreneurial opportunities. Furthermore, it suggests that selectees can be trained so as to increase their entrepreneurial capacities. This gives the macro theory a micro foundation. The macro theory is simply an aggregation of the individual capacities of the population for entrepreneurial behavior.

The value and flexibility of the theory is partly demonstrated by the fact that entrepreneurial capacities can be improved through training exercises. It seems reasonable to believe that a theory that permits not only interpretation of the world we live in, but also implies or suggests a way to change that world is likely to be more valuable than one that only allows for interpretation.

Behavior of Firms under Loose Equilibrium

Once we drop the maximization postulate and accept that individuals may be suboptimizers, we can acknowledge the differential qualities of potential entrepreneurs, and therefore the possibility of selecting those who are likely to be better entrepreneurs. Furthermore, the recognition that some individuals are frequently suboptimizers, and possibly inadequately motivated, allows us to incorporate into economic theory the possibility of training individuals to improve motivational capacities, as well as other skills necessary for entrepreneurship.

Visualize entrepreneurship as bundles of activities that can be carried out by ordinary people given some training, if necessary, and reasonable access to resources. Ordinary individuals will find it difficult to overcome the tight equilibrium of microeconomics in which firms are managed by carefully calculating, cost-minimizing managers or entrepreneurs.[3] Setting up a new firm in order to enter an established industry becomes exceedingly formidable if the existing firms successfully operate with the price of the product equal to the minimum cost of production. The very best the entrepreneur can hope for is that he will do as well as but no better than the existing firms. If he falls even slightly short of this standard he will face losses and eventual bankruptcy. Tight equilibrium requires unusually talented individuals to meet that standard. But if the entrepreneur faces what we will refer to as a loose inert area equilibrium range of costs, then the task becomes more manageable for individuals of fairly average or only slightly above average capacities. This is the approach taken in what follows.

Firms operating in an imperfect market can find a partial or complete haven from pressure to minimize costs by a variety of means including product differentiation, large size compared to market, and political means to limit competition. Some (probably most) of them are not minimizing costs. Selling their products at higher prices to consumers enables them to cover higher than minimum costs. This allows firms to expand their range of possible behaviors from the minimum-cost/minimum-price point of perfect competition to the wider area of the loose equilibrium. Then, as long as prices and costs remain within certain bounds, given the demand for the product, a firm will be in an inert area, that is, behave routinely with respect to input use, price-setting (markup or other) formulas, and quantity of output. When prices or costs exceed the inert area bounds, then the firm will be "shocked" into nonroutine behavior aimed at adjusting to the change.

The postulate of inert area behavior within the wider area of the

---

3. Benny Gilad, in a perceptive paper (1985), suggests that since there is no profit in equilibrium we must look to disequilibrium as the arena within which the entrepreneur operates. This is the traditional Austrian view developed most fully and precisely by Israel Kirzner (1973, 1979). In part, I agree. However, the point made here is that the entrepreneur can operate under the circumstances of a loose equilibrium as well. Note that this helps to explain how the disequilibrium may arise without having to postulate the existence of disequilibrium to start with. On the nature of this problem see Hébert and Link (1982, p. 99). See also Day (1984) for an analysis of the view that, despite Schumpeter, entrepreneurs emerge only in disequilibrium, under a system of adaptive economic behavior.

loose equilibrium says that such firms will not actively seek every profit-making opportunity they could possibly find. Instead of adjusting all the time to do the best they can to increase revenues or reduce costs, firm members will accept the "normal" effort levels of others in the enterprise.[4]

We assume the firm, in an imperfect market, operates without minimizing costs. Hence, in figure 9.1 we show a set of bounds for costs, marked $\overline{C}$ and $\underline{C}$, which illustrate the wide inert area within which the firm will not react to changes in costs. We assume constant costs with respect to scale. Costs greater than $\overline{C}$ will lead the firm to attempt to lower costs, while costs less than $\underline{C}$ will lead the firm to expand. Some firms may be in their inert area when they are operating at costs which are less than $\underline{P}$. This means that under the inert area conditions of costs and prices, these firms will not be looking for an opportunity to expand their scale of production.

For each firm there is a normal scale of output associated with any particular cost level.[5] Thus, the curves marked $\overline{C}$ and $\underline{C}$ are boundaries of an *array* of individual firms' cost segments for which the lowest cost firms are listed closest to the Y-axis.

We also assume there is some lower price $\underline{P}$ that will not induce firms to change their behavior toward attempts to lower costs. In addition there is an upper price level $\overline{P}$ below which firms will not be induced to expand the scale of the enterprise. Between $\overline{P}$ and $\underline{P}$ there is no inducement for firms to change the scale of their enterprise. Thus, we can visualize an equilibrium established by the bounds illustrated, $\overline{P}$ and $\underline{P}$, and $\overline{C}$ and $\underline{C}$, that does not induce behavior changes by the

---

4. In general, firms do not know what the maximum profit level is. They usually use some cost-plus pricing formula that yields a profit level that falls within inert area bounds. It is helpful for some purposes to view the firm as consisting of the sum of the actions of its individual members, rather than being some sort of entity in its own right. It is easier to see why a firm might not accept a profit-increasing opportunity when one thinks of it requiring everybody in the firm to change their behavior a little bit. Who in the firm is available to pressure everyone to change their behavior? Viewed as an "all-seeing" entity, it would be harder to see why a firm would ever not accept a profit-increasing opportunity.

5. Within the inert area of an individual firm the quantity that it sells may vary with costs, as for example when quantity varies with price and price is determined by a cost mark-up formula. The particular cost curve of the ith firm in the inert area will be a segment like the one in figure 9.1 bounded by $\overline{c}_i$ and $\underline{c}_i$. An array of all of these curves laterally results in the "fat" industry Cost-Quantity relation bounded by $\overline{C}$ and $\underline{C}$. The upper bound, $\overline{C}$, is determined by $\overline{c}_i$ for all i, and the lower bound, $\underline{C}$, is determined by $\underline{c}_i$ for all i.

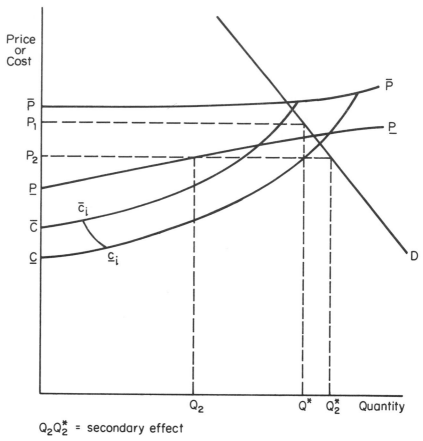

$Q_2Q_2^*$ = secondary effect

FIGURE 9.1

firms already in the industry. P_1 is the average price. The intersection of the demand function, D, and the average price yields Q^*, the equilibrium industry output level

We take care of the possibility of different inert areas for firms with different cost conditions by having a rising lower price boundary $\underline{P}$. The lower the cost, the lower the price boundary. This would make the firm react to an actual price below $\underline{P}$. It seems reasonable to assume that $\bar{P}$ rises as costs rise, that it takes a higher price to induce higher-cost firms to expand in terms of scale. Note that if ordinary entrepreneurs enter and the price falls from P_1 to P_2, this cuts the lower inert area boundary and puts pressure on the less-efficient firms. The primary effect is that at least some new firms produce at lower costs. In general this causes the existing less-efficient firms to attempt to lower their costs for a secondary cost reduction effect of ordinary entrepreneurs entering the industry. The firms represented by output $Q_2Q_2^*$ are the ones that have lowered their costs.

We can make the analysis more realistic by adding a disequilibrium area in which a subgroup of firms have costs above the actual price, and are attempting either to reduce their costs or leave the industry. As long as the disequilibrium firms' segments are not a significant proportion of the whole, they may not influence the other firms, leaving the boundaries of the loose equilibrium area unchanged. The potential entrepreneurial entrant into the industry will still see considerable possibilities for entry as long as the actual price is sufficiently above the cost level of the average firm.

Note that an entrepreneur can readily enter simply by attempting to copy the activities of existing firms, as long as there is some hope of producing at costs between P_1 and $\underline{C}$. Thus, entry by ordinary entrepreneurs becomes feasible once we get away from the tight equilibrium under which price is equal to a single, industrywide minimum cost. In this model firms copy or purchase from others the ideas or techniques that they introduce. We can visualize a gradation of innovations from very similar to very different. Further, we view entrepreneurs as introducing innovations into a relatively loose inert area equilibrium which has room for relatively cost-inefficient firms. Thus, for the most part, non-super-talented entrepreneurial types can be visualized as entering the industries that exist in the economy.

Summary and Conclusions

Entrepreneurial activities are a response to unfilled opportunities that first requires exploring for such opportunities. While establishing new firms or new ways of doing things in existing firms is an important subset of entrepreneurship the possible novelty element can be easily overstressed. Even the imitation of existing firms involves entrepreneurial action.

A basic motivational component of entrepreneurship is an individual's commitment to overcome the gaps and obstacles that exist in imperfect markets. The research associated with n Achievement theory indicates that it is possible to measure the varying strengths of entrepreneurial motivations in individuals, and that such qualities can be augmented through training. Therefore, selection and training might be used to increase the supply of entrepreneurs in a society.

Clearly, there is a need to fit entrepreneurship into microeconomics. Two difficulties stand in the way: the tendency to glorify the entrepreneur; and the use of a tight equilibrium where firms produce at minimum cost, and price is equal to minimum cost. We have suggested that utilizing the loose inert area equilibrium of X-efficiency theory enables us to see how entrepreneurs with average capacities might enter various industries and hope to succeed. If existing enterprises are not minimizing costs, then it is possible for new enterprises to be started by people without unusual skills, but with sufficient motivation to compete effectively. Of course, those with above-average skills would have an even greater probability of success.

This general approach suggests the importance of motivational and related capacities to the determination of the level of economic activity in general.

CHAPTER 10

An Implications Sampler

Implications, seen in proper perspective, are useful in suggesting aspects of the theory that can be tested. Also, some may suggest important policy considerations. It is important to look at implications, but implications are not everything. A good deal of work looks at implications as the be-all and end-all of what is being done. Hence, some cautionary remarks are in order.

In some fields the implications of a theory appear to be the bottom line of the efforts of researchers. Implications (or in mathematized fields, theorems) are frequently viewed as the real payoff of all the work that has gone before. In formal mathematics, or in mathematicslike structures, it is the deductive inference of implications that appears to be the essence of the work. This is also frequently presumed to be the essence of research in fields that have adopted (at least in part) a mathematicslike format, such as some of the work in economic theory.

But to focus entirely, or mostly, on implications is misleading in an essentially empirical subject. In a real-world, scientific field, implications have no separate life. Just knowing that a certain body temperature in humans represents health does not tell one very much about the health of an individual even if this fact is derived from some physiological theory. Even a set of such indices would not be especially informative without a sense of the overall nature of human functioning.

Similarly, focusing on the implications of economic theories is an extreme type of reductionism that can readily lead to misunderstanding real-world behavior. The point is that the behavioral content of the assumptions (the behavioral content in and behind the equations), and the mode of thinking about that content spelled out in the theory, as well as the ways in which these are expressed, are likely to be just as important as some set of implications.

In general one cannot really appreciate the relevance, or significance, or full meaning of implications without knowing the postulates from which the implications flow. In particular, the implications of economic theories cannot be fully understood without knowing the behavioral assumptions, or the behavioral equations that attempt to express that content. Furthermore, consider the differences in the significance and applicability of economic theories with such different modes of thinking as these: using the individual's viewpoint versus considering interactive behavior, taking degrees of motivation into account or not, observing certain kinds of behavior versus others, classifying specific contexts for behaviors or not, or using a static equilibrium form of thinking versus a dynamic form, and so on. Likewise, there are important differences in the ways in which different theories are expressed. Some may be less fully expressed, leaving many aspects of the theory unclarified, perhaps giving few examples and suggesting very little about the nature of the behavior involved. Some may be more fully expressed, with a fuller discussion of hypotheses, assumptions, behavior equations, and so on. A good theory is a vision of how things work, including some of its implications. In essence, the overall theoretical structure and the implications are inseparable. They are all part of a larger whole.

Even the mere formalization of the system is likely to result in the loss of content since the formalism leaves out the complexity of the world. A good deal of the richness of the fabric of reality gets lost in this process. Of course, a good deal is gained through the process of simplification, formalization, and derivation of implications. But this has frequently been emphasized, if not overemphasized, in scientific endeavors. Frequently missed are the possible losses of this approach. And the losses can be especially strong if we focus mainly, or only, on implications and do not pay attention to the other important aspects.

There are two additional aspects that have to be kept in mind: (1) we frequently cannot state explicitly *all* the postulates in a formalization, or quasi-formalization, and, (2) we usually cannot state *all* the implications. Certain postulates or conditions surrounding the discussion of a system of thought are presumed to be understood, but we can never be sure to what extent such postulates are really understood, and to what extent a consensus exists about what the unstated postulates really are. We can never even be sure that we are aware of all the implicit assumptions being made. Thus, almost all scientific descriptions are incomplete in this sense. Equally important, this implies that all the implications can never be derived. At best all we usually have are some of the implications, and we hope that those we have will be important and interesting. Hence, all we attempt to provide in what follows is a sample of the implications obtainable from the postulates and discussion of ideas presented up to now.

Summary of Basic Postulates

The postulates used to derive the inferences have already been discussed in considerable detail. Here is a brief list by title and a word or two of explanation. The seven postulates of prime importance are as follows.

1. *Max/Nonmax:* People both maximize and deviate from maximization in their decision making. The ratio of max/nonmax decisions follows the Yerkes-Dodson Law. We emphasize the first half of the law where less pressure is associated with a lower ratio of max/nonmax decision making.

2. *Incomplete employment contracts:* Effort is open to discretion to some extent. This is also true of various conditions of work that are controlled by management.

3. *Motivation of work performance:* Effort put forth by individuals depends on motivations from both incentives (intrinsic value of effort, and any extrinsic rewards for effort) and pressures (peer or hierarchical sanctions, or environmental competition or adversity).

4. *Utility of effort:* The marginal utility of effort increases up to some point, then decreases, and beyond some point is negative. Also, there may be an additional positive marginal utility of effort under teamwork conditions, that is, individuals may feel as well off putting forth more effort if the team puts forth more effort. It is a team approval effect.

5. *Coordination:* There is value to individuals in behaving as others behave because more desirable results are achieved through coordinated behavior. Also, to some degree people care about the reaction of others toward them if and when they are not coordinating their behavior with others.

6. *Inert areas:* Many relationships, including conventions, are such that within certain boundaries inertia exists with respect to the dependent variable. This means that no change in behavior takes place within these bounds when the independent variable changes, especially when the values of the independent variable(s) are embedded in a low-pressure environment.

7. *Imperfect competition:* The company or companies in question are assumed to be sheltered from competition to some degree. The greater the shelter, the less the pressure on the firm.

Effort Convention Implications

If this was a formal mathematical treatment, some of these implications would be listed as theorems. However, we will use the somewhat looser language of implications. In most cases the chains of reasoning are rather short. Hence, the implication will follow almost immediately from the previous analysis and the postulates on which the previous analysis was based. The significance of these implications is most readily seen when compared with the implications of standard microeconomic theory. For present purposes the implications are also of interest because they say something about the nature of internal inefficiency and frequently touch on the causes of such inefficiencies.

The first three implications to be considered are connected to each other. 1. Effort conventions may be optimal or nonoptimal. 2. Nonoptimal effort levels may be observed and yet no attempt may be made to change them. 3. A nonoptimal effort convention may be stable.

That an effort convention may be nonoptimal follows from the nature of coordination, which is a basic component of conventions. Individuals adhere to conventions in order to coordinate their activities with others as opposed to following their own interests. Possible coordinations need not be optimal. There is no reason why the behavioral interest in pursuing coordination may not dominate any other interest.

Now, consider the next implication: nonoptimal effort levels may be observed and yet no attempt may be made to change them. There are three possible reasons. It may appear to all parties who follow such a convention that too much effort is involved in trying to change it. Or individuals may simply wish to mind their own business. Or, even if it is apparent that a gain would result if everyone shifted to a higher effort level, no one may be in a position to be a residual claimant to the overall gain involved.

The implication that a nonoptimal effort convention may be stable follows immediately from the second implication. Namely, if no one is interested in making the attempt to change the nonoptimal effort level, then clearly such a convention will be stable.

4. Neither the work/leisure mix nor "on the job leisure" is optimal for all or many firm members in equilibrium.

Since working hours are conventions, such conventions in general cannot fit all individuals' desires. The movement of employees between enterprises may improve the fit but will still not suit all individual desires, since working-hour conventions are likely to be similar in a given area or in a given industry. Effort is also likely to be determined by convention, and hence individuals are limited in shifting their effort level toward their own interest. Furthermore, other components that determine the desirability of the job are likely to dominate in importance those relatively inflexible characteristics determined by convention.

Note that standard theory does not yield suboptimal results. It is the mixture of the Prisoner's Dilemma tendencies of the production situation, and the use of conventions as a means of avoiding Prisoner's Dilemmas that generally yields suboptimal outcomes.

The implications are on an individual and a group level simultaneously. For example, we can interpret each of the first three implications on an individual level. Thus, an effort convention adopted may be nonoptimal for an individual. Similarly, the nonoptimality of the convention and the behavior may be observed and no attempt be made by the individual to change it. Finally, the nonoptimal conventional behavior of the individual may be stable. At the same time, all three of these implications hold for interacting groups of individuals carrying out similar or related activities. Of course, it is because of the group aspect that conventions exist and are in fact meaningful.

The basic importance of these implications is that employees can, in fact, put forth more effort. Under some circumstances they would not mind putting forth more effort, but they are unlikely to do so because a special type of coordination is required to shift from one convention to another. Thus, the integrated culture of the system does not require employees to do more. Most important, it usually requires a shock to the culture for the group to even consider a new set of effort levels— that is, new conventions.

Firm-Level Implications

Some of the most important implications can be stated about firms as a whole. In general, these follow from division of what goes on inside firms, and involve generalizations from individuals and groups to the firm as a whole. The implications are as follows.

5. There is no well-defined, externally determined production function between purchased inputs and produced outputs that represents the state of the art for any specific firm.

One cannot speak of a well-defined production function as long as employees are given discretion with respect to their effort level. How such discretion happens to be used determines the relationship between inputs and outputs.

6. There may be a production function frontier that approximates the practice in the best-practice plants. However, most firms will not operate on the frontier.

Since the way in which employees use their discretionary powers will be different for different firms we should not expect output levels to be the same for all firms, and hence some firms, usually most, will not be on the production frontier.

7. For a nonfrontier firm, for a given output, costs are not minimized.

This follows immediately from the previous implications. Clearly, if output is not maximized (for given inputs) for a nonfrontier firm, then costs are not minimized for the given combination of inputs.

8. In general, firms can increase output without increases in labor, knowledge, or other inputs, even if in equilibrium they do not do it.

This follows from the general idea of the existence of X-inefficiency, that is, that the effort conventions and the working-condition conventions are not optimal. In that case, output can be increased, in principle, without increases in labor, other inputs, or knowledge. At the very least, increased effort would increase output. Similarly, effort is involved in using additional knowledge in the enterprise.

9. Cost of production may depend on price, in part.

Note that this implication differs markedly from the one that follows from standard theory. In the standard theory, the price of a commodity has no influence on its cost of production. However, in this version higher prices (other things being equal) imply less pressure, that is, a more sheltered environment. Lower pressure contributes to lower effort and higher production costs.

10. Firms in equilibrium do not operate at a Pareto-optimal quantity.

The inert areas surrounding conventions that determine the equilibrium of the individual do not require that firms be optimal quantity adjusters. Where markup pricing conventions are used, the quantities to be produced need not be coordinated with the markups. Furthermore, inventory policies are also likely to be determined by convention, or rules of thumb, and such inventory conventions need not lead to producing optimal quantities.

The implications on the firm level differ especially sharply from standard textbook theory. In that theory the firm is essentially a black box; it is in effect a production function. Firms are, in general, presumed to operate efficiently, and hence on their production function. Clearly, here we are concerned with internal inefficiencies.

11. The form of ownership is likely to be an influential element in determining the cost level.

This differs from the standard theory within which the ownership form does not influence the profit-maximization criterion. However, in our model pressure is a significant variable and the form of ownership is likely to determine incentives and pressures that are transmitted. Thus, owner-managers could be expected to operate differently than hired managers who own very little stock in the enterprise. Owner-managers are likely to care primarily about profits, whereas hired managers are concerned with other considerations such as growth, salary, and the possibility of moving laterally to other enterprises. State-owned enterprises will have other incentives and handle pressure in a different manner; for example, accountability considerations may predominate. Furthermore, profitability concerns may be blurred considerably by political considerations.

12. Firm group equilibrium includes firms with nonoptimal costs and outputs.

We have argued earlier (implication 7) that costs need not be minimized. In addition, we have argued with respect to implication 10 that output need not be optimal. Hence, the firm group equilibrium can exist with neither costs nor outputs being optimal.

13. Available profitable innovations will frequently not be put in if pressure is low.

This follows the ideas developed earlier with respect to ordinary opportunities to lower costs, or to control other aspects of the production process. Just as inertia, within bounds, results in a lack of push toward reducing costs, or superior quality control, or increasing sales, and so forth, so in the same way it results in a lack of the introduction of profitable innovations. With respect to innovations, an additional element may be the uncertainty that surrounds them, but the point here is essentially that inertia may exist when pressure is low, and continue to exist as long as the lack of introducing the innovation does not increase the pressure. Of course, eventually one would expect that if enough competitors introduced the innovation and improved their operations in the same way, that this in turn would put pressure on the firm in question.

Two examples are the introduction of modern systems of quality control and the introduction of robotics. In both cases the Japanese introduced the innovation of what were essentially American or Western inventions. Quality control came to the Japanese through the lectures of W. Edwards Deming, an American professor of statistical quality control, who earlier gave similar lectures in the United States. But it did not result in any adoption here. The same occurred with respect to robotics which was introduced in Japanese manufacturing on a large scale before its adoption in the United States, despite the fact that the techniques were largely developed in the United States.

14. There may be an inadequate supply of entrepreneurship; that is, there may exist a stock of unfilled entrepreneurial opportunities.

Two elements are involved here: (1) the nature of the culture, which may determine the extent to which people are induced to enter entrepreneurial activities, and (2) the motivational elements of individuals determined by the economic environment. The main point is that there is no a priori reason, given the postulates presented earlier, to have a stock of entrepreneurs that always fills the entrepreneurial opportunities available.

These are not the only inferences. Many others could be deduced from the postulates and related concepts and ideas; however, the implications in this sampler suggest something of the significance of the theory. Later chapters, which emphasize the problems of hierarchy, will lead to some additional implications to be discussed in the summary chapter.

CHAPTER 11

The Power of Hierarchy

Hierarchy is a ubiquitous phenomenon. If all we mean by hierarchy is a ranking, or graded ordering of various units vis-à-vis each other, then hierarchy can be seen in every aspect of nature from molecules to ecosystems. Hierarchy may also refer to the specific schemes of social classification found in insect, animal, and human societies, as well as in subunits of such societies.

It is easy to recognize hierarchical schemes in human organizations. Of course, hierarchy is not all there is to organizations, but it is an extremely important aspect. In fact, it is difficult to think of any human organization without thinking of hierarchy. It is therefore surprising, given its importance, to consider the extent to which hierarchy is ignored in many discussions of human organization. For our purposes it is particularly interesting that hierarchy is completely absent from standard economic analysis. The two basic units, the household and the firm, are handled without concern about their hierarchical structure. General equilibrium theory, the most rigorously developed branch of economics, ignores hierarchy completely. Similarly, the central probe of economic studies, the question of efficiency, is handled as if hierarchy did not exist.

This chapter and the next three are, directly or indirectly, concerned with hierarchy inside firms. We will argue that hierarchy is part of the solution to the "firm-size" problem of organizing production. In brief, there are advantages to firms that are large, and beyond rather small-sized firms, hierarchy is part of the organizational solution. That is to say, hierarchy is an ubiquitous characteristic of the variety of organizational solutions that can be applied to large firms. In Chapter 12 we will consider the connections between specialization and hierarchy, and the inefficiencies that frequently result from the particular types of hierarchical solutions that are applied. We will look at the inefficiencies attributable to different kinds of hierarchies and try to determine the particular kinds of hierarchical characteristics that are likely to lead to less efficient solutions than others. There then follow two chapters that, essentially, contrast the Japanese Management System with Western management systems. Here we show that the hierarchical characteristics associated with the Japanese Management System are frequently more internally efficient than some Western alternatives. We may view the discussion of the Japanese Management System as an aid in interpreting further the ideas developed in this chapter and the next.

From Adam Smith to the present, economists have been concerned with economies of scale. But for the most part we have passed over the organizational counterparts that would describe how such economies have been achieved. It is true that starting with Adam Smith there has been a detailed analysis of the division of labor, and the relation of the division of labor to efficiency. It is tempting to suggest that hierarchy is the reverse side of the coin of the division of labor. One cannot have one without the other. But somehow economists have succeeded in discussing the division of labor and ignoring hierarchy. It is of interest that in recent years hierarchy has entered explicitly in the work of Alfred Chandler (1962; 1977), an historian of industry and of the changing structure of large enterprises. Chandler's interest has been in determining how these giant enterprises were gradually forced to change their structure in response to the adoption of technologies that involve both economies of scale and economies of scope. In his work, hierarchy, and various forms of hierarchy, enter as significant results of these technological and economic changes.

Perhaps the most noteworthy contribution to the literature on hierarchy by an economist in recent years has been the work of Oliver Williamson (1975). For the most part, his contribution takes up the central question, raised by Ronald Coase in 1937, Why do firms exist? Williamson, following Coase, answers the question by viewing transaction costs as the basic explanatory variable. In other words, through establishing a hierarchy firms save on transaction costs from what would otherwise be a complex web of individual exchange contracts. While reduced transaction costs may certainly be an important benefit of hierarchies, they do not necessarily explain why firms have a certain degree of hierarchy in their structure. The view taken here is that while we do not want to minimize the transaction costs element, we do want to focus primarily on other aspects of hierarchy.

The main interest in this book is internal inefficiency. What are the possible connections between hierarchy and inefficiency? To what extent do efficiency considerations call for the introduction and expansion of hierarchy? Conversely, to what extent does hierarchy contribute to inefficiency directly or indirectly? Thus, we will concern ourselves with why hierarchy exists. If it is advantageous to have hierarchy, can we say anything about the minimal necessary hierarchical arrangements? On the other hand, are there, frequently, unnecessary hierarchical structures? Are hierarchies augmented for reasons that are not strictly economic?

Earlier we have attempted to explain internal inefficiency on the basis of a simplified two-level structure, say, between employer and employees, or bosses and workers. Now we will apply these arguments to three, four, or N-level structures. The question is, What difference do additional levels make? Do they have a tendency to attenuate or exaggerate the importance of the variables concerned? Is everything that is relevant for a two-level structure also relevant for an N-level structure? Do some elements disappear and do others arise as we go beyond two levels? For example, do the hidden Prisoner's Dilemma problems and free-rider incentives continue to play a critical role in multilevel hierarchies? Is the need for coordination more significant under N-level structures than under two-level structures? How do the central ideas developed so far, such as nonmaximizing decision procedures, conventions, sanctions, and nonoptimal solutions, work out under N-levels? We will attempt to trace the role that these various elements play in larger hierarchies. But we need to focus, first, on the advantages or power of hierarchy.

The approach to be taken at this juncture is that hierarchy does not exist for its own sake. Hierarchy is part of the solution to an economic and organizational problem. We will identify the essential problems that hierarchy solves. Furthermore, we will consider whether there are alternative solutions to those problems. Can we do without hierarchy? In Chapter 12 we will examine whether intraorganizational practices associated with hierarchy are unique, or if there are superior and inferior variants. In other words, are there alternative ways of handling the details of human interactions within hierarchical structures?

The transaction-cost approach lends itself to the view that hierarchy is to be contrasted with a set of individual, nonhierarchical exchange contracts between individuals. But strictly speaking this is not quite the case. We can think of a class of *individual* contracts that are essentially hierarchical and that exist without the benefit of reduced transaction costs. These are master-servant contracts, which involve master-servant relations. Such contracts involving participants of unequal authority, inferiors and superiors, are distinguished from contracts involving equals, as for example a contract between a housewife and a milkman. Master-servant contracts may be explicit, but frequently exist implicitly. Examples are the relations between housewives and household servants, and the relations between craftsmen and the people who work for them.

Consider the one-man firm that hires somebody, a "servant," to do part of the work that the one-man firm, the "master craftsman," has contracted to do for someone else. There are several possible forms of such a master-servant contract. The exchange may consist of well-specified work for the master, and nothing but the well-specified work. This may come close to a non-master-servant relationship. In other cases the contract may be explicitly an authority contract in which the range of activities of the "servant" are specified, but left subject to the direction of the "master" as to when to carry out each particular activity. In most cases, however, the master may have some discretionary power to change some aspects of the work, so that the activities expected of the servant are not fully specified initially, but left to the discretion of the master to some extent. Clearly it is immaterial whether the authority being used by the master is explicit or implicit. What is important is that the master is recognized as having such authority while the servant does not. This is an asymmetrical relationship which can be seen in the case of authority spillovers. Authority spillovers occur when a superior tries to use his position to get an inferior to do work that goes beyond the bounds of normal practice, that is, the implicit contract. Even if the authority is fairly explicitly bounded, there may frequently be authority spillovers. That is, the master may choose to give instructions beyond the bounds and the servant is put in the position of deciding whether or not to accept the improper use of authority. Even in this two-person situation, it is quite clear that a hierarchical relation exists.

The situation may be complicated further if we expand the previous case to the situation in which the servant finds it necessary to employ a helper, say an apprentice. In this case we have a three-level hierarchy, even though only individual two-party contracts are involved. While the servant's helper is not directly under the authority of the master, and has no direct relation to the master, nevertheless it is recognized that the helper is not at the same level as the servant. To what extent there may be authority spillovers between the master and the servant's helper will depend on specific circumstances. The point of this example is that we can readily describe a three-level hierarchy that depends only on two-person exchange contracts.

One question is whether the people involved in the situation above constitute a firm. It is obviously a boundary-line case, where it becomes hard to define whether a single firm does or does not exist. What is interesting is that this is a case where the activities that are carried out can be done on a nonhierarchical basis. (We will examine the details of such a possibility later.) There are, however, other cases in which the elimination of hierarchy is not possible.

Now to summarize the general approach that will be taken in the rest of this chapter. We shall argue that the basic reason for hierarchy in human organizations is that hierarchy is a solution to the problem of size, which is the tendency for the activities of a large group of individuals to be uncoordinated. In economic, political, and social contexts there are advantages to organizations of large size. Greater power, or greater capacity, is a consequence of size. In order to solve the size problem and take advantage of greater power, the authority and influence relations of a hierarchy usually have to be introduced. Of course, hierarchy itself is not the only aspect of the solution of organizing groups of large size. It is simply one characteristic of the solution, but an extremely important characteristic.

Frequently related to size is the characteristic of complexity. Hierarchy also helps to solve the problem of coordinating the many parts of a complex endeavor. Thus, whenever there are units that are of significant size and projects of sufficient complexity the organizing solution will contain a hierarchical structure. Nevertheless, such structures are usually not unique. We will see that a variety of hierarchical structures can provide solutions (but not equally good solutions) to the problems of organizing groups.

A related issue is that members of hierarchies will usually have feelings about the hierarchy. Some of these feelings may be positive and others negative. The fact that of necessity the hierarchy represents inequalities will in a great many instances cause resentments of one sort or another. But this is not necessarily the case. Hierarchies also allow for certain kinds of opportunities, especially career opportunities. As a consequence, this positive aspect of hierarchical solutions must also be taken into account. We will show later that both of these elements are likely to be related to internal inefficiency.

The Power of Size and Hierarchy

In a number of contexts there are a variety of advantages to size, for a great many reasons. Here we review some of these advantages in a rather general way, with no attempt to be complete or to give anything like an exhaustive treatment. All we need is to show that the size of the group is important. In a sense this must be so because there are, in fact, a great many large, organized groups. We review some of the possibilities in order to suggest something of the variety of ways in which size carries an advantage. Of course, in almost all cases our aim is to argue at a later stage that hierarchy is associated with size.

Consider the case of an army or a military unit. A mob of people by itself may have no value. But if the mob's energies can be channeled in certain directions, the mob will have power for good or ill. We may view military power as the activities of a mob whose focus is channeled. Clearly, there are advantages to an army in yielding protective capacities entirely apart from the equipment that it uses. Consider the case of an army without arms and a small group of individuals similarly without arms. The focused activity of the large group of people could readily overcome that of the small group if that were in any way necessary for protective purposes. The same holds true if each side were armed with very primitive weapons such as bows and arrows, or simple lances. Clearly, as a general rule, the capacities of armies in ancient times did not depend primarily on the arms they controlled or on the fact that they had arms superior to those of the groups they fought. What really mattered was organization, and part of the organization was the ability to focus a large group of individuals on specific objectives.

Note that the previous argument does not require the internal specialization of the group. Of course real armies, almost from time immemorial, have been organized along the lines of specialized units. Whether such units were made up of foot soldiers and horse soldiers, or bowmen and lancers, does not really matter. Even without specialization large units had clear-cut power advantages. It may be argued that the very fact that energies are focused in a given direction involves a type of specialization, even if there is no internal specialization of activity. At best this would be a borderline case, but it serves to point out that the power of the group does not require a number of specialized activities internally. Furthermore, the large group need have no specialized training and no specialized commitment except the willingness to focus its activities from time to time at the behest of some directing agent. Thus, we are arguing that power is associated with size even in a case where minimal specialization is involved.

For economists the interest is likely to be in productive economic units, and in such cases specialization is usually of the essence. Economies of scale are of course a basic consequence of organized internal specializations. In the pin factory example made famous by Adam Smith there are a variety of advantages associated with specialization such as job training, repetition, and as a consequence increased dexterity and increased quality. The important point is that the advantages that result from internal specialization can only be achieved with a certain minimum size; they cannot be achieved otherwise. Once again the focus is on size as the factor that eventually requires hierarchy.

A relatively large enterprise may also be needed in order to take advantage of necessarily bulky equipment, or other capital goods. In other words, technology itself may require units that are above a certain minimum size. Various large pieces of equipment can be irreducible units. They may also require relatively large complements of people to operate them. Consider the case of a cargo ship or a passenger ship. With increased size, up to some point, come other desirable qualities such as increases in speed and disproportional increases in cubic capacity compared to the cost of construction. Also, considerable manpower is usually required to run a large unit such as a ship. This manpower is of necessity organized in hierarchies. Similarly, railway systems or assembly lines must be units of a minimal size.

What is a minimum-size unit? Consider the case of a bridge to carry automobile traffic over a river. The automobile lanes clearly have a minimum width. Furthermore, the bridge span has to cover the entire width of the river. There cannot be half a bridge. Similarly, if we were discussing a tunnel we cannot have half a tunnel. In this sense size is clearly a function of technological requirements. A railway line also has to go from point A to point B, and does little good if it only goes halfway. A more complex question is the extent to which a subway system would require a minimal size to be viable. One could argue that the subway system would have to contain a minimal number of connections in order to be viable at all. Otherwise the system would not have enough traffic flow because of the lack of flexibility in its use. One could think of other cases in which the probability of covering a sufficient number of connections creates technological and economic needs for a certain minimum size.

Size is also likely to be a significant factor with respect to the marketing capacities of an enterprise. In other words, there is such a thing as marketing power, which we will argue depends in part on size. A good deal of economic literature has stressed the fact that market share, a function of the size of an enterprise, yields market power advantages. With a sufficient market share there is likely to be a reduction in competitive pressures to reduce price or costs, and thus less pressure on profits.

There are other marketing advantages that are frequently less noticeable. The marketing ability of an enterprise often requires the ability to gain attention. People frequently have to know quickly, and in a fairly striking manner, where a certain commodity is likely to be available. Size by itself, beyond some minimum level, is attention-getting. For example, a department store, simply because of size, gets more attention than a local retail outlet. A department store that is part of a chain of department stores is likely to get more attention than a single unit. For instance, it will usually be noticed whether or not there is a Sears in town. All this is part of the idea that size yields some types of information in an attention-getting fashion.

An additional element that will bring advantages to a large firm is that there are likely to be certain fixed costs for the development of both information to be distributed and information to be collected. Thus, in working out an advertising campaign there is a fixed cost simply in the creation and development of the advertising copy. This fixed-cost component falls per customer reached as the number of potential customers increases. Similarly, in developing marketing surveys to determine the nature of the market for a given product, or set of products, there are setting-up costs involved in the planning of the survey. Once again, the fixed cost per unit is reduced as a function of size. For instance, a given sample size may yield the same information about a market for a relatively large firm as it will for a very small one.

Uncertainty is a major problem in economic life, one that has to be faced by every enterprise. Large size provides a firm options to reduce uncertainty. A large enterprise can choose more scope, that is, a greater range of activities, products, or services. It can diversify its product lines in ways a small firm cannot. It can choose a wide-scope portfolio that reduces risk simply as a consequence of diversification. In addition, it can balance risky activities against relatively stable ones. The other side of the coin is that it can afford to gamble on some potentially high-profit, high-risk activities that a small firm cannot afford to try.

Related to this is the ability of the large firm to adjust the scope of its portfolio. As market or internal circumstances change the enterprise should, ideally, adjust to these changes. These changes may involve prices in different markets, demand in different markets, production procedures, and so on. A large firm can try to adjust by transferring activities from one part of the enterprise to another, by expanding profitable activities or product lines and contracting unprofitable ones. In addition, as circumstances change the large firm can, more readily than the small one, sell off units that are not doing well and purchase other units that are more profitable. Small firms will find it difficult to carry out such large activities.

Finance is another basic problem area. Here it would seem fairly clear, on a priori grounds, that the larger the going concern, the greater the financial options available to it. Other things being equal, the capacity to borrow from commercial banks is likely to be greater for the large firm, and certainly no worse than that of its small counterpart. The large firm, simply by the fact of size, is a highly valued customer in a way in which the small company cannot be. To the lender the small company is one of many, while the large company is one of the few whose withdrawal can be a significant loss. Perhaps more important, the large enterprise has available to it many more instruments of finance than the small one. The large firm can issue not only stock, but also a variety of stock instruments, as well as other financial instruments not readily available to the small firm, such as corporate bonds. Clearly the greater number of financial options increases the flexibility of the large firm in ways not readily available to the small one.

In the market for personnel some additional advantages of size come to mind. Other things being equal, the large firm should be able to attract higher-quality personnel than the small one. To start with, it can offer prospective employees a greater variety of activities. In addition it can offer options and guarantees that, if attempted by a small firm, would not appear as credible. For example, it can offer the stronger possibility of job security upon adequate performance since the actual life of large firms, on average, is very much greater than that of small ones. In addition, it can offer career paths inside the firm, which are in part a function of size and in part a function of variety. In addition, since size and hierarchy are connected, hierarchy can operate as an incentive system in the firm. To start with, higher levels can be associated with higher pay, and in addition, promotion to a higher rank and status will most frequently serve as an incentive mechanism. Also, the large firm can offer long-term income security, whereas such prospects in the small firm are likely to be more variable. The possibility of developing various fringe benefits for employees is likely to be greater in the large enterprise. In addition, various intangibles such as the possibility of identifying with the power and promise of the large enterprise are also likely to be important advantages.

Last but not least, large firms can credibly promise to undertake large-scale activities that small firms cannot readily do. Military contracts provide a clear example. A small firm coming in with a very low bid on a large-scale project cannot be taken seriously. Obviously the large firm's capacity to deliver is much more credible even if it has had no previous history with this particular type of activity.

So far, we have discussed only the advantages of size. Obviously there are significant disadvantages, or else what firms remain would be of mammoth size. But these disadvantages lie mostly in the area of bureaucracy and its close relative, hierarchy. We shall examine these matters in Chapter 12.

The Israeli Kibbutz: Size and Hierarchy

Let us now digress somewhat to consider the case of the Israeli kibbutz. The kibbutz is interesting because it operates under different incentive schemes than normal enterprises do; also, it resists hierarchy. The latter is especially why we want to consider the special case of the kibbutz here. However, before we do so a few general remarks about the nature of the kibbutz are in order.

Kibbutzim vary in size from 200 to 1,000 adult members, the average size being 439 (Don, 1985). All adult members vote in the general meeting that determines policies and plans, and elects people to the most important leadership roles. The kibbutz started and still exists as an organizational form based on socialist principles. The basic idea is that for the most part consumption is carried out in common while production activities ideally depend on member capacities and desires. What it comes down to is a strong egalitarian principle with respect to consumption. Three-quarters to four-fifths of consumption is carried out in common whereas the residual is given to members in money, which they can spend according to their wishes. The basic idea is that the consumption standard does not in any way depend on an individual's contribution to production.

How production is carried out in the kibbutz is somewhat more complicated. As a general rule individuals are allowed to choose their jobs.

Those jobs that have to be done and for which there are not enough applicants are filled by rotation. The less-desirable jobs are shared approximately equally by all members.

The kibbutz was already well established by the 1920s, some sixty years ago. Until recently the kibbutz has outperformed the Israeli economy as a whole in terms of various indices of efficiency and growth. The recent data are less clear. However, one has to be cautious in drawing conclusions from the kibbutz example because the kibbutz system is unrepresentative of the Israeli economy. It is only 3 percent of the work force and membership is voluntary. Thus, there is a self-selective aspect. Those who do not care for the system and the philosophy behind it can, and frequently do, leave.

On the whole it is surprising that the kibbutz system has done so well since in theory and in practice there is almost a complete lack of differential economic incentives in the kibbutz. The normal incentives available either in private enterprise in capitalist economies or in government service are completely nonexistent. We now consider briefly the lack of economic incentives. The most clear-cut aspect is the lack of differential pay for differential contributions. Thus, people who do very different types of work, which in the private sector would receive highly differential wages, receive exactly the same real income. Of course, most of the kibbutz income is provided in kind. Thus, kibbutz members usually take most of their meals in a common dining room, are allocated housing in accordance with their family size, and receive equal, small amounts of money for the sorts of goods and services that the kibbutz cannot provide. There is no hiding the fact that the contributions of different members are very different, both on similar jobs, and on different types of work.

Along with the equal consumption principle there is also no promotion system. Since hierarchy is repressed it is even impossible for individuals to receive a promotion as a consequence of unusual contributions. Of course, promotions and career systems are major incentives outside of the kibbutz system.

The question of hierarchy poses a difficult and unique problem. A strong egalitarian bias in the system implies that nobody in the system should be singled out as being superior to anyone else. Nevertheless it is recognized that work done by a large group of individuals requires somebody to be in charge. Thus, at least for functional purposes, a superior-subordinate relationship is necessary. The kibbutz ethos is to minimize the inequality of that relationship. The principle used is that all managerial or superior jobs should be strictly temporary and should be rotated. Ideally every individual should have the capacity and opportunity to take on these jobs. An individual should be selected from time to time for a managerial post and then after his or her period of duty is over, say after two or three years, the individual should go back to being a normal, ordinary working member.

In practice rotation is indeed carried out. However, some managerial posts are held for more than the "normal" three-year period. Furthermore, it has recently been discovered that while rotation takes place the type of rotation is "horizontal." That is, individuals with managerial skills are shifted from one hierarchical job to another with an occasional, usually brief, period as an ordinary low-level member. In view of the fact that there are differences in innate managerial skills, as well as knowledge, an extreme rotation system (one that permits everyone to be a manager an equal amount of time) would be at the expense of efficiency. Thus a question that arises is whether rotation, as it is actually practiced, eliminates hierarchy. This is one of the beliefs frequently expressed by kibbutz members. In fact, however, for those who serve only in subordinate roles rotation does not eliminate hierarchy, even though the actual superiors change from time to time.

We have already considered the fact that many of the more interesting jobs possible in factories are likely to have a managerial component; hence, the availability of interesting jobs might require a relaxation of the antihierarchy principle. In addition it has been pointed out that frequently people want jobs that have a career path of some sort. Many people want something close to a professional or managerial job, or a job outside the kibbutz in which high-level skills are involved. But the availability of such jobs clearly involves a violation of the antihierarchy principle. It seems clear there is bound to be conflict between practicality and hierarchy as the kibbutz moves more and more toward industrial and service activities. For present purposes the main conclusion is that an organizational form, the kibbutz, in which membership is completely voluntary, and whose philosophy is dedicated to the elimination or minimization of hierarchy cannot seem to do so in part or entirely in consequence of the needs of size.

The Hierarchical Solution to the Size Problem

The imposition of hierarchy in response to size has an ancient lineage. We find it mentioned in the Old Testament where Jethro (Moses' father-in-law) laments that Moses will wear himself out if he continues to try to lead all alone. He then recommends that Moses appoint captains of thousands, captains of hundreds, captains of fifty, and captains of tens (Exodus 19). Jethro is probably the first organization theorist in recorded history. In general we may view the problem as involving two major steps. To impose a certain degree of unity of purpose on a large-sized group of individuals requires that the group be organized in some way and that the group become responsive to certain necessary aspects of organization. The essence of the solution is to subdivide the large group into smaller groupings, which in turn are subdivided into still smaller groupings, and so on, until a smallest functional group size is determined. At that point hierarchy may be introduced as leaders of the smallest subgroups are appointed, and leaders of those leaders are appointed, and so on. Thus, hierarchy is not the entire system of organization; it is simply a characteristic of the organizational solution.

In what follows we will assume that a size-of-group problem exists and that hierarchy is used to solve the problem. In the real world, size and hierarchy are in some sense solved simultaneously. Furthermore the solution, whatever its value, is likely to evolve gradually in accordance with a system of trial and error. Nevertheless, there are some real situations in which we can observe the imposition of a new hierarchical solution on a large group when a previous solution has failed. This seems clear in Alfred Chandler's account of the growth of various large enterprises, such as Dupont and General Motors, where at some point in their history the firms appear to be stuck with an inappropriate hierarchy given their size and scope (Chandler, 1962). At such junctures the directors of the firm are forced to take stock of the situation as if they were examining the problem anew, and attempt to impose an appropriate hierarchical solution.

A significant element of hierarchical solutions is that they are not in any way unique. There are a great many possible divisions of a large group of people into smaller groups, and there are many ways of arranging these subgroups vis-à-vis each other. Hence, a great many hierarchical structures are possible. For example, the steepest hierarchy for any group of individuals would be a complete ranking of every individual in which, apart from the lowest and the highest, everyone had somebody above them and somebody below. An extremely shallow ranking would be one that had one leader and everyone else was viewed as an equal. In addition to such characteristics as steepness or shallowness, hierarchies may be composed of various structures, from one that is unitary to others that involve mutually independent segments. In general we should not expect hierarchies to be determined on the basis of completely functional considerations. Instead, the result is likely to be a partial consequence of history and culture. Thus, there are a great many hierarchical solutions that will work for a group of a given size, even though they may not all work equally well.

While an essential element of organization is to break up the large group into small units, the relations between the units can vary along several continua, for instance, complete autonomy at one extreme and complete control at the other. Because of the different degrees of autonomy that subunits may be given, two entities of the same size may have different numbers of levels, or different hierarchical steepness. In addition, sets of subunits, hierarchically organized, may be given complete autonomy. In typical large enterprises this autonomy may be along product lines (as is frequently the case in automobile industries), or along functional lines (for example, a marketing department may be largely autonomous from other areas of the company), or some combination of the two. In general, the more autonomy different units are given, the less the need for detailed control and the shallower the possible hierarchy.

The way the entity is cut up into subunits will determine the degree to which it makes sense and to what degree it is possible to give specific subgroups a high or a low degree of autonomy. The hierarchical nature of such units is determined by, and in turn implies, the functions and responsibilities assigned to the subgroup. A subgroup can be autonomous only to the extent that it has the capacity to scan the environment, and possesses the resources to make decisions on its own, and hence is in a position to get positive results. Otherwise, the unit in question will be seriously dependent on other units and levels in the hierarchy. A subunit may be dependent on resources, information, decision-making authorities, or access to markets for inputs or outputs, and so on.

Degrees of autonomy and degrees of dependence are mirror images. Their magnitudes sum to unity. The greater the dependence, the less the autonomy, and vice versa. It also follows that the greater the dependence of the unit on other units and on higher levels, the greater the need for a steeper hierarchy, other things being equal. By the same token, the greater the dependence, the greater the need for coordination, and again, this will usually imply a steeper hierarchy, other things being equal.

Hierarchy is also usually connected to the willingness of those on top, or the degree to which the hierarchical culture with allow those on top, to delegate responsibility to those below. Of course, this implies allowing for a degree of discretion on the part of subordinates, which in turn implies a certain degree of trust. A high degree of delegation and trust will permit less control, and hence a less steep hierarchical structure. This follows from the usual span-of-control arguments. The greater the trust, the less control required, which allows the subunit to have greater span of control. Other things being equal, the greater the span of control of the subunit, the shallower the required hierarchy.

Note that hierarchy need not work in a totalitarian way in terms of the transmission of information from the top down, or the gathering of information from the bottom up. Those at the top do not have to know how activities are carried out in detail, nor does knowledge have to be greatest at the top. It is quite possible for directions from the top to be vague, without detail, even confused, and yet for the hierarchy to work well. The reason is partly that those at the top can use very abstract language and allow lower levels to work out and implement detailed interpretations. The interpreters may be much more expert in choosing the appropriate detail than those who give the initial directions. All that superiors need is some feedback that indicates whether in some *aggregate* or *average* manner the intent of their directions was carried out. Clearly, there are various combinations of degrees of abstractness of the policies conveyed, and degrees of expertise in interpretation and implementation, so that a variety of hierarchical structures could also result on the basis of these variables.

Overall, the arguments presented suggest that there is probably an infinite number of possible hierarchical structures for a given size group and a given set of purposes. The outcome depends on the degree of autonomy that is given, or can be given, to subunits. This in turn depends on such elements as trust, need for control, the ability of an autonomous unit to know and to carry out purposes of larger units, and so on. The outcome is also likely to be a question of the attitudes of those at the higher levels, as well as the culture of the environment in which the enterprise exists. In other words, the result is unlikely to be determined entirely by functional considerations.

Because there is no unique solution, that is, a unique hierarchical form, conventions will become important parts of hierarchical structures. There are likely to be conventions for both structure and activities. As we have seen earlier, such conventions are connected with degrees of internal inefficiency. The relation between hierarchy and internal inefficiency is analyzed in Chapter 12.

Specialization, Hierarchy, and Internal Inefficiency

Just as hierarchy is a ubiquitous phenomenon, so is specialization. Nobody in a modern economy is self-sufficient. Without self-sufficiency some types of specialization are bound to exist. Although specialization is usually associated with efficiency we will see that specialization can also contribute to inefficiency through the fragmentation of certain "invisible" elements of human effort. The basic fragmented elements are motivational in nature; among the important aspects are commitment to others, trust, identification with the organization, cooperation, and a sense of common organizational objectives. Specialization requires the careful recombining and coordinating of these fragmented *invisible* elements to avoid low effort levels.

The approach taken in this chapter is to focus on such recombining and coordinating activities. Among the central questions are, What are the elements to be recombined and coordinated? What significant elements are left out, or not fully reintegrated, which turn out to be sources of inefficiency? In the process of recombining the "visible" elements of production, hierarchy creates distances between people at different levels. These distances tend to diminish cooperation at various levels. We will argue that such problems can be overcome by the development of "enlarged commitments" between individuals at different vertical levels. Also, enlarged commitments are a precondition for the horizontal cooperation that is needed to handle contingencies at the most efficient level. In general, it may be useful to view the firm as a network of vertical and horizontal relationships that can be connected in various ways. Both vertical and horizontal relations can be cooperative, isolated, or adversarial. We will see that the nature and distribution of such relations in the network determines the degree of internal inefficiency.

Specialization, Effort, and Motivation

Ever since Adam Smith's famous example of the pin factory it has been clear that there is a close association between specialization and economies of scale. In the pin factory example we have a description of the *visible* physical division of a previously integrated effort. The sequence of efforts that could be carried out by a single person attempting to make a pin is improved upon by separating the components of the individual's activities, *specializing* workers to perform the separate activity units, and then physically *reconstituting* the products of their separate efforts. Such specialization produces not only economies in the pace of effort, but frequently improvements in quality.

A few remarks about the advantages of specialization are appropriate here. First, there is an allocative advantage in the sense that if an individual or a piece of equipment has multiple uses, one could allocate activities to that use to which the person or piece of equipment is best suited. Second, there is likely to be a direct dexterity advantage. In other words, specialization leads to a greater pace of activity and, up to a point, greater precision with respect to quality. This applies to both individuals and to machines. Finally, there is likely to be a training advantage. The more specialized the activity, the shorter the training period and the more efficient the training. This is clearly more applicable to individuals than to machines, however, machines usually need a counterpart breaking-in and adapting period.

Little more than a century after *The Wealth of Nations,* the work of Fredrick Taylor took Smith's essential ideas a step further. He developed careful time and motion studies so that each activity unit of an individual would be carried out more effectively. What was missed by the early factory masters, as well as in Taylor's work and the work of others associated with the "scientific management" movement, was that the separation of activities and the allocation of activities to different individuals really tore at some significant, *invisible* elements of human effort. What was readily seen was that some sort of technical coordination of activities was required. What was usually not seen was that some type of coordination of invisible elements was also needed.

Let us compare the situation under one-man integrated production with specialized multiperson production. Suppose that a single individual purchases wood in the marketplace, works on the wood to make chairs, and then sells the chairs. Suppose that the individual produces one chair a day. The following scheme indicates the essential connection between the three types of activities.

Step I :   Purchasing ⟶ Work ⟶ Sales

$$?$$
Step II :   Sales Revenue $\gtreqless$ Purchasing Costs

This is a picture of a highly integrated scheme of activity, including a feedback element. The chairmaker makes purchases in the wood market, transforms the wood in his workshop, and sells the chair in the chair market. He then connects the sales revenues and the input purchase costs. Step II is a feedback relation that is very important in the process. If sales revenue falls short of costs then that fact should put pressure on the individual to reconsider his activities. Whatever motivational forces are at work, they are all integrated in one individual who pays all the costs and receives all the benefits.

We note that only two contracts are involved, the wood purchasing contract and the chair sales contract. If the chairmaker wants to maximize income then he works as hard as possible, but he can if he chooses work less hard, produce fewer chairs, and enjoy more leisure. We have here the possibility of a clear-cut trade-off between work and leisure since work is clearly connected to the two basic markets.

Let us now see what happens if we shift to a specialized mode of production. The scheme now becomes enlarged.

Step I :   Purchasing ⟶ Work (by employees) ⟶ Sales

$$?$$
Step II :   Sales Revenue $\gtreqless$ Purchasing Costs

The enlarged scheme is considerably more complex. The work that was subdivided has to be coordinated. Specialists in coordination (managers) have to be hired. Clearly there is now a wide variety of contracts. Not only are there contracts with the sellers of wood and the buyers of chairs, but there are additional contracts with "factory" workers.

The most significant aspect of this is that the motivational picture has now been changed markedly. The simple integrated motivational scheme in which the individual simply connected the wood and chair markets through his work and made a profit thereby is now complicated by a wide variety of contracts. In breaking up a simple motivational scheme we introduced new types of motivations that were either entirely absent, or almost absent in the initial arrangements. We introduced possible conflicts of interest between different individuals, as well as elements of trust and distrust surrounding such conflicts.

Suppose the owner hires ten people to carry out chair manufacturing, but he continues to do the buying and selling. He divides the activities so that his employees specialize—some will shape pieces of wood, others will glue the pieces of wood together, still others will pack for shipment, and so on. Obviously some degree of coordination of the separated physical activities is necessary. This coordination problem is a straightforward "engineering" question. But a number of other, non-engineering types of problems arise that did not exist before. What sorts of contracts will be given to employees? Will the employer attempt to specify the work in each case and offer a salary, or will he work out a piece-rate contract? Will the contract be the same for all employees, or will he allow individuals to choose? We can see immediately that certain motivational issues are involved. A piece-rate system has different motivational characteristics than a salary system for a specified effort output. Under a piece-rate system a clear-cut monetary motivation is operative. But can quality be maintained under piece rates? Will piece rates lead to "quality squabbles" between the owner and his employees? If everyone is to have the same contract should they all be under piece rates, or under salary?

Somewhat more subtle motivational aspects also enter. If a piece-rate system is adopted will employees emphasize quantity at the expense of quality? If a salary system is adopted will employees carry out their presumed contracts, or will they shirk? Should those who do more work receive more pay? The owner also has to consider his own motivations. To what extent does he want to be involved in monitoring activities? Will he be concerned about the aura of distrust that frequently surrounds monitoring?

Thus far we have emphasized individualistic motivations. How about the interactions between individuals? Do employees as a peer group provide, in part, an additional motivation system? To what extent are the activities of employees connected not only with their contracts but with peer approval and disapproval? At the same time individuals may also care about the approval of the owner. Furthermore, there may be subtle interactions between owner approval (or disapproval) and the peer-group approval system. The point of these remarks should now be clear. When the owner does all the work the motivational considerations are very different from the situation that arises when the owner hires others, introduces specialization, and creates at least one level of hierarchy as he himself operates as manager-coordinator. The initial division of activities not only tears at the previously integrated activity structure, but at the same time it also tears at the previous motivational structure. New types of motivational elements enter.

In the initial situation the major motivational decision the owner had to make was between work and leisure. Now the elements involve the possibility of shirking by subordinates, the possibility of cutting corners with respect to quality of effort, as well as interpersonal attitudes such as trust or distrust. We will also see presently that there are significant latent conflict-of-interest problems. These will exist both in the contract-making stage and during intracontract performance, but especially during the latter. Thus the basic motivational problems turn out to be very different once specialization and its motivational concomitants are introduced inside the organization.

We can easily imagine a further expansion of the enterprise and greater subdivision of activities. Thus, as output increases more individuals are employed in the basic tasks, these tasks become narrower, and hence more finely specialized. As a result there is need for further coordination, and this in turn results in more steps in the hierarchy. Visualize a system in which there are basic employees, foremen, and first-level middle managers who coordinate the foremen's activities. In addition, various functional divisions may be set up so that there is now a marketing director, an office manager, a purchasing director, and perhaps a vice-president in charge of finance. Note especially that all of these are activities that the owner previously did by himself when the enterprise was smaller. Now the enterprise is more specialized and the owner no longer carries out these activities. If anything he keeps an eye on those activities and when necessary coordinates them at the highest level. But in this case the tears in the motivational fabric are likely to be even greater than in the case when the owner did everything himself.

Process Cuts, Specialization, and Recombinings

In the discussion of the gradual increase in size, specialization, and complexity of a chair manufacturing firm it was clear that what was once a unified production process gets cut, as it were, into a number of separate, specialized activities. It is obvious that all these specialized activities have to be recombined so that the product as a whole is produced. There is a technical aspect of the recombining process that is a part of engineering. Somehow the specialized activities have to be scheduled and the outputs recombined at various levels to produce a finished product. Thus, if the specialized activities are A, B, and C, there is likely to be a higher-level activity that recombines A, B, and C into a product. If further specialization takes place (say, A_1 and A_2, B_1 and B_2, C_1 and C_2) then further recombinings, have to occur. The important point is that these technical recombinings, occurring at different levels of the hierarchy, are of a clearly visible nature.

What we have to examine is whether everything that is divided up by the cuts gets to be recombined, or whether some things that are not so clearly visible get left out. The answer is related to how fast and how well the various basic and recombining activities occur. This appears to be the central internal efficiency question.

A major element likely to be left out is motivation, probably because it is essentially invisible. In cutting the activity stream, specializing activities, and assigning these activities to different individuals, the previous motivational structure is destroyed. Is something put back that is equally effective?

The one-man firm who carries out all the activities by himself does not have to worry about a motivational problem. The process of production does not change his motivation. If he carries out some degree of sequential specialization, as long as he does it all by himself it is unlikely to result in a motivational change. But, once additional individuals have to be brought into the process they are unlikely to have the same kinds of motivations as the original owner-manager-employee, whatever his motivations were.

The divisions in the production process to produce specialization cut up the motivational pie, so to speak. The initially integrated motivational scheme of the one-man firm is no longer necessarily an integrated scheme in a multiperson firm. Where there are ten people rather than a single person, these ten do not behave as if they are one person somehow enlarged. In fact, each one of these ten people is likely to have different motivations from every other one, and the question is how all of these differences add up in terms of motivating behavior within the enlarged structure. If nothing is done to recapture an integrated motivational scheme, how effective will the multiperson motivational scheme be compared to the one-man firm?

Consider the extreme case of nothing being done to marshall individual motivation into a coordinated whole when the firm shifts from the single individual to one in which ten specialized people are hired. The employees are likely to be given incomplete instructions as to how their jobs are to be carried out. What interpretations of the incomplete instructions will result? In part each individual will interpret his job on the basis of his specific previous experience. Through trial and error, and through some negotiation with the owner a mutually tolerable interpretation will be worked out. Nonetheless, it is most likely that the results will be mixed. Work quality will probably vary considerably between individuals. Coordinating differences in quality in producing individual chairs will turn out to be fairly difficult. What was a simple integrated standard of work quality for the owner-craftsman is no longer so for the employer. A standard with a fairly wide range of variations is likely to be established. Similarly, different paces of work are likely to result, at least at the outset.

One can examine such technical or engineering aspects of a firm's production by looking at the product and its subunits, or by looking at observable activities, but still something important will be left out. The major aspect of production that is omitted is the extent to which in- dividuals care about cooperating with the larger entity, namely, the enterprise. At the outset it is likely that none of the employees will care about changing their performance except through pressure from, and negotiations with, their superiors about their views of their implicit work contracts. Some individuals will grudgingly yield to the authority of the employer to some degree.

One thing is clear. Diverse motivations means that people no longer have a sense of being integrated by a single set of goals and interests. Individuals have a sense of being separated from each other by diverse motivations and interests, and thus, free-riding incentives with respect to effort are bound to arise. At the very least, individuals now recognize two sets of interests: company interests and personal interests. Pre- sumably there is no reason for any individual to put company interests above his own, hence there is a motivation to shift away from company interests to personal ones. Earlier we considered only two-level hier- archies—employees and management. The question that now arises is, How do multiple levels change the picture?

A strong argument could be made that multilevel hierarchies exag- gerate the problems associated with free riding with respect to effort. Consider two levels at a time: those of subordinates and superiors. The superior, not being the owner, is no longer the ultimate boss. To what extent do the superior's expressed desires to subordinates represent the interests of the company? After all, superiors also have their own interests, and subordinates may be asked to serve superiors' individual interests. Thus, the net result is apt to be an attenuation of company interests in various ways. At each step in the hierarchy people are likely to be serving, to some degree, someone else's private interests. The perception of company interests must of necessity become distorted when special private interests intervene at each step. Furthermore, as one descends the steps of the hierarchy the distortions are likely to increase. Thus, if individuals have free-riding incentives with respect to company interests, they are likely to have even stronger free-riding incentives with respect to the private individual interests of other employees.

Similarly, multilevel hierarchies may aggravate problems arising from adversarial feelings between those at one level and those at the level above. Will people have adversarial feelings against either private interests of superiors, or the way superiors interpret company interests? After all, there is a sense in which company interests represent the common interests of all employees regardless of their status in the hierarchy. The company provides the jobs and the incomes to meet the needs of its members. The greater the success of the company the easier it is to provide jobs and incomes. But if the objectives of the company now appear to be distorted and confused by the private objectives of those at higher levels, then the common interest aspect of the company becomes attenuated and adversarial concerns no longer appear to attack what is envisioned as the common welfare. Rather they take on an adversarial stance against what are viewed at least in part, as the private interests of those in dominant roles.

An alternative "solution" is possible—the optimally cooperative community. If each and every individual were optimally motivated then each would try to find out what the superiors at the next level *really* wanted and what would be optimal from the viewpoint of the enterprise. Likewise, each person at a higher level would try to communicate the required behavior in terms of "company interests," that is, in terms of the interests of the entire membership of the company. Under such circumstances individuals might no longer be concerned about the boundaries of their particular jobs and whether or not their implicit contracts appear to be violated. Instead they would try to find out what they could do cooperatively, that is, how each might best fit into the group effort. The level of communication and the flow of information would now be very different from the situation considered above. In each case there would be an attempt to interpret, as far as possible, the company interest at that level of the hierarchy, and to communicate that interest to the level below. At the same time, those below would attempt to interpret such communication, also with reference to the company interests. This represents something like an optimal motivational scheme under a hierarchical system. We are not concerned here with the realism of such a scheme, nor how to achieve it. It is presented simply as a means of assessing the deviation between an optimal scheme in a multiperson organization, and what is likely to exist in the actual situation as a consequence of cuts in the production flow necessitated by the introduction of specialization.

Related Invisible "Cutouts"

In addition to motivation, but tied to it, there are a number of related human attitude variables that usually get cut out in the process of specialization creation. Let us look at them on the basis of table 12.1, which compares the integrated nature of the components when only one individual is involved to the situation under the multiperson hierarchy. Note that all of these components are of a nontechnological nature. Furthermore, all are essentially invisible. Perhaps most important, all of these components are naturally integrated in the individual and equally naturally separated in the hierarchy.

TABLE 12.1.

Single person	Hierarchy
Integrated motivation	Fragmented motivation
Integrated identification	Fragmented identification
Integrated trust	Fragmented trust
Integrated commitment	Fragmented commitment
Integrated cooperation	Fragmented cooperation
Integrated information on objectives	Fragmented information on objectives

If we go through the components one by one, we find that the points to be made are true almost by the definition of an individual. The individual identifies with himself or herself. He trusts himself. He is likely to be committed to his own objectives. He cooperates with himself and he has access to necessary information about his objectives. None of these are likely to be true for the hierarchy. Members of a hierarchy do not necessarily identify with it. Nor do they necessarily trust each other, trust those at a higher level, or even trust the hierarchy as an organization. Clearly, firm members need not be committed to the objectives of the organization. Furthermore, they may not cooperate with their peers, their superiors, or in some sense with the enterprise as a whole.

The point is that these natural attributes of the self-contained individual have to be fostered and created in a hierarchy. It does not come naturally to individuals to behave in the way that would most benefit the enterprise. The enterprise has to create an environment in which people identify with it. Creating conditions under which trust is the rule is likely to be extremely difficult. As before, we have in mind trust between peers, between individuals at different levels, and trust of the hierarchy as a whole. Such conditions are likely to be very difficult to establish. Furthermore, trust is likely to be a fragile relationship.

The same difficulties regarding trust and its fragility also hold for commitment at every level. The opposite of commitment is the pursuit of personal interests where these deviate from the organization's interests. Obviously every organization may desire a cooperative spirit to pervade its activities, but cannot count on it, and when it does occur the organization has to work to maintain it. The degree of commitment to others in the organization is critical to how well it functions. (More on this later.)

While information is a very complex variable, what is meant here regarding the last component in table 12.1 is the information that is likely to be available to an individual about what his own objectives are, and about what may be desired in order to pursue such objectives. Once an individual has this information he necessarily has access to it, but it is exactly this type of information and access that can no longer be taken for granted in the hierarchy. It is not even clear where the hierarchy is to obtain its sense of objective. If a committee structure allows the hierarchy to enunciate objectives, there is a problem of how to distribute this information, and a problem of determining the exact nuances that the hierarchy may wish to convey about the objectives. In any event, it is clear that for the hierarchy information of this type generates both information-gathering and distribution problems.

A review of the elements in table 12.1 suggests that in the hierarchy they are all likely sources of internal inefficiency. Fragmented identification is likely to imply a lesser concern with the firm's objectives on the part of firm members. The same holds true for the divided commitment of individuals as well as for incomplete trust. Similarly, a limited cooperative stance by employees is likely to result in less effective effort than a fully cooperative one. Finally, the more fragmented the information about the hierarchy's objectives, and the more limited the access to it by those who may need to know, the less effective the outcome. Hierarchy either fragments or limits the cooperation of these components unless countermeasures are taken. The greater the number of levels in the hierarchy, the greater the fragmentation that is likely to occur.

Hierarchical Levels, Distance, and Separations

Now we consider what the existence of hierarchy does to the relationships between individual members of the hierarchy, especially those at different levels. In general, the hierarchy is intended to bind together the different visible, specialized activities in the organization. At the same time hierarchy creates a distance between certain individuals. It limits or eliminates access and creates separations between groups. We will examine these characteristics of hierarchy one at a time.

A hierarchy usually has a head. By this we mean a unit at the highest level that determines priorities, objectives, and constraints for the organization, and that is in some sense responsible for these elements of policy. In a completely authoritarian organization the head would be the chief executive officer or the owner-manager. In other cases it may be the CEO plus the board of directors, or some significant committee. The point is that the hierarchy creates a distance between the top and other levels. The more levels the greater the distance. In a two-level organization there is closeness to top policies. The basic employee can easily see the boss. In a ten-level organization it may be impossible, or close to impossible, for him to do so.

Hierarchy also creates separations between levels. After all, the whole point of hierarchy is to assign different functions and different responsibilities to different levels, and hence to demarcate different levels. At the very least the separations created are functional, but very frequently there are likely to be nonfunctional spillovers to other aspects of life in the organization, and even outside it. Usually some sense of status, class, or caste will either exist or be interpreted by others to exist among members of a hierarchy, even if this sense is sometimes subtle. To some degree hierarchy limits access between individuals who are members of different levels. The extreme case is probably that of the Indian caste system where a complex religious scheme determines separation of every aspect of economic, social, and communal life.

Some of the relationships between members of different levels involve asymmetry. One example is the authority relation. Some have authority over others, but not vice versa. The same holds for evaluation. Some at higher levels evaluate the performance of those at lower levels, and usually not vice versa. This also holds for responsibility for performance. In addition, some at higher levels may have authority to convene meetings of lower-level employees, but again not vice versa. In general there are likely to be decision-making activities that allow those at a higher level to make decisions that determine the activities, or influence the outcomes (pay, promotions, privileges) for those at lower levels. Finally, partial power relations between individuals are likely to exist, and to some degree to be directly associated with levels in the hierarchy.

We have already considered the consequences of distance and separation. Both motivational aspects of intrafirm activities and near-motivational aspects such as identification, trust, commitment, and cooperation are likely to be influenced by distance and separation. All of these are likely to be reduced because of distance, and because hierarchy separates the organization into groups that are likely to develop strong horizontal bonds. These horizontal bonds may be used to avoid or to limit the vertical, asymmetrical, powerlike relationships to some extent. As a consequence it becomes more difficult, because of both distance and separation, for those at the top of the hierarchy to transmit pressure for improved performance to those below them.

Controls, Incentives, and Motivations under Hierarchies

Thus far we have argued on the assumption that the organization was not aware of the invisible motivational factors and would not counter the consequences of cutting up these invisible elements. This was a useful device to isolate the nature of the motivation problems. But of course there is no pretense that this assumption is realistic. Leaders of enterprises are likely to be aware directly or indirectly, at least to some degree, that motivations and incentives play a role in productive behavior; hence, they have to somehow take these factors into account in "designing" and "redesigning" the nature of organizational activities and structures. Usually such awareness arises in response to problems. In the experience of most executives of almost every enterprise frustrations arise because in some way employees are not working as attentively as they should, or as carefully as they should, or as effectively as expected, or as cooperatively as required. It will frequently be gleaned that somehow the incentive structure is at fault. As a consequence some procedures or other changes meant to counter or influence motivations will be introduced in the hope of attaining improved performance. We now consider some of the means employed.

One way to handle the situation is to try to minimize individual discretion. In order to do this those in charge have to try to anticipate all possible work contingencies and to establish a procedure, or rule of behavior, for every predictable situation. This means that almost everyone's job in the organization has to be specified in as much detail as possible, in advance. In a sense every demand on a person's time has to be preprogrammed and classified so that an appropriate response can be determined for every contingency. Needless to say this will result in a completely bureaucratized organization.

Does bureaucratization work? To a considerable degree it does. By minimizing discretion it minimizes the errors and costs that employees can impose on the firm through discretionary behavior. It enables those at higher levels in the hierarchy to be able to predict what those below them will do. Such an approach is likely to be augmented by a system of monitoring and sanctions. However, if this is all that exists, the work environment is likely to be somewhat dehumanized. This approach represents an attempt to fashion the organization in the image of a machine. Most important, it is likely to be suboptimal. It does not use positive motivational factors, such as enthusiasm, inherent in human beings. At best it gets from the work force only what can be safely blueprinted in advance. In addition, as argued earlier, many of the preprogrammed responses may be inferior to individualized responses to special circumstances. In other words, a mixture of routine *and* discretion is likely to produce more efficient behavior than routine alone.

Another way of handling motivation is to emphasize negative motivational factors through monitoring of people's activities or output and imposing penalties for presumed shortcomings. Penalties may range from admonitions, to lack of wage increases or promotions, or deprivation of privileges, to firing the individual. Such penalties may occur when performance was satisfactory but the individual did not follow accepted rules or procedures. Frequently, encouraging individuals to follow rules and procedures may become an end in itself entirely apart from seeking behavior that is in the interest of the organization.

The third means of handling motivation is to create a system of positive incentives with both pecuniary and nonpecuniary benefits for superior performance. However, creating the differentials in rewards between individuals to provide incentives for performance has its limitations in a nonhierarchical system simply because such organizations are likely to be quite small. It is especially noteworthy that hierarchy increases the possibility of creating positive incentives. To start with, hierarchies allow for the possibility of multilevel internal careers. As a consequence some employees will have the incentive to perform well in order to be promoted from one rank to the next. In addition, the reduced number of posts available with each step up in the hierarchy creates the possibility of competition for promotion. Furthermore, each level of the hierarchy allows for differential nonpecuniary benefits such as office space, carpets, staff, and the various trappings of status. Thus, hierarchy allows greater complexity in the system of pecuniary and nonpecuniary payoffs. Whether such a system gets the most effective effort out of those in different posts depends on circumstances.

We have seen that hierarchy plays a role in each strategy for handling motivations. Under the bureaucratic strategy hierarchy allows those at different levels to better understand and predict how the "machine" is operating. Under an internal career system, hierarchy widens the range of positive payoffs, as well as the range of possible sanctions, in part through the denial of career privileges.

If the reaction to every created incentive was well understood then one could compute an optimal incentive structure for every degree of hierarchy. However, this is unlikely to be the case. The reason is not only a lack of knowledge about responses to various incentives, but also the interdependencies between individuals at the same level and at different levels. Free-riding incentives or feelings of peer-group solidarity, and the cooperative or adversarial nature of vertical relations will influence responses to each type of voluntary or monitored incentive system. Isolating incentives and gauging individual responses is not sufficient for determining what happens, because of such group interdependencies.

It is useful to separate incentives from motivations. The hierarchy supplies incentives, firm members have motivations. The incentives supplied need not match the demand for incentives that result from the motivational forces that govern the behavior of firm members.

Motivational Interdependencies and Hierarchy

Groups create incentives for individual behavior, as we saw in the chapter on conventions. Membership in a group will lead individuals who identify strongly with group aims to be more productive than they would be if they were concerned only with their own interests. The reasons for such behavior are well established. People usually seek signs of group approval, the avoidance of group disapproval, and especially the avoidance of group sanctions. Thus, if the influence of a subgroup reflects the goals of the hierarchy, individual effort levels may be greater than under purely individualistic incentives. By the same token, if the subgroup influence is antagonistic to the interests of the hierarchy this will limit or reduce individual performance.

We need to distinguish between two types of groups, horizontal or peer groups, and vertical groups. A vertical group is not restricted to a single level while a horizontal group is limited to members of a given level of the hierarchy. Also, there are different types of horizontal relations. Those in a horizontal group may cooperate for a variety of objectives. Thus, it is important to distinguish horizontal cooperation for adversarial purposes from cooperation for productive purposes. This distinction is especially critical when considering the effect of horizontal cooperation on various types of inefficiency. Different types of cooperation are likely to work in opposite directions. Horizontal groups also can be neutral with respect to the hierarchy, or serve to shelter group members from some of the pressures of the hierarchy.

Neutral horizontal groups usually involve situations in which the group purpose is not connected to central and basic hierarchical interests. Where it is connected there is no reason (in the absence of certain vertical relations to be discussed later) for the horizontal group to reflect hierarchical interests since it does not contain members of another level who would have other-level interests. The most important example is a trade union that limits membership so that those with higher-level interests are excluded.

Another important example is a profession whose members are employed within hierarchies but do not rule their firms' hierarchies. Examples of such groups are physicians, lawyers, economists, accountants, and actuaries. In most cases standards of behavior for such groups reflect their professional membership rather than the standards of the corporation that employs them. Usually such individuals will resist the imposition of behavior that goes against such professional standards.

Of course, in reality there are cases in which members of a given profession rise in the hierarchy and attempt to disassociate themselves from their profession. They take on their corporate coloration. Nevertheless, in general, professions are at least to some degree directly or indirectly in conflict with hierarchies and attempt to retain their own unique modes of behavior in the face of hierarchical pressure to do otherwise.

Whether horizontal groups are sheltering, or antagonistic, or cooperative toward the hierarchy is very likely to influence an important aspect of horizontal relations, the degree to which peers cooperate in carrying out activities that could be categorized as falling *between* the accepted definitions of different jobs. Such interstitial job activities could be successfully carried out by firm members in different types of jobs, possibly at different levels. If routine jobs are well defined then cooperation may not be critical for routine circumstances. But an interesting question is, What is the best way to handle nonroutine problems? In business endeavors things do not always work out as anticipated. A certain number of nonroutine circumstances arise in many types of work. Nonroutine situations are apt to call for interstitial job activities.

An argument can be made that nonroutine problems should be handled at the lowest possible level, for two important reasons. First, the lowest working level is where the most detailed knowledge of the situation is likely to exist. It is best to handle problems where the most knowledge is available. Second, if we assume that rates of pay are lower at lower levels, then it is also likely that the cost of handling nonroutine problems will be lowest at the lowest possible handling level.

In a great many cases nonroutine problems are handled at a higher level. Masahiko Aoki (1986) has argued that in American firms, where strong job demarcations dominate, nonroutine problems are handled at higher levels, but that in Japanese firms this is not the case. In Japanese firms, peers are not concerned with strict demarcations of their jobs; they are highly cooperative from a production viewpoint. Furthermore, job rotation enables individuals to have lots of information about different jobs, and about possible interstitial job activities. Hence, workers are able to handle nonroutine problems at the lowest possible level. Also, it was pointed out to me by engineers who have worked in similar firms in the United States and Japan that the Japanese had relatively few employees assigned to interstitial jobs compared to the United States. Clearly, an important aspect of this dichotomy is the motivation to protect specific jobs versus the motivation to cooperate in interjob activities. We will consider this problem more fully in the next section, when we discuss vertical relationships. There we will take up the question: To what extent does horizontal cooperation for production goals depend on vertical relations?

Vertical Groups

Of special interest for the study of hierarchy is the role of vertical groups, the nature of such groups, and their relation in the firm. The focus will be on mutually cooperative vertical groupings. By this is meant a subgroup whose members are at different hierarchical levels and establish special cooperative relationships with each other. For example, a subordinate may make it clear that he will do the bidding of his superior in an enthusiastic manner but in return he expects his superior to be especially helpful in gaining promotions or other forms of vertical movement for the subordinate. Thus, those at different levels can clearly see mutual benefits from their relationship even if the sense of mutual benefit does not occur simultaneously.

The elements that enter into mutual vertical cooperation are most of the elements encountered earlier (see table 12.1), namely, a sense of common identification, a sense of trust, cooperation, and a sense of common objectives. What all of these involve critically is an attitude of commitment to a person or persons at a higher level. Similarly, those at a higher level have enlarged commitments to those at lower levels. Where these commitments for performance are mutually recognized there is a mutual commitment scheme, which is likely to be the basis of the various types of activities that come under the heading of mutual vertical cooperation.[1]

Now, commitments to others may be limited or open. A limited commitment is one that is strictly within predetermined bounds. Thus, a

---

1. While this chapter was being revised a paper by Wintrobe and Breton (1986) appeared that argued that hierarchical vertical trust is likely to be associated with efficiency whereas horizontal trust will be associated with inefficiency. From the present point of view this would seem to go only part of the way in explaining efficiency versus inefficiency. In part, this is because trust is only one element; commitment also has to be involved. Clearly, trust without commitment will not necessarily yield cooperative productivity results. Furthermore, as will be argued later in connection with the Aoki proposal, there is a relation between vertical and horizontal cooperation, which partly depends on commitment. The relation is that vertical mutual commitments are a necessary prior condition for horizontal cooperation on production goals.

commitment to be responsive to a certain category of requests, but none outside of the category, is limited, while a commitment to accede to any request from a superior, or to any observed opportunity that would improve output would be an open commitment. Openness is a matter of degree. Thus, a limited commitment would involve a sense of a rigid job demarcation, while an open one would imply flexibility with respect to jobs and the willingness to consider new job boundaries if that helps productivity. A completely open commitment would mean openness to any request, or acceding to any possibility, or suggesting any observed opportunity to improve output.

Consider the case of a three-level vertical group. Those at each level expect some sort of benefits from those at other levels. For present purposes it does not matter whether those at Level I (the lowest level) have to go through Level II to achieve some benefits from those at Level III, or whether direct access is possible between Levels I and III. What is important is that a sense of potential mutual benefit leads the entire group to perform effectively with a high degree of team spirit. It is both the cooperation and the motivation generated by team spirit and augmented by the sense of mutual benefits that are likely to result in highly effective performance.

Now carry the basic idea one step further. Suppose that on top of the three-level vertical group there is another three-level group linked to it with at least one member in common. Thus we conceive of a higher group made up of a Level III person and of Level IV and Level V members. Because these two groups are linked we have a subhierarchy, so to speak, which (assume for the moment) contains all the hierarchical levels except for the chief executive officer. Now visualize a firm composed of a set of such linked vertical groups that cooperate. If disputes arise among them, the CEO acts as a referee and resolves differences in order to retain cooperation. Clearly, a system of this sort is likely to solve, at least temporarily, the hierarchical problems of the enterprise. In other words, with vertical groups of this type, the divisive character of hierarchy can be modified or eliminated. Something like this exists in the *idealized* Japanese company.[2]

2. It is possible that if vertical groups are highly cooperative (that is, if there is enlarged commitment) so that everyone relates to the same set of common objectives and identifies strongly with the enterprise, then we may have something approaching "mutual altruism" as a limiting case. Taylor (1976) has made the point that mutual altruism solves Prisoner's Dilemma problems and hence may solve the kind of P.D. problems considered earlier. Oded Stark has made a similar point recently in an unpublished paper (1986).

In discussing mutual vertical commitments we assumed implicitly that a superior has something he can offer to a subordinate in exchange for the subordinate's effort. In other words, there is some basis for an implicit or explicit exchange relation. While this may be true for superiors at the top it need not be true for superiors at intermediate levels of the hierarchy. The outcome will depend on the power distribution inside the firm. By "power" we have in mind the resources available to influence others. Consider an extreme case. Suppose every promotion requires a "budget" that is determined entirely by top-level managers. Furthermore, potential candidates for promotion are nominated only by top-level managers. Under such circumstances managers at intermediate levels cannot make reliable commitments to subordinates since they do not have the power to do anything for those below them. The opposite possibility is the case in which, at every level except the bottom, firm members have the authority and resources to select those directly below them for promotion. In this case, if a superior wants to make an implicit commitment to a subordinate he has the power to do so. Of course, promotions are not the only type of benefit that a superior can offer to a subordinate. Usually, in specific cases, observable behavior will suggest what powers individuals have to offer tangible and intangible benefits to those below them. The general implication is quite clear. Power, in the sense used here, must be distributed from the top throughout all but the lowest steps of the hierarchy if strong mutual commitments are to be possible throughout the vertical chain of relations. How much power should exist at each level may be difficult to determine at any one time. However, if it can be guessed at as a result of experience, then normal marginal analysis will determine marginal shifts of power between higher and lower levels.

Another potential difficulty is that there may be stronger incentives for a firm member to form mutual commitment relations with those above him, than with those below. In other words, it is likely that someone at a middle level would have a greater interest in making worthwhile connections to help his own career advance, than in aiding the advance of someone at a lower level. If this were true of everyone except those at the very top, it would pose an insurmountable difficulty to the establishment of a mutual commitment chain throughout the hierarchy. Somehow, this almost natural asymmetry of incentives has to be counterbalanced so that people are assessed, in part, by how well they are able to obtain creative and voluntary efforts from those below them. This potential for asymmetric incentives has to be recognized as a potential source of inefficiency in the organization.

We should also recognize that not all mutual vertical commitments are for the creation of "goods." Some may be for the creation of "bads," in terms of organizational interests, or the pursuit of organizational objectives. This situation may exist when a high degree of factionalism is part of the company culture, and mutual vertical commitments in response to factional interests go counter to the production and profitability interests of the company as a whole.

Another difficulty with achieving or maintaining vertical cooperation lies in the fact that asymmetrical power to influence and direct activities is likely to exist between levels. This is likely to be true even if the power granted to the superior is purely of a functional character. Once asymmetrical power exists it is very tempting for superiors to use it for personal interests rather than the firm's. In other words, it requires unusual restraint on the part of the superiors not to use power for their own personal benefit and possibly against the interests of subordinates in handling superior-subordinate interactions. This can contaminate the spirit of cooperation and the positive motivation that results from mutual vertical cooperation. It may be difficult for superiors to refrain from using the power they have, or to refrain from overstepping the bounds of a purely functional use of power.

Vertical cooperation, when it works well, is likely to depend more on cooperative commitments to specific individuals than on commitments to different posts. Hence, there may appear to be little point in making such commitments if people move from one firm to another (or one post to another) since it may not be possible to count on longer-term payoffs. In other words, where the payoffs for cooperative exchanges do not occur within a relatively short period of time, then a great deal will depend on whether superiors and subordinates remain within the same organization. Difficulties are especially likely to arise when subordinates "pay off" by cooperation in the short run, but superiors pay off in a much longer period of time. Such payoffs may be lost to subordinates if superiors move between firms. The lifetime employment ideal of the Japanese enterprise helps reduce such difficulties, and thereby helps maintain vertically cooperative commitments.

The Commitment Network

Let us return to the problem of horizontal cooperation. Here, we want to raise the question of the interactions between vertical and horizontal relations. Suppose we have a case of adversarial vertical relationships. It is likely that this will be associated with a lack of mutual objectives in individuals at various levels, and hence a lack of a sense of joint effort. Thus, there will be a lack of reasons to do anything that improves the output of other individuals. This would seem to imply a lack of any reason to go beyond one's own job concerns. Hence, this situation would be associated with a keen sense of job demarcation and a lack of positive, "metajob" concerns.

On the other hand, we are likely to find that a high degree of mutual vertical commitment creates a sense of common objectives and a concern for the results beyond one's own job, which in turn is likely to support horizontal cooperation on production goals. In the latter case job demarcations become less significant and a horizontal team spirit is likely to flourish. Thus, while I agree with Aoki on the importance of horizontal cooperation I would argue that where horizontal cooperation on production goals flourishes it is likely to be a consequence of a high degree of mutual vertical commitments. To the extent that factionalism exists we should expect horizontal cooperation within factions but not between factions.

It may be useful to think of the organization as a network of invisible, attitudinal relationships, some of which are vertical, some horizontal. We may distinguish three possible relations: isolated (neutral), adversarial, and cooperative. These relations may exist between individuals who are vertically connected in the hierarchy, or horizontally connected. Now, let us speak of "enlarged commitment" as combining the properties of (1) commitment to some other individual, (2) plus the reciprocity of the other individual, (3) plus trust, (4) identification with the group or firm, and (5) a sense of common objectives. Note that when these other elements of enlarged commitment, that is, trust, identification, and common objectives, are absent, then the significance of the commitment is reduced or negated. For instance, commitment without trust is likely to be fragile; the commitment is likely to disappear when it is revealed that trust was unfounded. Likewise, trust without a commitment is not especially useful because trust alone will not achieve any mutual objectives. A lack of identification with others is likely to lead to low motivation for performance beyond individual self-interest. A lack of common objectives may lead to activities that are either unrelated or at cross purposes.

Table 12.2 indicates the likely consequences of horizontal and vertical connections if held by all or most firm members. Some of the consequences are clear-cut, while others are ambiguous.

Factionalism is not considered in the table. However, factionalism

TABLE 12.2.

HORIZONTAL RELATIONS

VERTICAL RELATIONS

	Cooperation on production goals	Cooperation for adversarial goals	Isolated (neutral)	Adversarial horizontally
"Enlarged commitment" cooperation	Higher productivity	Contradictory	High productivity	Unlikely
Isolated (neutral)	Limited productivity	Contradictory	Effort free riding	Effort free riding and low productivity
Adversarial vertically	Workers are idealistic and managers have private goals (could happen in government); likely to be unstable	Even higher effort free riding	Effort free riding and low productivity	Effort free riding and low productivity

and firmwide cooperation on production goals are contradictory. Factionalism is likely to be associated with comparatively low productivity unless the factionalism is handled extremely adroitly by those at the top of the hierarchy. Otherwise, factionalism is likely to mean a lack of agreement on overall firm objectives.

Given the three types of relations, the clearest conclusions are the following: (1) isolation from both horizontal and vertical others is likely to lead to a high degree of free riding with respect to effort; (2) strong horizontal relations that are adversarial with respect to those vertically connected are likely to result in even greater free riding with respect to effort—the adversarial component may even lead to a desire to damage those at a higher level; (3) if the relations are vertically cooperative, then enlarged commitments are likely to mute or reduce free riding and thus lead to higher levels of productivity; (4) in addition, strong vertically cooperative relations are a precondition for the high productivity associated with horizontal cooperation on production goals. Vertically cooperative relations are likely to lead to higher levels of productivity if the commitments are more rather than less open. While these four conclusions do not exhaust all the possible combinations, the others are likely to be either self-contradictory, ambiguous, or involve effort free riding (see table 12.2). For example, vertically cooperative relations and horizontal cooperation with respect to adversarial objectives are contradictory.

Internal Entrepreneurship and the Commitment Network

In addition to the nature of its commitment network, the efficiency of the firm will depend on internal entrepreneurship, which is the extent to which individual firm members have the capacity and take the initiative to put forth ideas that improve output, broadly defined. It will not matter if the hierarchy has a smooth system of procedures for making changes if individuals do not suggest any changes. Thus, ideas for improvements, and ideas for new projects to be undertaken by the enterprise depend on the capacity and willingness of individuals to be creative and to push such ideas. This in turn may depend on the extent to which the network stimulates and encourages such ideas and their implementation; it will certainly depend on the extent to which the network discourages, resists, and represses them. Thus, in a vertically cooperative network with relatively open commitments we might expect entrepreneurial efforts to come, to a considerable degree, from the bottom up. But, in a vertically isolated or adversarial network we would expect that entrepreneurial initiatives would come only from the top.

For entrepreneurial initiatives to be undertaken energetically by those at lower levels, the entrepreneur has to believe that the ideas will be taken seriously by those higher in the hierarchy, and that if they are valid the entrepreneur will be adequately rewarded, in some sense, in both the short and the longer run. In cases in which an entrepreneurial initiative is not valid, it will have to be handled with sufficient tact so that it does not spoil the existing mutual vertical commitments. This suggests that such ideas as "quality circles" cannot be expected to work automatically, but will depend, to a considerable degree, on the nature of the commitment network within which they are tried. If the vertical network is adversarial, then individual members of a quality circle are likely to feel it is useless to make serious suggestions, since they will question or fear the reception their ideas will receive. Of course, the same lack of suggestions or initiatives may occur when no formal arrangements exist for making suggestions or putting forth initiatives.

Factionalism

A major difficulty with the picture just painted is that the problem of factionalism is assumed away. Usually it is factionalism that will determine what are frequently referred to as the internal politics of the organization. In other words, individuals will be promoted, or receive some benefits, not because of performance, that is, because of their contribution to the enterprise as a whole, but simply because they are loyal to their faction, and the leadership of the faction happens to have maneuvered itself into a powerful position in the hierarchy. This situation is likely to go counter to objective criteria and motivational supports for performance. In fact, it is apt to do the exact opposite, namely, provide incentives for loyalty to the faction irrespective of performance, or even in the absence of performance. In other words, performance for the faction becomes the motivational substitute for performance to the enterprise as a whole.

The word "factions," as normally used, refers to competing vertical groups. However, the existence of vertical groups need not imply that factionalism is the only possibility. The situation will depend on both the history of the company (that is, the company culture), and on whether those at the highest levels allow power to be the major consideration in the determination of position and status. If the company culture is made up of established conventions where contributions to the company welfare (rather than raw factional power) determine position and status, then cooperation between vertical groups may be the norm. People will still feel a sense of affiliation to the vertical group, partly because it is easier to arrange a sense of mutual responsibility to a group made up of, at most, several dozen individuals, than to have such meaningful arrangements for the company as a whole, made up of hundreds or thousands of individuals. Thus, group identities and trust may still serve important motivational functions even where senior members of the group can only guide their subordinates rather than reward them for loyalty to factional objectives that differ from company objectives. Indeed, where the vertical groups do cooperate the group objectives and the company objectives are likely to become very close to each other, if not identical.

Autonomous Internal Organizations

We have seen that some problems of hierarchy can be solved by creating largely autonomous suborganizations within the larger one. Such cases are, by now, well understood in the light of Williamson's work on the M form, and the work of Chandler and others. This point is especially true if the autonomous unit can be judged by some "bottom line" that summarizes the unit's performance. Here there may be difficulties. The objectives of the organization may not be completely reflected in the objectives of the autonomous units. Furthermore, it may be more difficult to transmit pressure into and throughout the autonomous units than it would be in an integrated organization. Although these are important considerations, they do not necessarily outweigh arguments for the creation of autonomous units when these are feasible, when the units have the characteristics needed to form a viable, separate entity apart from the larger organization. The reverse would be the case if the autonomous unit would find it easy to create shelters against the pressures of the larger organization.

Summary

Now we will try to bring together the various threads of the argument. Specialization creates cuts in the continuous fabric of production. These cuts, dividing up activities into small units, increase efficiency per specialized activity. However, there are counterpart losses in efficiency. These result from the cost of setting up the hierarchy to coordinate, control, and reconnect the separated activities; and the possible costs that arise from invisible motivational losses.

Specialization creates the need for hierarchy since the separated activities have to be "recombined," that is, coordinated, controlled, and connected to the purposes of the enterprise. Specialization at Level II requires control, coordination, and connection at Level III, and so on. At the same time, cutting up activities into smaller units has a tendency to cut out invisible motivational elements and related components. We may consider these losses on two levels: the horizontal and the vertical. On the horizontal level there is likely to be a loss of efficiency due to following free-rider incentives, or due to adversarial behavior. In the vertical direction motivational losses occur because of a lack of connection to organizational purposes determined at the top of the hierarchy, and because of attempts at each level to insulate that level from pressures from above.

In summary, the latent horizontal and vertical diseconomies arise because hierarchy creates distances from the top between individuals and separations between groups.

The hierarchy will try to handle motivational problems in one of three ways: (1) by minimizing discretion through the creation of bureaucratic procedures, (2) by applying sanctions to deviations from approved behavior, and (3) by creating hierarchically based rewards both of a pecuniary and nonpecuniary nature. The outcome of the hierarchical structure will depend in part on feelings of affiliation to subgroups and on the nature and purpose of such subgroups. Horizontal subgroups tend to isolate vertical pressure and to interpose horizontal group interests against organizational objectives. Vertical subgroups have a tendency to interpose their interests which involve factional struggles.

In general, the extent to which the hierarchy is efficient or inefficient will depend, in part, on how the hierarchy's employees affiliate with each other. If the affiliations are primarily positive horizontally for adversarial objectives and antagonistic vertically, then this is likely to be a source of inefficiency. If affiliations are primarily positive vertical groupings, and especially if they are linked vertical groups, then the outcome will depend on whether the essential conventions that make up the company culture result in cooperative vertical groups or in factional divisions. The latter is also likely to be a source of inefficiency.

We can visualize an ideal vertical group setup such that the vertical groups are internally connected all the way up the hierarchy through "enlarged and open commitments" that involve mutuality of interest and that include, by definition, mutual trust and a sense of common objectives. At the same time, cooperation between different vertical groups is achieved through the political and refereeing activities of the chief executives of the enterprise. This results in a sense that there is an equitable division of organizational quasi-rents between different vertical groups.

Of course, real companies are likely to be mosaics of some horizontal groups at the bottom, some partial vertical groups toward the middle, a variety of management factions struggling for influence, and, in general, various groups that work at cross purposes to the organization as a whole. Usually there will be enough cooperation and control so that despite the hierarchical sources of inefficiency the enterprise manages to survive in the marketplace. After all, survival does not depend on some absolute level of internal efficiency but on the relative degrees of internal inefficiency of competing enterprises, and the degree of shelter from competition that the enterprise has achieved.

CHAPTER 13

On Japanese Ethos, Culture, and Management

One of the questions that invariably arises in any discussion of the Japanese Management System is whether the presumed efficiency of the system depends on management practices or on Japanese culture. Here we will examine the cultural aspect and attempt to see to what extent culture rather than practice is the dominant influence. Chapters 13 and 14 form a unit; they are interrelated and should not be viewed as separate treatments of the problem.

Does the high level of efficiency have anything to do with management practices? Perhaps Japanese workers are "made" or "programmed" to be efficient before they ever pass through the factory gates. Perhaps it is Japanese traditions and the Japanese nurture system that create hardworking and efficient employees, and the management system has nothing, or very little, to do with it.

If this is true, it has significant consequences. To start with, it would suggest that if we wanted to understand Japanese efficiency we should not try to understand what goes on in the factory, but instead study the homes and schools, that is, the system of nurture. This fits the human capital approach. Perhaps the Japanese invest more in their children before the children get to their jobs and that is why they are more productive.

Also the Japanese nurture hypothesis complicates the question of transferability. If it is nurture and culture and not the management system that is important, then it may turn out that even if management practices may be transferable, the cultural system may not be. The cultural system may depend too much on the unique history of Japan, and on practices that developed as a consequence of that history. In any event we can see that an analysis of the culture is important, but we have to do more than simply try to understand some connections between management and culture.

Various writers on the Japanese enterprise devote a section or a chapter in their books to *some aspects* of Japanese culture, mores, habits and practices, and so on. The intent is frequently unclear. In general, they are interesting. They attempt to show some of the threads between history, certain cultural influences, and the nature of the present Japanese Management System (JMS). This helps the Western reader to see the continuity of certain practices, and to see the management system and its peculiarities within the general context of Japanese history, ethos, and culture. There is a sense in which by being told something about the society, we are made comfortable with the bundle of practices referred to as Japanese management. But this can be only the beginning.

A number of related questions are part of our concerns. Among the most important are: Is the culture supportive of the management system? Can the success of the large Japanese firm be explained by the degree of supportiveness of the culture for the management system? Does supportiveness depend on the *managerial group* or also on others in the firm? To what extent are the management system and the culture separable? The last is an especially difficult and important question. If the two are separable, then transferring the Japanese system to firms in other countries would be much easier.

A related question is, What do we mean by culture? Perhaps a better set of terms would have been values, norms, and practices. Of course, this includes the family nurture system, and all the traditions of the past that are transmitted to the present generation.[1] We shall be concerned with those aspects that either describe current behavior or shed light on why current behavior is what it is. Thus, we shall look at social and cultural history, Japanese religions, Japanese nurture practices, and descriptions (usually by anthropologists) of norms, practices, institutions, and representative behavior patterns.

It is easier to speak about Japanese culture than about Western culture, partly because the Japanese population is very much more homogeneous than American or European populations. In addition, Japan's isolation during the Tokugawa period is a unique historical

---

1. Clearly, certain cultural aspects may be so ephemeral that it may not be necessary to consider them. For example, do Japanese art and aesthetic standards influence the firm? One could argue that restraint and understatement is part of the Japanese artistic aesthetic, and as a result, this aesthetic also characterizes individual behavior within the firm. However, the arguments that we shall present will not be as abstract and tenuous.

experience. Furthermore, Japan represents a unique culture despite its borrowings from many cultures in a way that no European country can be seen as having a unique culture.

One of the interesting elements of Japanese culture lies in the ability to reflect Japanese character and significant day-to-day human relationships by a half-dozen Japanese words. Thus, cultural anthropologists and psychologists frequently focus on such Japanese concepts as *amae, giri, on, chu, ninjo,* and *wa.* There is no Western counterpart to this phenomenon, no brief set of words that explains relationships between various individuals within Western cultures. Certainly the Ten Commandments or the Sermon on the Mount convey important ethical precepts but they do not suggest how individuals in a small group will relate to each other and behave toward each other. Thus, it probably follows that the Japanese nurture system and education system inculcate much more detailed behavior patterns than their Western counterparts.

Borrowing

A theme that runs through Japanese history is borrowing. But this idea must not be misunderstood. The Japanese are not unselective borrowers. What is borrowed is usually adapted in some way or other to the core of Japanese culture, so that to a considerable degree the core itself is retained. This is especially true with respect to the borrowing of technology or of technical ideas. Here it is clear that the intent is to adopt the technology but not to change any of the essentials of Japanese culture or of the basic Japanese belief system.

Of course, all countries have been borrowers to some degree during their history. The alphabets used by European civilization had their origin in Asia Minor. The major European religion, Christianity, came from outside Europe. Clearly, the same holds true for various aspects of language, technology, and so on. But in most cases the borrowing that takes place is not carried out as part of a national policy. Rather, it is usually individuals who carry ideas from one country to another, and some of these ideas or techniques catch on and spread. Thus, in general, the process may be viewed as a general intellectual exchange rather than borrowing.

The Japanese are frequently accused of being primarily borrowers. However, much of the cultural borrowing by the Japanese has resulted in unique refinements, which in themselves are contributions. Most important, the borrowings have somehow, through various adaptive devices, resulted in the retention of a core of beliefs and practices that are almost uniquely Japanese. This is epitomized by one of the slogans used during the Meiji period, "Japanese spirit and Western technology."

A few examples of Japanese borrowings will indicate the general nature of the argument. The Japanese borrowed most of their writing system from the Chinese sometime around the sixth century. Since China was the cultural colossus in the area, this seems understandable. Whether the Chinese writing system would have been borrowed if the Japanese had made a worldwide search of alternatives is questionable. But given the physical closeness and the cultural ties between Japan, Korea, and China, this is not the way it happened. The Chinese characters were and are to a considerable degree unsuitable to the spoken Japanese language. Chinese languages are monosyllabic, Japanese is multisyllabic. Certain ideas simply had to be *sounded out* and the Chinese written language clearly did not allow for this. As a result, the Japanese developed two syllabaries of about fifty characters each that permit the writing of Japanese or foreign words in a phonetic manner.[2]

The Japanese adopted Buddhism in the sixth century as part of their religious system, but they did not drop Shintoism. Japanese religion is not exclusive—Buddhism and Shintoism exist side by side. Some family rituals and ceremonies use Shinto shrines while others use Buddhist temples and are performed with the aid of Buddhist priests. For example, marriages frequently use Shinto ceremonials and funerals use Buddhist ritual. Even Christian ceremonies are frequently adapted into this framework so that Japanese who are not formally Christians find it quite reasonable to get married in a Christian church. At the same time, Japanese Buddhism has been transformed so that many of the Buddhist sects have practices and philosophies not found elsewhere.

A similar story can be told with respect to the Japanese use of Confucianism. During my stay in Japan, I asked a Chinese anthropologist who was visiting Kyoto about the relation between Chinese Confucianism and the Japanese interpretation. "There is practically no relation," was his reply. While this may sound extreme, it is possible to

2. The Japanese could have kept the syllabaries and dropped the Chinese characters. It is worth noting that what is frequently referred to as the greatest classic of Japanese literature, *The Tale of Genji* (ca. eleventh century; Waley, 1935), was written entirely in the Hirigana, one of the two syllabaries. For reasons of cultural prestige, the Chinese characters were maintained. By now they are very much a part of Japanese culture. If the Hirigana had been adopted as a substitute, no doubt various ways would have been developed to handle many of the homonyms in Japanese.

find Japanese scholars who hold similar views. Michio Morishima distinguishes sharply between Chinese Confucianism and Japanese Confucianism. The remarks that follow are based on Morishima's analysis (Morishima, 1982).

Confucianism is not a religion as that term is understood in the West. Rather it is a guide to behavior contained in a variety of maxims and exhortations. It emphasizes certain virtues and more or less demands that individuals recognize these virtues as a guide to their behavior. In the original Chinese version the main virtues (in order of priority) are benevolence, justice, ceremony, knowledge, and faith. Benevolence was viewed as the virtue that is at the heart of human relationships. Benevolence was based on the extension of the affection that exists between different family members. Additional virtues were filial piety, and the discharging of one's duty as a younger brother. An essential virtue was the achievement of harmony between members of society.

Japanese Confucianism emphasized loyalty, ceremony, bravery, faith, and frugality. Loyalty was by far the most important. Certainly, it is the virtue most frequently emphasized periodically by Japanese leaders speaking in behalf of those in power. Furthermore, the concept of loyalty was not the same to the Japanese as it was to the Chinese. To the Chinese loyalty meant being true to oneself, or being sincere to one's conscience. In Japan the loyalty that is emphasized is loyalty to an institution or an individual, such as loyalty to the Emperor or one's lord. According to Morishima (1982, p. 7), "Confucius' words 'act with loyalty in the service of one's lord' were interpreted by the Chinese to mean 'Retainers must serve their lord with a sincerity which does not conflict with their own consciences,' whereas the Japanese interpreted the same words as 'Retainers must devote their whole lives to their lord.' " Quite clearly this type of loyalty is likely to conflict with the element of individualism in the idea of being true to oneself,[3]

We can sum up these ideas with a quotation from Richard Storry's *History of Modern Japan* (1960, p. 31). After discussing Japanese behavior in the seventh century, he makes the point that, "Here we can

3. After the Meiji restoration, some Japanese became interested in British individualism, and in that variant of it encapsulated in the self-reliance literature. Thus the classic, *Self-Help*, by Samuel Smiles was translated into Japanese and became a best-seller. It also was interpreted in various ways by important Japanese literary figures. However, the end result of the flirtation with the self-reliance literature was the determination that the purpose of achieving self-reliance was service to the Emperor, and to Japan generally. Thus the individualist aspect was ignored.

perceive that characteristic of the Japanese that has been active whenever they have been brought into contact with a civilization differing from their own; namely, a quite indefatigable curiosity, a passion to learn, and an aptitude for choosing, borrowing, adapting, and 'japanizing' foreign ideas and techniques." The same holds true for all of Japanese history.

More on Confucianism

Various writers have argued that both the Tokugawa emphasis on Confucianism as well as the emphasis in the Meiji era explains or helps to explain Japanese economic success. This is quite similar to Weber's argument that the Protestant ethic explains the rise of Western capitalism. Indeed, Morishima is quite explicit in seeing the analogy between Weber's theory and his own. There is really no way of judging the significance of such extremely broad assertions.

What is clear is that the Confucianist influence theory contains large gaps when we try to understand the relation between Confucian behavioral precepts and day-to-day behavior. Confucianism was a philosophy that applied to the Samurai class. Even if the Samurai did take it very seriously, they represented only about 5 percent of the population during the Tokugawa period. If we want to look at the majority ethos, we might be much better off by examining the behavioral forces of the peasantry and the tradesmen who formed 95 percent of the population. Thus it makes sense to adopt the view of Chie Nakane and look at behavior from the viewpoint of relationships formed within agricultural villages (Nakane, 1973).

There is little doubt that above all else the inculcation of feelings of loyalty was the main aim by the Tokugawas in emphasizing Confucian doctrines. This is very clear from Sansom's review of the cultural aspects of the Tokugawa. "The rationalizing element in their legislation is rather to be found in certain ethical principles which they held or professed. Chief among these . . . was the principle of loyalty, the bond of duty subsisting between master and man . . . in the Edo period, during the years of peace, it became the common ideal of all classes and was regarded as the touchstone of conduct not only between lord and vassal, but also between farmer and laborer, merchant and clerk, artisan and apprentice, and even gambler and pupil." (Sansom, 1981, p. 463). However, this still raises the question of loyalty to whom.

While the Tokugawas were primarily interested in loyalty to the Shogun, the history and practices of the period could hardly have developed that type of loyalty. From the very onset duplicity was part of the general practice.[4] In addition, the system was undermined by the ambiguity as to whether ultimate loyalty was to the Shogun or to the emperor (see Storry, 1962, chapter 3).

A few additional snippets of Japanese history (based mostly on Sansom) should put some critical aspects in perspective.

Even before the Tokugawa period, a major concern of various regional lords was the safeguarding of their domains. As a consequence the lord (Daimyo) was primarily concerned with the variety of duties to be carried out by those below him. No attention was paid to rights. The authorities carried to an extreme the principle of joint responsibility by punishing for the offense of the individual not only his family but sometimes his neighbors, and even an entire village. An edict issued in 1445 states "All quarrels and disputes are strictly forbidden. If this is disobeyed, both sides will be put to death without inquiry into right and wrong." Internal dissension was viewed as a source of weakness. Clearly, rules of this kind will induce harmonious relationships, at least on the surface (Sansom, 1981, p. 430).

However, loyalty to a *variety* of groups was always a problem (Sansom, 1981, p. 463). It is clear that the Japanese recognize various conflicts that interfere with feudal loyalty. Thus, the conflict between loyalty to one's family and loyalty to one's lord, especially the obligations and loyalty involved in filial piety, and the conflict between ninjo (human feelings) and giri (moral duties).

The authorities did not wish to be concerned with internal disputes. As a consequence they attempted, as much as possible, to deal with groups rather than with individuals, and to be concerned with group responsibility and as a result to discourage individual responsibility. This made it much easier to police the carrying out of duties and related obligations of various sorts. Thus, there was a general neglect of the duties of one individual to another at the extreme micro level, and at

---

4. The orginator of the Tokugawa Shogunate, Ieyasu, won the battle of Sekigahara by arranging for some of the Daimyo to change sides in the course of the battle. It is also clear that for the two-and-a-half centuries of the Tokugawa regime the Shogun and his advisers never really trusted the Daimyo that were supposed to be loyal to him. Hence, the system of keeping wives of the Daimyo as hostages in the castle at Yedo (modern Tokyo) and in checking access roads so that no wives went out and no guns came in. Furthermore, the Tokugawa developed a system of spies throughout Japan so that they could check on any possible stirrings against the Shogun.

the other end, the duty to society at large. A high standard of corporate or group morality was offset by a ruthless unconcern for the rights of persons outside the group.[5]

The matter of loyalty to a direct and clear-cut benefactor is a very different matter. Thus, it would seem that the spirit of loyalty lay between the Samurai and their Daimyo, but the relation is also buttressed by the possibility of mutual gain. The Daimyo had it within his power to help the Samurai materially and the Samurai were absolutely necessary to maintain the position of the Daimyo. Once this relationship atrophied and the Samurai had to look elsewhere for their welfare, they frequently went so far as to marry into the lowest class; namely, that of the merchants. Thus while the Confucian ethic unquestionably played a role, its role was greatest when buttressed by a mutual-gain vertical relationship. On the general influence of the Confucian ethic, the Japanese anthropologist Eiichiro Ishida is quite clear. He sums up his views with the sentence, "Yet the influence of a Confucian ethic or world view is rarely seen amongst townsmen and is almost nonexistent among farmers" (Ishida, 1974, p. 101).

In general, we must not view the ethic promulgated by the Tokugawa rulers only by selecting those aspects that appear to fit Japanese behavior within the Japanese enterprise. We must also consider those aspects that clearly contradict such behavior. The very nature of the four-class system, with the merchants at the bottom, is by itself antagonistic to the development of a strong business class. Whereas in the West there developed clear-cut philosophical underpinnings for the pursuit of profit and the virtue of exchange, no such literature developed in Japan. There is no Japanese counterpart to Adam Smith's *Wealth of Nations*. On the contrary, the peasants were viewed as productive and the merchants as nonproductive. The type of Western individualism espoused by the classical economists still has not taken root in Japanese culture. It certainly is not part of the Confucian ethic in either the Tokugawa or Meiji period.

The development of industry was initially through the aid of government and the motives espoused were to help the Japanese state. Profits as such were viewed as incidental to the system and not as in

---

5. A classical instance is the story of Sakua Sogoro, a poor farmer, who on behalf of three hundred of his fellows, oppressed by their lord, presented a memorial to the Shogun himself, in 1651. The guilty baron was punished by the Bakufu for his misrule, but Sogoro and his wife were crucified, having first seen their children beheaded.

any way meritorious. Even the use of money was not well developed. Well into the nineteenth century the basic exchange unit was rice, even though in practice the use of rice was clearly awkward and money had superseded rice as the unit of exchange. While much is made of the Samurai as a group who became the early entrepreneurs during the late Tokugawa and early Meiji periods, it is not clear that in fact this had anything to do with their Confucian ethical training, or whether it occurred despite such training. A good case could be made for the latter position.

The era of peace under the Tokugawa, and the abolition of the Samurai after the Meiji restoration, simply created the necessity for the Samurai to find means of support outside of their ancestral occupation. This they could do by marrying into rich merchant families or using their connections with government in order to have government finance their entrepreneurial efforts during the Meiji period. To show that Samurai values may possibly have been dysfunctional, it is worth repeating an incident in the life of Fukuzawa Yukichi. Yukichi, the founder of Keo University, "tells . . . in his autobiography how he was taken away, by his *Samurai* father, from his teacher because the latter was giving instruction in elementary arithmetic. Fukuzawa's father said that it was 'abominable that innocent children should be taught to use numbers— the instrument of merchants' " (Storry, 1960, p. 74).

The Social Anthropology Approach

The approaches we have been examining are to some degree historical. Another way of looking at the matter is to examine the attempts to describe existing critical (that is, important) social patterns. While such descriptions appear to be ahistorical, they are not necessarily nonhistorical. This is especially true in the work of Chie Nakane on which this section primarily rests (Nakane, 1973).

Nakane is interested in *enduring* social relations. She is sensitive to the avoidance of ephemeral behavior. The question she attempts to answer is: What is it that really endures in social relations behind the changes we call "modernization"? Furthermore, these enduring elements uniquely (or almost uniquely) distinguish Japanese social structure from the social structures of other countries.

A basic distinction upon which Nakane's analysis rests is that between "attribute" and "frame." People can be organized in a variety of ways. Organization by a common attribute or characteristic is a readily understood idea. The concept of "frame" is somewhat more difficult, but essentially it implies the locality or institution to which one belongs, entirely apart from personal characteristics or common attributes. For instance, organizations of landlords or tenants are *attribute*-type organizations. But the members of X village or of Y university are members of a *frame* organization.

Of course, all countries or peoples have both types of organization as part of their social structures, but the relative importance of these organizations will differ in different societies. We have raised the question, loyalty to what? Are we primarily loyal to an attribute type of organization, or to a frame organization? A simultaneous question is how we identify ourselves. Do we primarily think of ourselves in terms of an occupation or in terms of an organization to which we belong? There is the tendency among Americans to introduce themselves by indicating what they do, that is, the nature of their occupation, whereas a Japanese will indicate that he is a member of the, say, Sanyo Company. Clearly the American identifies himself in terms of the attribute and the Japanese in terms of the frame.

The frame idea and its importance in Japanese social relations is an extension of the Japanese family system. This system is quite different from that of India or China as well as that of the West. In it, biological kinship is less emphasized than in the West, and membership in a specific residence or residential group is more important. Thus the Japanese *ie* (household) contains the significance of location. The important members are all those who live in the household and hence belong to it. This will include all those related biologically such as the children of the parents, but also the daughter-in-law, or an adopted son-in-law, or non-kin-related servants and retainers. At the same time, sons who have started other households and daughters who have married and gone to live elsewhere are not part of the household. Their importance to the household will be considerably less than household members, whatever their biological relation. When a group develops in terms of the frame rather than the attribute, a very high degree of emotional closeness develops through continual contact. The one-to-one relations within the group are likely to increase the sense of oneness. At the same time it is likely to create a feeling of estrangement between the frame one belongs to and competing or parallel frames.

Nakane compares family structures in Japan and India. In Japan when a new wife joins her husband's household, she loses the close relationship with her former household. At the same time, she does not develop a common "attributelike" relation with other wives. If she has trouble with her mother-in-law, there is no one to come to her aid from outside the household. In India wives will temporarily leave the husband's household and return to their former households. At the same time they may get support from neighboring wives in daughter-in-law/mother-in-law arguments. The kinship relations, despite different households, remain very strong in India but are very much weaker (relative to the household) in Japan. There is a Japanese saying that the husband leads and the wife obeys. At the very least this will be the image conveyed to outsiders. Thus one frequently hears stories about neighbors overhearing the husband's strong assertions to guests without any wifely participation, but the husband receiving a strong dressing-down after the guests have left.

The business enterprise is likely to be the other main area of strong emotional interest. In some cases the emotional participation in the business may even be stronger than that in one's family. This is reflected partly in the fact that employees will frequently not take vacations, or stay very late at work, or not see their children during the week because of devotion to the company to which they *belong*. At the same time, the company itself takes cognizance that they are training people morally and mentally as well as technically. Furthermore, these moral and mental attitudes within the company have an important bearing on their productive power. This requires that people join the company at a highly malleable and formative stage in their career, hence the desirability of recruiting people just after they leave school rather than at some later point in their work experience. "Men who move in from another company at a comparatively advanced stage in their working life tend to be considered difficult to mold or suspect in their loyalties" (Nakane, 1973, p. 16).

After World War II the occupation authorities fostered the spread of unionism as part of the imposition of the new constitution and various elements of democracy into postwar Japan. Unions quickly enrolled something over nine million members. The authorities did not foster any particular kind of union movement since the United States at the time had both craft unions and industry-wide unions (for example, automobiles). However, the unions that developed in Japan were a form of company union where the bargaining that took place was entirely or primarily within the company, that is, a framelike organization. The most important union success was gaining of the right of appeal against summary dismissal. To quote Nakane, "Here is demonstrated a radical divergence between Japan and America in management employment policies; a Japanese employer buys future potential labor and an American employer buys labor immediately required" (Nakane, 1973, p. 19).

One could cite many other examples of "familialism" within the enterprise. The emotions involved have been used and fostered directly by Japanese managers. Thus they call for "the feelings of love for the company" and recognize that it is exactly such feelings that determine the abilities and talents of the management staff. This is clearly the exact opposite of the cold, technological view frequently taken by Western managers. The other side of the strong emotional involvement with the family or enterprise is competitiveness or hostility to those outside the frame. In its extreme, total emotional participation within the group results in a high degree of isolation between it and other groups. This may explain the lack of craft unionism. Even where there are cross-frame organizations, they are clearly less important than intraframe involvement.

In my visits to various Japanese universities, I was frequently entertained at meals and drinking parties in traditional Japanese restaurants. The relaxed atmosphere seemed to me a good setting to raise a particular type of question: "Would my hosts, economists at X University, prefer to be highly regarded within X University, but relatively unknown among Japanese economists; or would they prefer to be highly regarded among Japanese economists, but not well regarded within their university?" It seemed clear and obvious to me that in the United States, as well as in Europe, the latter option would be clearly preferred. Among Japanese economists the former option (to be well regarded by their university colleagues) was invariably the preferred choice.

There is probably no society in which the sensitivity to rank is as well developed as in Japan. Part of it is a carryover of the parent-child relation within the family. What is perhaps surprising is the thoroughness of this carryover to almost every aspect of social and economic life where ranking is a possibility. For a Japanese the world is clearly divided between seniors (*sempai*), juniors (*kohai*), and colleagues (*doryo*). Of course, there are situations where people do not know each other and where interactions are necessary without a sense of ranking. However, Nakane argues that these are exceptions to a general rule.

To emphasize her general point Nakane (1973, p. 30) says that "In everyday affairs a man who has no awareness of relative rank is not able to speak or even sit and eat." Speaking is difficult because the language requires the use of relative degrees of honorific expressions appropriate to the rank of the person addressed. At meals seating arrangements will depend entirely on relative ranking in relation to the place of honor, with the back to the *tokonoma* (alcove for flower arrangement and painted scroll). The Japanese custom of exchanging name cards is used to facilitate an estimate of relative rank so that social intercourse can take place with ease. In seminars, and in other meetings, it is customary for the highest-ranked individuals to speak first and for those in an inferior status not to speak until higher-status people have had their say. Disagreements and a general dialectic style of argumentation are rare. (However, I have observed exceptions to this rule among scholars who have received part of their graduate training in Western universities.)

Part of the rank consciousness, based on nonmerit criteria, leads to the feeling "I can do it too" by those who are peers; for example, those who have graduated from the university at the same time. Thus, according to Nakane, objective ranking of one's ability is minimal.

The day-to-day relations between members of the same group will be through the ranking structure. Thus if three individuals are ranked in a hierarchy in terms of A, B, and C, then C will not directly confer with A but will arrange access, when necessary, through B. If B and C are on the same level and A on a higher level, the relationship of B and C will be mostly through A. In part, such arrangements are facilitated by the custom that when someone enters a firm or other organization he will be assigned a parentlike individual who will both help him and direct him in his activities. Thus various groups will have a sense that the group operates primarily through a hierarchical system in which those lower down owe loyalty to those higher up, and those higher up have a very strong sense of responsibility to those lower down.

In the Nakane system it is important to get a clear idea of the nature of the critical hierarchical relationships. In Japanese it is referred to usually as the *oyabun-kobun* relation—*oya* for parent and *ko* for child. Some examples are those between patron and client, landlord and tenant, master and disciple, section chief and subordinate, and so on. In the West we usually view hierarchical relations as strictly functional when they exist in a pure form. Thus a supervisor may give work orders to a subordinate during working hours, but the relation ends when the working hours are over. In Japan the relationship is closer to a complex mother-child relationship. It is not narrowly functional. In the West there are, of course, spillovers from the functional aspect of the relationship, but these are frequently viewed as a type of exploitation. Such considerations do not enter into the Japanese relationship. The nature of the relation is tersely stated by Nakane (1973, p. 42) as follows: "The essential elements of the relationship are that the *kobun* receives benefit or help from his *oyabun,* such as assistance in securing employment or promotion, and advice on the occasion of important decision making. The *kobun,* in turn, is ready to offer his services whenever the *oyabun* requires them." These relations are not contractual, and quid pro quo considerations are not of the essence.

While the oyabun may have a number of kobuns under him, he himself may be the kobun for somebody at a higher level. The longer the relationship lasts, the greater the closeness of the ties and the wider the requirements that the kobun may be called upon to serve. The consequence of such a hierarchical system is that it leads to factionalism. If the group gets too large, it is frequently natural for it to split up, but the factions will maintain amicable relations. The leader in such a system has to be able to produce for his followers. It would seem natural that with a very large number of followers the leaders cannot offer everything the followers may desire. The general feeling is that every individual is under someone, but there is no way of easily expressing dissatisfaction. There is likely to be a conflict between what an individual can do for himself, especially if he is capable, and what he can do for the group as a whole. But the group must come first. Otherwise, someone who increases his reputation or performance beyond group standards will incur the envy and hostility of his colleagues. Clearly such situations can lead to ostracism of the individual or the formation of independent similar groups. Usually, according to Nakane, an effective group will be made up of one or two dozen members. Thus a large organization may have a number of factions. This is clearly the case in the major political parties. The existence of such factions may interfere with the objectives of the larger organization. However, in the case of an enterprise that is reasonably successful, it is the enterprise as such that will be viewed as the main frame. Higher levels of management will have as part of their job to see to it that the various factions can be reasonably rewarded out of the revenue of the enterprise.

One consequence of this system is that frequently an appointment of a single individual cannot be made. Rather an appointment will involve the senior person bringing with him many or all of the lower-level people who are his direct or indirect kobuns so that it is essentially a team rather than an individual that receives the appointment. The advantage of such a system is that in carrying out plans they can frequently operate as a well-oiled team and respond quickly to orders from the team leader. On the other hand, cooperation between teams may sometimes be very difficult to arrange.

While the cost of receiving loyalty is quite high, it does mean that the leader of a group does not have to know a great deal about how his underlings do their jobs. His major concerns are their loyalty and his capacity to reward them for loyalty. He can, in a sense, count on them to try to figure out what they really have to do to carry out demands from above. In fact, one of the problems subordinates have, or so I have been informed in Japan, is to find out exactly what it is that the leader wants. This is frequently a task in which different members of the group may cooperate. This last especially becomes a critical problem whenever the formal *Ringi* system is involved (see Chapter 14).

The argument is frequently made that leaders in Japan do not stand out in the same way as they do in the West. Their identity is almost fused with that of their group. It is how the group as a whole works that really matters. Thus the leader's qualities and the leader's functions will frequently be much less clear than they would be in the case of his Western counterpart. This is all part of the basic idea that the connections within the group are much more emotional than functional. From this it follows that it will frequently be difficult to bring in outsiders because such an outsider would find it hard to fit in with the emotional ties even if outwardly it appears clear that he fulfills a missing functional link or functional capacity.

One advantage of such groups is that they will frequently be highly adaptable in adjusting to changing situations. Since the basis of membership is not a clear-cut division of labor, each member may feel almost equally capable of carrying out any task. Thus efforts do not have to cease because of the absence of a presumed expert in some activity. Others easily enter to fill the breach. This is the exact opposite of what happens in some work situations in Western firms where everyone has clearly defined tasks with well-demarcated boundaries. In such cases people feel that they have "property rights" in their jobs. No one dares cross the boundary into someone else's domain. Here the absence of an individual may mean the incapacity to fulfill the work required.

The general emotional relationship involved in group membership also implies a different attitude toward contributions of effort. The ethical principle is to contribute to the group as much as one can. This permits great variations in the amount of the contribution. In counterpart Western situations there is concern about the fairness of contributions and hence a concern about approximate equality of contribution.

The Theory of Amae

We can obtain some further insights into the kinds of ideas developed by Nakane if we consider some closely connected ideas considered by Doi in his theory of amae (Doi, 1971). Doi is a Japanese psychiatrist who received some of his training in the United States. He was very much impressed by the differences in behavior patterns between Americans and Japanese. He came to the conclusion that a central aspect of this difference is described by the Japanese word amae—usually translated as "dependence."

The concept of amae, the feelings implied by amae, helps to explain the high degree of group loyalty felt by Japanese and the sort of groups to which they are most likely to be loyal.[6] While the basic relation is one of dependence, it means more than that. It could be applied to both intrafamily relations or to groups made up only of adults. The concept of *amae,* especially as it translates as dependence, has a negative sound to Westerners, but takes on an affirmative sense to the Japanese. This is so because it presumes the desire to "amaeru" and the hope that this will essentially be indulged. In a sense we might think of the vertical relationships emphasized by Nakane involving both the dependent "indulgee" and the superior or group representing the "indulger," so to speak. Nevertheless, a rejection of such behavior has its costs, and it arouses feelings of hostility.

Doi sees Japanese developing circles around themselves on the basis of sensitivity to amae. For those within the circle, constrained behavior is not necessary since any untoward behavior is expected to be forgiven. The boundary of the circle is where *enryo* is involved; that is, where behavior is constrained in some way. Beyond the boundary there is a sense of indifference since one is dealing essentially with strangers

6. Amae is usually described as a concept that is untranslatable or not easily translated into English. It is a word that Japanese would normally use, but does not have its counterpart in a Western language. Thus, it is argued, the relationship involving amae is something which is significant and well understood in Japanese life, but at the same time it involves feelings that are repressed in the West.

rather than individuals involved in the special relationship within the circle. A question of guilt versus shame is reconsidered here in the sense that guilt involves a possible sense of betrayal of the group, while shame involves an adverse opinion of others within the group. Because of both aspects, Japanese behavior easily leads to artificial apologies and attempts at easy reconciliation. In the West, such apologies are rare and, when given, are usually given reluctantly since that implies acquiescence to guilt itself.

The greatest shame or dishonor for an individual is to be ostracized from the group as such. Thus, everything possible is done to avoid such ostracism. Hence loyalty to the group is easily obtained. Any type of behavior that is believed to imply any degree of disloyalty is avoided in order to escape the possibility of ostracism. Thus, for the traditional Japanese, acting alone is likely to be seen as verging on treachery since it is likely to involve behavior that does not consider the group as such.

The concepts of *on* and *chu* are concerned with specific interpersonal social exchange relations—usually between nonequals. In general, on requires an individual to have a sense of indebtedness (on) to a person or entity that provides the individual with resources. The act of creating this obligation is signified by chu, which essentially implies an obligation of loyalty. The creation of the obligation is usually viewed as the laying on of on. Thus, the individual would have a specific sense of indebtedness (on) to the firm, which in turn expects loyalty (chu).

Giri: This concept represents a diffuse sense of obligation which need not arise out of any specific act by others. Thus the general sense of obligation to friends, neighbors, and relatives involves giri. But giri may also involve obligations that contain some sense of favors to be received and returned. This is a sense of obligation that will frequently exist among equals or without regard to rank differences. It is frequently important in cementing peer group relations. According to Harumi Befu, "a breach of this obligation is a breach of the moral codes of society and results in sanctions of various kinds and degrees. People will lose trust and confidence in such a person as a moral individual . . . The . . . substance of this concept is its moral compulsion to force people into behaving properly even though they personally may not wish to do so" (Befu, 1971, p. 169).

Ninjo: This concept is usually translated as "human feelings." It represents a person's natural inclinations and desires. Taking ninjo into account involves an understanding and appreciation of the difference between a person's giri behavior and his normal desires. Thus while individuals are not expected generally to succumb to ninjo, behaving in consideration of ninjo permits the type of indulgence required in dependency relations.

Wa: This concept represents the generalized sense of harmony that serves as an ideal for all types of behavior. When the ideal of wa is pursued, it will have a tendency to repress conflict, individualism, and competition.

The archetypical relation of dependency is that between the child and its mother. Of course, this is true in all cultures. However, in Japan the child-mother relation is likely to be closer than in the West because of a variety of institutionalized aspects of the system of nurture. The Japanese child is likely to be in much closer physical contact with its mother than its Western counterpart. The mother usually carries the child on her back for a good portion of the day while she carries out her chores. In an interesting article on "who sleeps with whom," it is pointed out that the Japanese child usually sleeps in the same room as the mother and at a later age than Western counterparts. This will be true even if there are enough rooms to give each child a separate room. Furthermore, Japanese children are usually fed on demand not only in the early period when they are breast-fed but later on as well. Japanese children are usually encouraged not to cry, and they will usually be given sweets of some sort when they do cry, or seem about to. Thus the nurture relationship is one in which there is a very high degree of indulgence of the child's wishes, and very little experience of the separation anxiety that takes place in Western families. As a result, the nurture experience is not only dependency on the part of the child, but one that is highly satisfying to him, since most of his needs are met almost immediately. At this stage dependence almost invariably implies indulgence. Thus this is viewed by Japanese as a very sweet time in their lives. The concept of amae also denotes a sense of "sweetness."

Even in Japanese families the demand for indulgence by children can go too far. Some types of childhood behavior have to be circumscribed or discouraged. The normal means of discouragement is the threat of ostracism from the family. Thus the child may be threatened by the idea, sometimes presented semiplayfully, that "someone" (a bogeyman of sorts) will come and take the child away from the family; that is, away from the warmth and sweetness of life that exists for the child in the Japanese family.[7]

The newspaper columnist and management consultant Masaaki Imai reports recent surveys in which 74 percent of Japanese children want to remain children, while more than half of American children want to grow up as fast as possible (Imai, 1981). Thus he argues that Japanese adults look back on their childhood as the happiest part of their lives. As they become adults and are weighed down with more and more responsibilities, they would like to return to the dependent relationships of childhood, which they found extremely satisfying. Consequently, as adults they have a tendency to seek somewhat similar dependent relationships which they hope will, in some way, be equally satisfying. As an adult one has to find some group that will bestow resources (indulgence) that somehow will generate similar satisfactions. But in order to achieve this one must make a contribution to the groups that one joins. Thus one will learn to be completely loyal to such groups, and the group will be expected to provide the resources that can somehow yield the satisfactions involved.

A question to which Doi's work does not direct itself explicitly is why the Japanese should put almost all of their emotions, efforts, and loyalties, primarily into two organizations; the household and the firm.

7. I noted an example of this practice in front of a supermarket in Kyoto. A child of about three had apparently taken some candy from the supermarket. The mother got on her bicycle, the child's seat empty, and rode away with the child chasing her on foot, screaming and apparently in a panic. The mother rode the bike just fast enough so that the child could not catch her. The child, running as fast as he could, cried and called after her. About 100 meters from the store the mother stopped and spoke to the child, at which point the child started running happily back to the store, where he returned the candy. The mother then permitted the child to get into his customary seat on the bicycle and they left, the child happily reunited with the mother. It is interesting that my Japanese colleagues, when told of this incident, inquired whether this was not the way that children were nurtured in the United States, and were surprised to learn that this is not the case.

After I returned to the United States, I also observed a situation the reverse of the one in Kyoto. In Cambridge, a mother dressed in jogging clothes and a three-year-old similarly attired were in the park. The mother attempted to get the child to jog along with her. Failing this, she decided to jog ahead and leave the child, hoping the child would pursue her. However, on turning around to see if the child was following, she observed that the child was waving good-bye and seemed entirely unconcerned at the mother's leaving her.

This differs from the Western practice where individuals spread their interests and efforts by joining a relatively large number of groups. Why the difference?

Some of the ideas developed around the concept of dependence help us to speculate and partially understand why the Japanese concentrate a very deep level of involvement in few organizations. Even if there are a large number of options for an individual, it would seem sensible for him (or her) to put all of his effort and emotion into the organization where he can get the greatest satisfaction from the play of *amaeru*. Since dependence fosters a sense of oneness with the group, it is unlikely that this sense could be maintained if it were distributed among a large number of groups. In other words, it is difficult to "feel as one" with many different groups, some of which may compete with each other.

Whatever privileges exist by virtue of being in the group have to be paid for, as it were, by devotion to the group, and it usually is difficult to spread such devotion thinly among a large number of groups. This would seem to be especially true since the amae sensibility is constantly stimulated and, in some sense, needs to be constantly rewarded.

It is interesting to note that many of the groups developed in the West such as social groups, athletic organizations, professional groupings, are not well developed in Japan. One possibility is that such groups are essentially groups of equals. Groups of equals cannot play a great role in satisfying the dependence relation. Dependence is a relation between unequals with different capacities. To a very great extent, the Japanese identify, and see others identify, with the groups they belong to. Once again it is difficult to have a strong identification with a large number of groups and to lose oneself through such identification within many groups. Thus, on the basis of such emotional identification, it would seem to make sense to concentrate on the relatively few groups where the emotional rewards of identification are likely to be the greatest.

Summary

All authorities seem to agree that Japanese borrowing is of a special partial and protective type. As far as possible the Japanese attempt to adapt what is borrowed so that they retain the essentials of Japanese customs and practices. As a result, while the current management system has borrowed Western techniques, as well as accepted practices imposed on it by the occupation authorities, it has retained critical cultural elements so that the end result turns out to be a unique management invention.

Although Confucianism is sometimes put forth as a major element in determining behavior, I have suggested that while Japanese Confucianism may have a background role in developing a broad ideology in conformity with existing management practices, it is not specific enough to explain the relation between the Confucian ethic and most of the specific practices. A variety of specific behavior patterns may fit reasonable interpretations of the Confucian ethic.

We have seen that Japanese history, the system of nurture, and the system of expected interpersonal relationships emphasized loyalty to the group, and a strong sense of duty between the individual and his superior. We saw that the general nurture system, as well as historical traditions, led to the choice of immense emotional attachment to relatively few organizations, such as the household and the workplace. There is much less involvement in organizations that depend on common characteristics or attributes, such as athletic interests, political interests, occupational or social characteristics, and the like.

We have seen that throughout Japanese history the nature of loyalty, its relationship to various obligations and duties, led to the funneling of feelings and attitudes toward entities so that a sense of obligation could be carried out. The emphasis on a general sense of shame rather than a morality based on guilt is important; however, one must not overemphasize the dichotomy since in all cases, and especially in the Japanese case, these are psychological and cultural attributes that are supportive of each other, rather than completely separate.

Especially useful in understanding the cultural role is the work of anthropologists and psychiatrists that relates some unique aspects of the Japanese family nurture system to later behavior. Nakane's emphasis on loyalty to the "frame" rather than organizations based on common attributes helps to explain the strong loyalty toward the household and the enterprise compared to common attribute organizations. The emphasis on hierarchy illustrates that the essential bond in which these strong loyalties are developed depends on hierarchical relations similar to the child-mother relationship. Doi's theory of "amae" (dependence) complements the ideas put forth by Nakane. The "sweet dependent" relationships in childhood, especially the mother-child relation, are sought in later life. This helps to explain the strong attachment of individuals to their groups. They become strongly dependent on these groups, and in turn these groups are normally capable of "indulging" economic and emotional needs.

The nurture system uses the threat of ostracism from the family, and this leads to the fear of ostracism from any group. Any sense of latent ostracism is therefore important as a negative element in fostering a strict sense of group cohesion. Hierarchical relations, especially within *limited-size* groups, and the debt of loyalty on both sides involved in such relations, is a major positive element in fostering group cohesion. Because of such strong attachments, the possibility of ostracism from such a group becomes the most feared possibility. As a result behavior that can lead to ostracism is most unlikely to take place. Thus the type of hierarchical relationship found in the firm, and the simultaneous interpersonal relationships, seem to fit very well modes of household and organizational behavior justified by Japanese history and culture.

CHAPTER 14

Japanese and Western Management Systems: The Contrasts

Can one capture the essence of the differences between Japanese and Western management systems in one or two sentences? This is a frequent, and not surprising, request of anyone who has presumed to understand the Japanese system and try to explain it to Westerners. Of course, so short an answer could not provide an adequate analysis. Furthermore, it could easily be misleading. Nevertheless, it contains an interesting challenge. Is there anything that can be said in a sentence or two that would convey the essential basic difference, even if it were far from self-explanatory? Something like the following might be said: The Japanese system emphasizes the motivational system of the organization first and foremost, and is concerned with the acquired skill aspects only secondarily, while the Western management system is concerned with the skill aspects first and foremost, and worries about the motivational system secondarily (if at all).

In their essentials the large Japanese and Western enterprises operate on the basis of very different principles. In this chapter we examine (and overemphasize) the contrasts rather than the similarities. It is by appreciating the contrasts that we will be led to understand why they are so different, especially in terms of efficiency. It is to be emphasized, perhaps more than once, that we shall be concerned only with large enterprises—say, those that have more than a thousand employees. In the West it is frequently argued that it is the medium-sized enterprises that are the most efficient. Hence it is of special interest that the Japanese seemed to have learned the secret of how to operate very large enterprises really efficiently, *especially when the quality characteristics* of the product are taken into account.[1]

Perhaps one of the most important things to be said about the Japanese Management System (JMS) is that it has a basic inner coherence. The elements of the system follow a certain connectedness and logic. It is not additive, it is organic. In other words, one cannot separate certain significant pieces of the system and still retain the value of the others. But not every part of the system is attached to the essential core. The essence of the core is that it works as a motivational engine.

What we shall present may be viewed as a stylized version of the system in operation. It is somewhat similar to the architectural rendering of a complex building. Not all elements of the building can be seen in the architect's drawing. However, the general nature of the building and its components, and how these components relate to each other, can usually be appreciated from the drawing. The building when constructed may differ from the drawing in important ways (for instance, the doors may stick and the windows not open), but the essentials are there. If some of the materials are poor and some less expensive details have been substituted for more expensive ones, and so on, the reality may differ from the architectural conception. Nevertheless, the building can be clearly recognized from the architect's rendering.

In the enterprises the author visited, the general managerial conception seemed to be the same even though the firms themselves produced very different products and handled some managerial details differently. But similar questions about aspects of management style received the same or similar responses. Thus it would appear that the higher echelons of management had very similar notions about how the system operated in principle, and how various principles of operation were connected to each other. Nevertheless, there is no doubt that in actual practice there were deviations between basic principles and practices. These deviations frequently involved responses to special situations that arose in normal business activities. An example will serve to indicate what is involved. Normally large Japanese enterprises do not "hire away" mid-career individuals from another firm. But we ran into one such

1. According to an estimate by Comanor and Miyao (1985), Japanese firms in the United States using the Japanese Management System produce approximately 30 percent more gross output per person than their American counterparts. While somewhat less of the product is produced inside Japanese firms, that is, more of it comes from suppliers, this probably does not account for more than 10 percent of the difference. It is hard to get estimates of the actual value added differences per employee.

case. A man with specialized training was hired by a firm in mid-career when the firm was enlarging its product line and needed someone with that sort of training. Normally, such an individual would have been obtained by sending one of the firm's regular members to receive the specialized training, but this probably would have taken several years. While others were being trained, it seemed useful to have on hand someone who had the requisite skills. The point is that this event was viewed as something that was clearly outside normal procedures. The general conception was still intact even if some practical deviations occurred in response to special circumstances.

Of course, the simplification of reality into a stylized system must have a relation to what actually goes on. If there is very little connection between reality and the presumed system, then there is no point in analyzing the system as such. In fact, the characteristics of the Japanese system that we shall discuss are in general representative of what actually goes on in large firms.

Why use a stylized version of the system at all? The answer is simple; we want to avoid a consideration of a large number of details that may differ from one enterprise to another. In a sense, we want to get to the essentials and not worry about differences that are irrelevant. If our aim is to examine the efficiency of the system, then we want to see what it is about the significant common elements that contributes to efficiency and not the less important differences which we hope to argue are unconnected to the essentials that *drive* the system.

One of the contentions made from time to time is that the Japanese learned their management techniques from American examples and that hence there is nothing uniquely Japanese about the system. Even if in some sense this were true, and even if a great deal of borrowing from some American experiences had taken place, this would not deny the uniqueness of the JMS. To start with, Japanese borrowing from the West, and for that matter from China, has usually been selective. Furthermore, borrowing has usually been adapted to Japanese circumstances, culture, and institutions. Hence, despite some degree of borrowing, the result could still be an amalgamation and transformation of ideas that end by being something quite original.

The Career Elements of the JMS

If one visited an American firm and a similar Japanese firm, many of the important differences would not be readily apparent. In both cases a variety of tasks are subdivided and these subdivisions might not be very different. People may appear to be doing very similar things in order to produce the same product. Even if differences were noted, it would not be these differences that were significant. Some differences would be apparent. For instance, Japanese workers frequently do group exercises and sing the company song before starting work. Also, Japanese workers wear similar clothes, something like a uniform, whereas their Western counterparts are quite differently attired. The differences of this type would not reveal very much about the sense in which things are, in fact, done quite differently. The essential differences come out most clearly not when we consider a cross-sectional picture of how different elements of the firm operate at a given time, but only if we look upon it from the viewpoint of a representative career.

The Japanese Management System is, in some respects, best understood by contrasting it with characteristics in the West such as those in the United States or the United Kingdom. The set of characteristics listed below, written in "telegraphese," is taken from the longer list developed by Rodney Clark (1979). There are, of course, many variations within each style (Japan versus the West), but in general it would seem useful to keep the stylized characteristics in mind in order to see if they lead to any general conclusions.

The brief list below contrasts the two types of management systems.

	Japan	*The West*
1.	Firm recruits people of particular age and education.	People recruited with particular skills (or experience) to fill specific job.
2.	Lifetime employment ideal.	No lifetime employment ideal.
3.	Company a community.	Less emphasis on community ideal.
4.	No sharp distinction between managers and workers.	Sharp distinction.
5.	Strong emphasis on general hierarchical ranks.	Management positions not standardized—related to function.
6.	Age and service length explicitly recognized as a promotion criteria.	Age and length of service only marginally relevant to promotion.
7.	Authority and responsibility diffuse.	Authority and responsibility ostensibly specific.

Japan	*The West*
8. Managerial authority limited by internal labor mobility.	Managerial authority challenged practically by trade unions.
9. Enterprise unions.	Trade unions.
10. On-the-job training for a variety of jobs.	On-the-job training for specific jobs.
11. Job rotation and boundary flexibility.	Focus on specific job with specific boundaries.
12. Emphasis on cooperation, harmony, and consensus.	Greater stress on individualistic behavior within bounds of narrow job definitions and commitments.
13. Bonus system.	No regular bonus system.

The essential career elements are (1) firm recruitment at a particular age, (2) lifetime employment ideal, (3) guaranteed increases in rank, (4) strong emphasis on hierarchy and standard ranks, (5) no major distinction between management and workers, and (6) all employees start at the bottom.

To start with, large firms recruit individuals at one of two points in a person's life: at the end of secondary school or at the end of university education. Thus, all permanent employees are recruited at the outset of their career without any particular concern for training or specific acquired skills. This, of course, is in very sharp contrast with the practice of the Western enterprise which is to recruit people with respect to particular skills and to fill specific jobs. In the West, skill (and sometimes membership in the appropriate union) is the requisite for access. In fact, Western countries are very much skill-oriented societies. It is not an exaggeration to say that to a considerable degree we identify ourselves by our skills and the jobs at which we practice these skills. But the Japanese, by recruiting at a particular age, can recruit without regard to skill or training. They can use very different criteria, such as the ranking of the university the individual came from, and information about his "character." This last is likely to give essential clues as to how well the person will operate as a member of a group.

Lifetime Employment Ideal

A great deal has been written about lifetime employment in Japanese enterprises. In some cases the lifetime employment arrangement has been discussed as if it were the essence of the system. At the same time there also exists a debunking literature which argues, frequently on statistical grounds, that lifetime employment does not exist any more in Japan than elsewhere. That, in fact, only a proportion of employees work for the same company throughout their lives. Both types of assertions really exaggerate on opposite sides, and miss the essential part of the argument.

What matters for our purposes is not whether there is lifetime employment, *in fact,* in all cases (or even in most), but that there is a lifetime employment *ideal* that is part of a larger set of expectations that exists within the enterprise. While the lifetime employment ideal is a necessary part of the JMS, it is not sufficient. By itself it does not solve all the motivational problems that exist in a firm. Similarly, if lifetime employment were adopted in British or American enterprises, it would not solve management difficulties that might exist in such enterprises. What really matters is that people behave as if this is a critical part of the institutionalized arrangements within the firm in association with other cooperating institutional arrangements. Thus in terms of the ideal, and in terms of behavior in response to such an ideal, it is not really significant if a certain proportion of employees do not stay with the same firm with which they start. This is especially true in those cases where young individuals might explore working conditions in several enterprises before they settle down to what they view as their lifetime career.

The next two elements are best considered simultaneously. Relatively guaranteed increases in rank obviously depend on the existence of a hierarchical system of ranks. This is clearly facilitated where the ranks are standardized. The Japanese as a people, and as a culture, have an unusual sensitivity to steps and substeps in a hierarchy. Usually there is a very large number of standardized ranks that have similar titles in different enterprises. Thus between any two different titles there usually is no ambiguity as to which one outranks the other. In other words, the hierarchy is clear-cut, well developed, and likely to be well known to all members of the enterprise. However, ranks are not well correlated with jobs. People doing similar jobs may have different ranks and people doing different jobs may have the same rank. The existence of the system of ranks facilitates the guaranteed progress of an individual through the ranks, or at least through a considerable portion of the ranks. Hence an individual starting out in the firm, given his educational level, can practically see himself proceeding more or less methodically, but not quite in lockstep fashion, through a series of ranks and ending up fairly high in the hierarchy toward the end of his career. Rank and salary are highly correlated so that guaranteed increases in rank also imply guaranteed increases in salary. In practice, persons who merely serve time will not necessarily progress at the same rate as those whose service is distinguished in some sense. The essence of the system is that up to some point, toward the upper management levels, age and experience are extremely significant and highly respected institutional criteria for promotion.

Because the ranks are rather narrow, and would be viewed as subranks within ranks in some counterpart Western scheme, they do not possess the sharp distinction that exists where ranks are few and closely related to actual jobs. Thus there is much less of a sense of distinction between management and workers than exists in Western firms.[2] Some artificial distinctions do exist in order to adapt the incorporation into Japanese life of certain Western institutions. This is especially true with respect to the company union. The problem is, who is to be a member of such a union? When do people move to the other side of the table to negotiate with the union on behalf of the enterprise? Here it is necessary to develop some purely arbitrary boundaries.[3]

A related aspect is that almost everyone starts on the bottom rung of the ladder. Thus, if the company is primarily a manufacturing enterprise, almost everyone will spend six months to three years on the shop floor. Furthermore, this will be true whether the individual has been recruited at the end of the middle school (ninth grade) or at the end of high school, or whether he is a university graduate. Also, when the university graduate does his work on the shop floor, he may find that his immediate superior is a high-school graduate, and further that the superior's superior may be a middle-school graduate. The impli-

2. Many of the appurtenances of that distinction do not have their counterpart in Japanese enterprises. There are no special executive dining rooms, or keys to the executive washrooms.

3. In one of the large firms my Japanese colleagues and I visited, one of the people sitting around the table, whom we interviewed, was the head of the company union. His office was in the company headquarters in Tokyo; he had come down to the plant we were visiting. When he was leaving I inquired whether I could see him when I visited Tokyo since I wanted to learn more about the role played by the company union. He said he would be happy to see me, but that I should come fairly soon—he was scheduled to be promoted within a month, and would then have to leave his union post and become part of management. This apparently was a usual and normal procedure.

cation of this is that the higher rungs of the administrative ladder are staffed by individuals who, from their own personal day-to-day experience, know what it is like to have performed the job at the bottom, as well as in many intermediate categories. Of course, this will also be true of the chief executive officer of the enterprise.

This is not to suggest that everybody enjoys the work at the bottom. In fact, some of the college graduates may find it onerous and boring, and certainly less interesting than the college life they enjoyed during the previous four years. Nevertheless, they will usually accept it as a phase of their career.[4]

Now let us look briefly at the Western counterparts to the Japanese system. Obviously, people enter large Western enterprises at a variety of ages. While some enter at the bottom and work their way up into certain jobs, this is neither the only nor even the prime vehicle of access. People also enter because they have special experience, special skills, or special attributes that lead to special skills. When a job becomes available, the "best candidate" to fill it may come from either inside or outside the enterprise. Whether or not those inside have some special advantage, those with the skill from the outside are usually viewed as not having a distinct and obvious disadvantage. While people of all ages may not have equal access, and while this may be true especially of those beyond middle age, people do enter the firm at a wide variety of ages. Thus access to entry and career pattern are not clearly related. In fact, some careers may be best pursued if the person hops from one firm to another as opportunities arise, rather than by staying within the same enterprise.

There are areas in Western economic life in which the lifetime employment ideal exists: the civil service, the military, and in academia. Nevertheless, even in these areas it is not quite the same as a lifetime employment ideal recognized by both sides in the employment relation. It is not necessarily the case that there is something especially desirable in working for the same employer throughout one's working career. But most important is that usually nothing like a lifetime employment ideal exists in private enterprise. People can be fired at any age even

4. We should note in passing that the various elements we have discussed are not matters of contract. It is more a matter of an institutionalized set of expectations. To what extent the enterprise would have legal rights to fire workers is not especially relevant. It is the institutionalized expectations that are the dominant force, not any sense of legal reality. Since Japan is not a litigious society in the sense in which the United States is, the matter of the legal status of such arrangements is not really significant.

if in many companies it may turn out to be a rare occurrence for senior and long-serving employees. A sense of security on the part of the employee is very different if he is aware that lifetime employment is part of the particular economic and social *culture* within which he operates, as against the situation in which he or she is aware that the opposite holds. Thus we should keep in mind that the general nature of the expectations is not the same in Japan and the West. Most important, we must connect the lifetime employment ideal, or its absence, with other characteristics of the management system.

Most Western enterprises do not have a system of standardized ranks nor a clear-cut formal sense of hierarchy. Rather, a presumed hierarchy is drawn from the relative importance of different jobs. It is not at all clear which of several vice-presidents stands in a higher position than others so designated, or whether they are really on the same level. Of course, rough hierarchical patterns do exist, and they are connected with beliefs about the importance of different jobs. But the situation is much murkier than in the Japanese case. This is very much related to the lack of an increase in rank simply on the basis of service and age. Because Western firms presumably place considerable importance on skill and merit, we cannot have a system that automatically promotes people just on the basis of sticking around. At the other end of the skill-merit-service axis, those with unusual capacities feel that they ought to be on the lookout for superior opportunities elsewhere without any feeling that this in any way goes against the norms or standards of the employment relation. Although, in fact, to some degree mere time-serving does play a role in Western enterprises, and merit does play a role in Japanese enterprises, it is nevertheless interesting to consider the comparison as if this were not the case. The importance and emphasis of these criteria are very different in the two cases. It is not simply a matter of degree; we shall see that it is a matter of a different view as to how the system operates.

It is almost self-evident that in Western enterprises there is a major distinction between managers and workers. Furthermore, those hired as managers will frequently (and usually) have no experience as workers. Those hired as workers will usually not believe that they have an equal chance to become managers. Whether relations between management and other employees are antagonistic or cooperative, the sense of a distinction is very clear. Furthermore, those who become managers can to some degree learn management skills on the outside—either in business schools or in other firms. Such training and experience become immediately relevant to the jobs they can aspire to. This is in sharp contrast to the Japanese system where such training is usually beside the point. In fact, under the Japanese system such training may be a barrier to entry.[5] Almost no Japanese who receive MBAs from American universities are able to obtain jobs with Japanese firms. In a sense they are, as a consequence, spoiled for the JMS.

Jobs, Training, and Unions

Associated with the unusual career characteristics of the JMS are the role of jobs, training, and unions. In Japan there exists a high degree of job rotation, on-the-job training, boundary flexibility between jobs, and enterprise unions. We now consider how these elements are related to the career system and to each other.

In some way or other people have to be trained for the jobs they perform. They can be trained outside, before they join the company, or within the company. As far as possible, under the JMS, people are trained *within* the company. Most of the training is on-the-job training. Thus a new recruit might be assigned to a somewhat more senior employee who will break him into the details of the work he is to perform at the beginning of his career or at subsequent stages. Two points go hand-in-hand. First, within the career the individual will proceed through a fairly wide variety of jobs. A person is likely to spend only two or three years on any specific job. To the extent that specialized training is necessary as the person moves through a sequence of jobs, this will be provided either on the job, in night school, or if necessary in training programs outside the company, but paid for and arranged by the company. Thus there is a sense in which the individual "owes" his training and skill to the company as he proceeds with his career.

An important element of job rotation lies in the fact that people do not stay long enough on any specific job to identify completely with the job as such. They do not develop anything like "property rights" *in* the job, as is usual with American, British, and European employees. In part, because job rotation is the normal expectation, there is no point in closely identifying with a job one happens to be doing currently since in a few years one will change jobs.

5. There is the case of a talented Japanese who received a Ph.D. from a school of business in the United States, and then went back to start his undergraduate career in Japan so that he may be able to enter a Japanese firm.

A significant element related to job rotation is boundary flexibility. In other words, employees do not develop a clear-cut sense as to where their job ends and somebody else's begins. Thus, there is very little likelihood of an individual's refusing to carry out certain activities on the grounds of "that's not my job." This general approach is augmented by a tendency toward group work and group tasks. Of course, some types of work, on purely technological grounds, are best assigned to a single individual. In other types of work a choice is involved; the work can be divided in a way such that groups of two or more individuals can do the job. Clearly if something is handled by a small group boundary flexibility is desirable. Each person can pitch in, or be asked to contribute, where he feels that he can put forth the best effort toward group goals.

Clearly group jobs and clear-cut job boundaries are likely to be incompatible, at least in some instances. This was made clear by a production engineer in an aircraft firm who worked for three years in a similar enterprise in the United States. In comparing the internal efficiency of the two enterprises, he argued that the American enterprise was almost equally efficient, except that it had to hire a fairly large proportion of individuals to do the interstitial jobs, and to check on the interstitial quality of work between job boundaries. No such individuals were required in the Japanese enterprise. Those who carried out work within the job boundaries were not concerned about doing what was necessary to coordinate with others, nor about the possible spillover into other people's jobs.

Since the ideal is for people to work for a single firm and not to move from one firm to another in mid-career, there is very little advantage for individuals to train for specific jobs before joining the enterprise. In a sense, if the stylized system we have described were carried out in detail in all firms without deviation, there would be no point whatsoever for individuals to obtain specialized training before entering their company. Such training could, at best, only be useful for relatively short portions of one's career. Since individuals cannot predict what jobs they will have, nor for how long, it clearly makes little sense to be specially trained for such jobs. Of course, similar arguments could be made against a good deal of technical training, outside the enterprise, that goes on in the West. But at least for those who obtain jobs in which their training is useful, they may expect to stay in such jobs for a long period of time. Nevertheless, it can readily be seen that in a purely technical sense it makes sense to train people internally for most jobs within the context of the JMS.

Whether the JMS needs unions or not is an open question. However, if unions are to exist then unions within the enterprise are much more consistent with the nature of the system than unions that cross enterprises. Thus, for the most part enterprise unions are the ones that have developed in large Japanese firms. Since there is no special attachment by employees to a specific job, or in some sense to a specific trade, then cross-enterprise unions associated with jobs would be unsuitable, because employees would be in any specific union for only a short period. It makes more sense, given the rest of the system, for bargaining to take place for those employees of a given enterprise below a certain rank.

There are other ways in which the unions may be viewed as enterprise unions. The relations between the unions and the enterprise are now closer than in their Western counterparts. For example, union offices and support services for union executives are provided by the enterprise. They are usually housed in the same buildings as other enterprise offices. Furthermore, union executives "normally" shift to management jobs within their normal career. Thus in some cases the same individual might bargain earlier in his career on behalf of the union and somewhat later move to the other side of the table and bargain on behalf of the company. No sense of disloyalty or awkwardness is attached to such procedures.

Nevertheless, this description of enterprise unions should not create the impression that the unions are exceptionally docile or that the bargaining process is not genuine. In all cases, in the firms I visited, there were stories of strikes and strife with the union at some point or points in the enterprise's history. The aftermath of such unpleasant experiences seems to have been a greater sensitivity on both sides as to how to carry out the bargaining procedures without excessively disrupting the normal productive activities within the firm, and within the Japanese ideal of cooperative behavior. There is a sense in which the role of enterprise unions is perhaps more important under the Japanese system than it would be under its Western counterpart. Because of the career aspects of the system there is frequently nowhere for an employee to go if he is unhappy with conditions within the firm. Given the lesser possibility of movement between firms, it is clearly helpful for lower-level employees to have a union system to operate as a countervailing force. The essence of the argument is that under Western arrangements, it is easier for employees to vote with their feet, as it were. The Japanese system permits "voting with the feet," but it is more difficult and costlier to the moving employee than it is in the West.

We can very quickly consider the differences in characteristics under the Western system. While they may be viewed as matters of degree, in essence they represent a different philosophy. Strictly speaking, individuals are not forced to stay with a single job in large Western enterprises. Movement exists. Nevertheless, individual employees usually do define themselves in terms of their job. They frequently have a clear-cut sense of job boundaries. For the most part these boundaries are fairly fixed rather than flexible. This is certainly true for the more permanent, higher-paying and frequently unionized skills. It is as if the craft system had been taken over from the preindustrial stage and retained in the industrial stage in the production of goods, despite the fact that a factory system may require a greater division of each craft into many more narrowly defined jobs. Of course, it is exactly this system that permits and encourages a considerable amount of movement between firms.

The essence of the argument is that there is a basic difference in marketability of "intracareer" manpower in the West as against Japan. Where individuals develop a basically salable skill, this skill can be marketed at various junctures in their careers. In the Japanese case, what is essentially involved at the mid-career level is a general capacity and willingness to work, to adapt to firm demands and requirements, and to show loyalty to the firm. These basic attitudes are, in some sense, hidden from view and are not readily demonstrated in the labor market outside of the firm to which an individual belongs. The latter attributes are clearly highly valuable to the firm employing an individual for some period of time, but it is not clear to what extent they are marketable. At the same time the individual is aware that his value to the firm for which he works is, in general, much greater than some sort of *demonstrable* value to outside firms. As a consequence, the Western employment system is one that encourages movement between jobs (that is, the sale of skills), whereas the Japanese system discourages such activities, since skill development is not the essence of the Japanese labor market system.

In Western firms there is also quite a lot of on-the-job training. However, the on-the-job training is usually for a specific job that the individual will perform more or less indefinitely. To the extent that there is a career system, it exists for individuals clearly slated for the management rungs of the ladder. Here initial outside training, such as that provided by a school of business, and the characteristics of such training will play a role in determining where an individual will work within the organization. All of these considerations are part of a system that very clearly demarcates management from other employees. In the West the representative chief executive could not assert that he had started at the bottom.[6]

The Japanese Payment and Bonus System

A sharp contrast between the Japanese firm and its Western counterpart is the bonus system. Japanese employees generally receive their income in two parts: the normal wage and bonuses twice a year, the value of the bonus being frequently about 30 percent of the normal wage. Thus, while the normal wage represents the lower bound of the income received, the wage plus the bonuses allows for an unusual amount of variation in employee income. There is almost no counterpart to this system in the United States, except at the higher managerial levels.

From the firm's viewpoint the bonus system creates the possibility of a high degree of wage and cost flexibility. This is true despite the fact that in practice the flexibility for union members usually has a built-in one-year lag. The reason is that normally the unions also negotiate for the bonuses as well as for the standard pay system. Hence the bonus for the year is determined at the usual annual April negotiations (*Shontu*). However, if the company did poorly, less revenue and lower bonuses would be available for the following year. In the managerial ranks the bonuses could be reduced during the same period if sales or profitability is low. As a result the enterprises have some degree of built-in flexibility to keep costs in line with economic performance.[7]

6. This is clear from the report of a writer, Robert Christopher, who lived in Japan for some thirty years, to the effect that, "Of the scores of Japanese senior executives I have interviewed over the years, I can recall only two who did not sooner or later make a point of informing me that they had spent their entire working lives with one company. And nearly all Japan's current crop of top executives are quick to tell you that they started out on the assembly line or in some equally humble job. (This is a fact that sometimes has rather anomalous results: it is doubtful, for example, that the chief executive of any American corporation can boast, as Mitsui Zosen's Yamashita does, that he was once the leader of his company's labor union)" (Christopher, 1983, p. 245).

7. From the viewpoint of employees and their families, the bonus system gives them a certain degree of flexibility different from their Western counterparts. The reason depends in part on the way the Japanese think about their income. The part of the income they can count on and on the basis of which they can plan expenditures is the normal wage. *The bonuses represent something extra.* Hence, for the most part, households attempt to arrange their day-to-day (and month-to-month) expenditures on the basis of the wage. The bonus system may help to account for the unusually high rates of personal

Community, Authority, and Consensus

One of the arguments in recent years has been the question of whether Japanese enterprises are run from the top down or the bottom up. This is similar to the issue of centralization versus decentralization. Except in very extreme cases, there is no answer to this question since most enterprises have elements of both occurring simultaneously.

To see the essentials of the Japanese system, it is necessary to view it within the context of the enterprise-as-a-community philosophy. The communitarian ideal implies that almost everybody in the firm agrees with general firm objectives. As a consequence, differences that exist and items negotiated are all constrained by this general ideal. We have seen that the bonus system creates a situation in which all firm members share in the prosperity of the enterprise. Therefore, all have to some degree an interest in seeing that work arrangements are such that internal efficiency and other elements of prosperity are maintained. Furthermore, firms are more interested in maintaining or expanding their share of the market than in increasing profits. This too fits a situation in which individuals have lifetime employment and in which career potentials are advanced as the enterprise is enlarged.

There is a sense in which the formal structure of the Japanese organization is centralized and authoritarian. The directors have the power to issue directives from the top down. This power is limited by the power of the unions to participate in the determination of certain decisions through negotiation. Furthermore, each side in the union-enterprise bargaining arrangements is very much aware of the limits to which it can push the other side. The close relations between unions and management make it possible for them to use common sources of information and to negotiate without upsetting common enterprise objectives. Furthermore, a very high degree of social relationships within the work force enables the union to know the kinds of grievances that may exist at any particular time, and to discover informal means of handling such grievances. On the other hand, this does not interfere with certain management prerogatives such as long-range budgetary

savings made by Japanese households. Thus the household does not get stuck with a standard of living that depends on anything more than their normal income. Reductions in the bonuses may affect savings or unusual expenditures, but they do not affect the normal living standards that the household counts on. Thus the bonus system allows for the absorption of economic shocks of various kinds, and adaptability to economic changes that do not have a counterpart in Western countries.

planning, and making some of the detailed budgetary decisions. This, in turn, is constrained by the fact that much detailed budgetary information will be obtained from various units in the firm, that is, on a somewhat decentralized basis.

It is interesting that one of the areas in which consensus is not sought is the assignment of employees to units within the firm or to various branches within the enterprise. This is normally left to higher levels of management or to the personnel department. There seems to be a general consensus that for the welfare of the firm it is desirable for higher management levels to have the right to assign subordinates to various units.[8]

There are two elements in the system that involve "bottom-up consensus" determinations. One is the *Ringi* system, and the other is informal consulting known as *nemawashi*. Under the Ringi system, a proposed change is developed (by a fairly low-level employee) by circulating a document of the proposed change and obtaining signatures from everybody who might be influenced by the change. Thus the approval system goes from the bottom up. In addition, any change in the document becomes a consequence of informal consultation. Although the Ringi document itself will usually be developed by the lowest-status individual appropriate for the task, informally the nature of the document may have been suggested to him by somebody higher up. Thus the Ringi document can originate almost anywhere in the hierarchy, although its form of procedure is bottom up. The small-group orientation of work, and small-group orientation of adjustment of individuals to group desires, involves essentially a considerable degree of informal intragroup consensus determination. It is in this sense that the greatest degree of consensus is achieved. Nevertheless, small groups by themselves cannot change the general course of the enterprise as such. This is usually decided on a somewhat more hierarchical basis through normal managerial procedures.

The complete degree of consensus and the boundaries between consensual and nonconsensual areas differ in different enterprises and probably depend on the internal history of the enterprise. With respect to proposed changes it is clear that various formal and informal means of obtaining consensus exist and are used to a very great extent. Perhaps

8. To what extent informal discussions, especially through third parties, is used to avoid an undesirable assignment is hard to determine. In any event, the literature suggests that enterprises have relatively little difficulty in assigning people where the managers involved feel it would be in the best interest of the enterprise.

the most important aspect is that a spirit of consensual action exists that can be employed under various circumstances.

At the very lowest level, informal consensus may be obtained by the conventional understanding that superiors are responsible for their subordinates in a much wider sense than is the case in the Western enterprise. Furthermore, subordinates will socialize to a considerable degree with their *immediate* superiors, and hence opportunities for informal exchanges of information exist. Some of these, which involve drinking parties, are also occasions where the veneer of deference and politeness is temporarily overcome so that views that one would not ordinarily dare express are expressed under the cover of inebriation. As a result, at the very least, an information flow is available so that management can determine to what extent consensus exists. In general, the strong antiadversarial element of the system (emphasis on harmony) has as its counterpart the requirement to obtain at least apparent consensus wherever that is possible.

The Industrial Group

The Japanese enterprise is usually a part of a circle of cooperating firms that help each other in various ways. The circle (*Keiretsu*) will usually include one or two fairly large manufacturing enterprises, a bank, one or two trading companies, subsidiaries of the larger companies, and a group of smaller firms that operate as suppliers of various parts for the larger firms.

Various forms of cooperation will take place within the circle. For example, the manufacturing firm may "place" some of its retirees in jobs with subsidiaries or with its suppliers. Long-term credit for expansion may be easily obtained from the bank or banks that are members of the circle. Such credit will not be viewed as depending on short-term performance, and hence the manufacturing firm may undertake projects that are known not to pay off for even as long as ten years. At the same time, enterprises considering long-range plans may seek advice both from the sales organization or the banking organizations. Suppliers will almost of necessity be required to take very seriously the demands and specifications as well as the cost concerns of the firms within the circle to whom they sell.

All the firms in the circle are meshed in one way or another in a series of generally informal cooperative arrangements. However, if there is a considerable gap or disadvantage in dealing with a firm within the circle as against one outside, dealings with the outsider will take place. An article in the *Wall Street Journal* (1983)[9] explained how an American supplier producing a unit, needed as part of a manufacturing process, that lasted twice as long as its Japanese counterpart was able to win a long-term contract in competition with an in-group supplier. The in-group supplier might have had an advantage if the cost differences had been low, but when they were considerable, it did not. All this reflects the fact that it is the firm itself that is the basic unit of concern, and whose welfare is prized by its members, and not the larger circle to which it belongs. It is the motivational system *within* this basic unit, and its reaction to its surroundings, that is the main determinant of actual behavior.

Summary and Conclusions

We have considered a number of elements of an idealized version of the Japanese Management System, including lifetime employment, hiring after secondary school or college, all careers starting at the bottom, mostly on-the-job training financed by the company, job rotation within ranks, age-determined increases in rank, emphasis on group responsibility for work, flexible boundaries between jobs, emphasis on harmonious intragroup relations, informal and formal consensus procedures, imprecise division between workers and managers, intracompany unions, and seniority as a major element in promotion.

On the other side of the employment relation, firm members receive a salary determined mostly by age or length of service, significant twice-yearly bonuses, and a variety of fringe benefits such as contributions to an intrafirm retirement fund, health services or insurance, subsidized housing, facilities for athletic and social outlets, and expense accounts at higher managerial levels. It is interesting to note that despite the fact that there are inequalities of rank and salary at any given time, *over the course of a career* there is a rough equality, or at least very much greater equality. This is because all permanent employees rise within the system, up to a point, through promotion by years of service.

With respect to decision making, our focus was on effort free-riding. Although there may be some free riding under Japanese conditions, it seems clear that because of the strong sense of belonging there is a lack of practical distinction between the company agenda and the in-

9. Regrettably, I could not find the exact page in my notes at the time of writing.

dividual's private agenda. As a result very little free riding is observed in the average case.[10]

While standard procedures for everyday activities are common, there also exist extensive procedures for the introduction of changes through informal and formal means. Thus, gaps and obstacles in the procedure set can be fairly easily filled and overcome by informal means. This is facilitated by the frequent communication that is part of the consensus-building system, and possibly by indirect, subtle peer monitoring.

Of course, the latent Prisoner's Dilemma possibility exists in Japan as elsewhere, but it infrequently comes to the fore. Although most enterprises have had a severe strike at some point in their postwar history they seem to have learned from this experience so that it rarely or never happened again. The system of organization is well oiled by a passion for harmonious relations, and a set of conventions and procedures that foster such relations. Clearly, institutionalized arrangements, such as an emphasis on consensus building of both the informal variety and the more formal Ringi system, lead to the repression or elimination of adversarial horizontal alliances along management or worker lines.

Strong vertical bonds also minimize or eliminate adversarial horizontal alliances so that labor-management disputes are not significant. The output-cost aspect of production has been amply discussed, but an equally or more important aspect is quality. Here it seems clear that the group decision mechanism, and the fact that jobs are not narrowly specified, help considerably to maintain high quality standards. If each member of a group feels responsible to the group, and if the group is held responsible for the quality of the work, then individuals will have an incentive to check and cover for the quality performance of other members of the group. This is obviously the exact opposite of what would happen where there is a narrow job definition and each individual cares only about the performance of his own job (to the extent that he may care about that) and not at all about how any other member of the group performs. A similar mechanism operates with respect to the quantitative aspects of production.

Perhaps the most important aspect of the whole system is the almost seamless web of elements, in part cultural and in part unique to the Japanese Management System, that supports and buttresses the strong

10. The case of those working for the National Railways in the early 1980s may be an exception.

vertical and mutual hierarchical bonds within the organization. Cultural and nurturing aspects of Japanese life create an emphasis on loyalty to the group to which one belongs, and loyalty to one's superiors. Almost all the elements mentioned earlier contribute in one way or another to a system in which vertical bonds are much more significant than latent adversarial horizontal ones. These vertical relations also help to create a mechanism for the effective transmission of pressure for internal efficiency from the top of the hierarchy down through the ranks, and thus from the outside of the firm to the inside.[11]

At the same time, note that the vertical bonds help to support the horizontal bonds with respect to production. Thus, vertical cooperation, and the fact that people move from job to job and can expect to rise through the hierarchy create an atmosphere in which people find it easy to cooperate productively horizontally and take care of unanticipated problems at the lowest effective level (see Aoki, 1986). All of this is consistent with our discussion of the relations between vertical and horizontal cooperation considered in Chapter 12.

Among the components worthy of special note are the career aspects of the system under which people start at the bottom, operate in terms of a lifetime employment ideal, receive guidance from a mentor appointed to help them, and become involved in frequent social occasions with their immediate superiors. Each individual member can count on a superior to ease his career path. It is important to observe that there exists a two-way stream of mutual support, direct and indirect, up and down the ranks. Also, the lifetime employment expectations means that, in a sense, implicit psychological contracts are made vertically between individuals who are expected to stay around a long time. Hence, mutual fulfillment of expectations can be achieved over long periods. The system of consensus building is also mostly vertical and works both up and down the ranks. Understanding and communication are facilitated by the fact that those on the higher rungs of the ladder know what it is like to be at the bottom. Job rotation and the lack of job boundaries reduce the incentives for horizontal bonding. Essentially, it is the strong vertical bonds of the hierarchical system that minimize the distance between organization and private agendas.

---

11. Of course the Japanese firm has also achieved success through the introduction of manufacturing techniques, such as the "just in time" system. However, other firms could easily incorporate such techniques. It is the incentive aspects of the system that make it possible to fine tune the system so that "just in time" production techniques will work. See Schonberger (1982).

A qualifying remark is in order. Of course, repressed competitive feelings between peers and tensions between those at different levels exist. Furthermore, the competition among peers and near-peers to contribute to the group effort can lead to excessive working hours and undesirably truncated vacations. Thus, while the system is efficient it may not maximize on-the-job happiness. The latter is hard to assess.

To my mind one of the frequently unrealized, important strengths of the Japanese Management System lies in the imaginative use of hierarchy in the cause of internal efficiency. This is supported by the various bonds of mutual obligation that exist between those at different levels. At the same time the bonus system gives individuals a sense of sharing in the fruits of the success (or lack of it) of the enterprise.

CHAPTER 15

Putting It All Together

The purpose of this chapter is to show how the ideas discussed in this book all fit together. First, we will present a model of production within firms that integrates the various concepts and components we have discussed into a unified theory. We will describe a basic model that can be further elaborated to various degrees without changing its underlying nature. Then, we will glean from the model and the earlier chapters some of the major sources of internal inefficiency in firms.

The Basic Model

The following schematic set of relations indicates the major connections among the basic variables:

$$\text{EPr} \longrightarrow [\text{HPr}] \longrightarrow [\text{E}] \longrightarrow [\text{Per}] \longrightarrow [\text{PR}]$$

where EPr = external pressure, HPr = hierarchical pressure or internal pressure, E = effort, Per = performance, and PR = pressure reaction.

In words, this set of relations states that the pressure in the market and the environment is transmitted to the hierarchy, which in turn transmits the pressure internally. Internal pressure[1] determines effort levels, which in turn determine the firm's performance. (The efforts in the firm determine costs and revenues and hence determine profits—an index of performance.) "Pressure reaction" results as a consequence of performance. The pressure reaction is the hierarchical pressure that takes into account performance and the external pressure. Thus, it re-

---

1. We shall use the expressions "hierarchical pressure" and "internal pressure" interchangeably.

flects the amount of pressure that the hierarchy will continue to transmit as a consequence of its most recent performance and the nature of the environment. The outcome will depend on whether the pressure reaction approximately equals (within inert area bounds) the internal pressure (the translated external pressure). If it does, then we have an equilibrium; the firm will be essentially satisfied with its activities and no attempt will be made to change firm behavior.

Now, let us look at the basic variables in somewhat greater detail. Note that there are three aspects to pressure: (1) external pressure in the environment including the market, (2) internal pressure as translated by the hierarchy from the outside to the inside of the firm, and (3) the internal response to translated pressure, which is effort toward performance to bring about "pressure reaction."

By the hierarchy we have in mind everyone in the organization ranked in terms of their superior-subordinate relations. We also have in mind the usually invisible vertical or horizontal commitments, and *chains* of commitments, that various organization members have made to others in the organization. As explained in detail earlier, it is the nature of these invisible relations that largely determines the extent of the latent Prisoner's Dilemma problem in a firm and the kind of effort-convention solutions that will exist. It is especially important to note that particular effort conventions will depend, in part, on the *history* of the particular enterprise, and on the width of their inert areas.

In our scheme, [E] is an effort vector whose components are the effort levels of every individual in the organization. Effort takes on a vast variety of forms. Some of the major effort categories are: production efforts, including both quantity and quality aspects; price-setting and price decision-making efforts; marketing efforts; packaging and shipping efforts; post-sales customer relations; personnel, efforts to improve market position or increase monopoly power; and finally, coordination efforts that attempt to make sure that the other effort levels are in some reasonable balance vis-à-vis each other.

Actual performance depends partly on the various effort levels, including the efforts put into price and quantity decisions, and partly on price parameters for both inputs and outputs. Note that some price decisions are made by following conventions, namely, by using conventional pricing formulas. Assessment of performance further depends on conventions. Standard accounting conventions determine how values are estimated (for example, depreciation conventions), and how data is amalgamated so that performance results are transmitted to the hierarchy (for example, the bottom line).

In the section that follows we will examine in some detail the crucial relation between pressure and the effort response to pressure. What goes on inside the firm to accomplish the translation of pressure into effort, and especially into productive effort, is critical to the outcome of the firm's performance. We will then return to looking at how this relation fits into the larger set of relationships, which includes the flow of output and the revenues and costs associated with the output flow. These factors determine the performance characteristics of a firm, which in turn influence the felt internal pressure.

Pressure, Hierarchy, and Effort

The main connection between external pressure and internal performance is through the hierarchy. The extent to which a particular firm responds to external pressure, if at all, once pressure is transmitted inside, will depend on the nature of the commitment structure of the hierarchical commitment network.

To start with, recall certain behavioral postulates discussed in earlier chapters. These are: the voluntarism hypothesis (Chapter 8), effort free riding (Chapter 5), the discretionary effort range (Chapter 5), and inert areas (Chapter 4). Now, consider the following list of factors, which suggests the basic structure of commitment relations that lies behind the theory of hierarchy presented in this book.

I. Commitments to:
  (1) Oneself (for example, work ethic)
  (2) The firm (for example, minimum effort, effort conventions)
  (3) Others in the firm
      (a) Vertically
      (b) Horizontally
II. Vertical commitment structure:
  (1) Whether superior-subordinate commitments exist
  (2) The nature of commitment chains
      (a) Complete chains
      (b) Asymmetry of interest
      (c) Gaps, obstacles, breaks
      (d) Factions
  (3) Strength of vertical commitments
      (a) Distribution of power (rights to hire, promote, reward, dismiss)

 (b) Quality or degree of augmentation (trust, identification, common objectives)
 (c) Openness (to suggestions for improvements, to requests for performance)
 (4) Transmission through the vertical commitment chains of:
  (a) Objectives
  (b) Pressure for performance
  (c) Performance requests
  (d) Bottom-up information

III. Horizontal commitments:
 (1) Horizontal cooperative commitments for productivity
 (2) Horizontal cooperation for interlayer adversarial purposes
 (3) Relation of horizontal to vertical commitments

Behind the effort decisions of the members of a firm there are a number of broad motivational forces. The voluntary effort hypothesis suggests that, if motivation is sufficient, more can be achieved through obtaining voluntary effort than through explicit, monitored effort contracts. This, among other considerations, implies that effort discretion exists, and within bounds firm members have the option of responding to effort free-riding incentives. The response to such incentives will depend on whether informal relations are generally adversarial, neutral, or cooperative. Whether free riding will be resisted, and to what extent voluntary efforts will be made, will depend on the quality and degree of openness of the commitment relations between firm members.

People enter commitment relations in the same sense in which they enter other exchange relations, but the rules and procedures are more subtle and less obvious. In general, commitment relations are entirely or partially implicit. Just as we can conceive of all possible mutually beneficial exchange relations for goods, so we can imagine all *possible* mutually beneficial commitment relations between firm members. But actual commitment relations will usually fall short of latent possibilities. If the commitment relations are consistent with the firm's objectives, then the more extensive these exchanges the more integrated the organization will be.

The strength of each commitment relation has two aspects: a degree of augmentation and a degree of openness. The degree of augmentation is determined by such elements as trust, identification with other members, and a sense of common objectives. By openness we mean the degree to which the parties to these implicit exchanges are willing to meet requests for performance and respond to suggestions for improvements in the firm, rather than being limited to preset boundaries of behavior.

We can visualize the vertical commitment structure as being made up of a series of chains of commitment relations. These chains may be strong or weak. Some of the weaknesses in the chain may manifest themselves in obstacles to communication, or in obstacles to obtaining performance responses, or in actual breaks in the chain. Also, degrees of weakness may reflect less openness or lower degrees of augmentation. Chains may also be weakened by biases in performance, when individuals are more eager to fulfill their commitments to those above than they are to those below. In part, the extent of mutual commitments will depend on the distribution of power through the hierarchy, which determines the extent to which firm members at a variety of levels have something to offer to those at lower levels. The strength of commitment relations will determine the extent to which firm members transmit firm objectives, pressure, demands for performance, and information vertically in both directions.

Commitment chains may be separated from each other longitudinally so that each chain, up to a certain level, operates on the basis of separate objectives. This describes the classical instance of factionalism. Each faction has greater loyalties to its factional interests than to some overall objective of the firm. This implies that those at the top of the hierarchy cannot reconcile the different factional interests, or themselves belong to one faction and use their position to obtain some type of advantage over another faction or factions. Of course, this represents a weakness in the overall integration of the enterprise.[2]

We should also keep in mind that horizontal commitments between peers are likely to be equally as important as vertical relations. The same categories that are relevant for vertical commitments are likely to apply to horizontal commitments. Also, strong vertical commitments are likely to be supportive of productively cooperative horizontal commitments. On the other hand, weaknesses in the vertical commitment chain are likely to be associated with either horizontal isolation or horizontal cooperation for adversarial purposes. In general, the extent and the strength of the horizontal and vertical commitments will determine

2. See Halberstam (1986) for a vivid description of factionalism in the Ford Motor Company in the 1960s.

the effectiveness of the effort response to both environmental pressures and the hierarchical transmission of firm objectives.

Now let us look at these hierarchical networks in greater detail, keeping in mind the possibilities listed in table 12.1. In a response to pressure, either from the outside, or from an individual at a higher level, three types of activities are involved: the transmission of the firm's objectives; the transmission of pressure; and the production activities at some level that result in value added to the product. Figures 15.1a, b, and c indicate three possible superior-subordinate relations. For instance, in figure 15.1a we assume a strong cooperative relation. Essentially, the individual at the higher level makes a request for performance of the one at a lower level, who interprets the request and responds in accordance with the extent to which he is motivated. In demand and supply terms, the one at the higher level may be viewed as demanding performance from the one at the lower level, who supplies the performance. However, the performance may simply be transmitting pressure to someone further below, who in turn may be required to transmit pressure to a still lower level. In figure 15.1a, in which a highly cooperative relationship is assumed, the response is fairly close to the demand even at high pressure levels. This would be especially true if the supplier of performance also cooperated productively with those horizontal to him.

In figure 15.1b the respondent is isolated vertically. His level of performance is the same irrespective of the pressure response of the one above. Figure 15.1c would fit an extreme adversarial situation in which those at a lower level resent any increased pressure and respond with less effort. In less extreme situations the adversarial subordinate re-

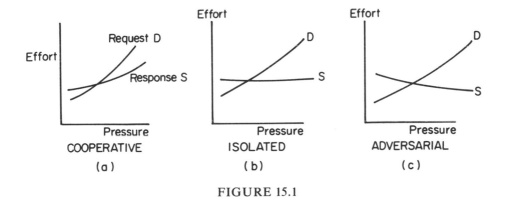

FIGURE 15.1

sponds to pressure reluctantly, producing a greater gap than in the non-adversarial case illustrated in figure 15.1a. However, it is quite possible that for all pressure levels the supply of performance is below demand, that is, the curves need not cross.

For some pressure levels one may get a demand equal to supply, as illustrated in the figures. This implies that for very low pressures the supply of performance is greater than demand. We may interpret this to mean that the work effort and the effort conventions of the subordinate are greater than is demanded at these low pressures. The superior is pleased with the performance level, but he would also have been happy with a lower performance level.

It is interesting to consider the possible attenuation of pressure as it is transmitted down the hierarchy. In figure 15.2 we show this possibility occurring. P_0 is the initial pressure level. Note that a performance E_1 supplied at S_1 is the same as the demand for performance P_1 at the next level, D_2. That is, demand is essentially putting pressure on the level below. In consequence, the movement of pressure follows the path *abcde*, and pressure becomes attenuated from P_0 to P_2.

The elements of vertical commitments that are important determi-

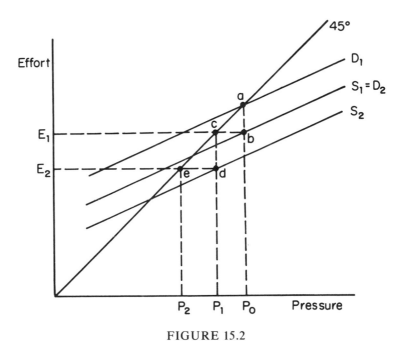

FIGURE 15.2

nants of the height and slope of an effort curve are: (1) the extent to which the rewards and sanctions that a superior gives in response to the efforts of a subordinate are supportive of a cooperative relation; (2) the mutuality or asymmetry of commitments; (3) the strength of the commitment-enlarging elements, such as trust, a sense of common objectives, and identification with the enterprise at large; (4) openness; and (5) the upward transmission of information. The stronger these elements are, the higher we should expect the degree of effort to be.

It is important to keep in mind that the extent to which rewards and sanctions are offered by a superior depends on the vertical distribution of power through the hierarchy. A superior cannot offer rewards if he has not been given any rewards to offer. In general, the more widespread the distribution of power, the more numerous the ties that can be made throughout the hierarchy's vertical chains. In addition, the criteria for rewarding employees must counter the possibility of an asymmetric bias against "downward" commitments—that is, the possible bias that people at middle levels may have to prefer to enter mutual commitments with those above and avoid such commitments with those below. Thus, the criteria for judging superiors has to be based in part on the strength and outcomes of their mutual commitments with subordinates. Where mutuality and openness of commitments are weaker we would expect that the effort-pressure slope would be shallower (as in the supply curve in figure 15.1b).

The effectiveness of the transmission of pressure among more than two individuals will depend on the extent to which there are gaps in the transmission (that is, deviations between the request and the response), and complete breaks in the transmission. Once a break occurs, then transmission ends, and whatever transmission took place at higher levels ceases to be of any consequence.

Another important aspect is the symmetry of relations between superior and subordinates. Up to now we have considered the top-down relations, as it were. We ought to simultaneously look at the bottom-up relations. Do subordinates provide information about the nature of problems that exist at lower levels to those at higher levels? Where the provision of such information is blocked because of a lack of access, or lack of incentives for those below to communicate information to those higher up, then sustained inefficiencies at lower levels could develop without any attempts to correct them at a higher level. Under these circumstances, where there is essentially a lack of feedback from those below, we would expect that effort would deteriorate at lower levels, and the effort level would be determined mostly by long-run, horizontally determined effort conventions. Note here that motivation is likely to be involved in responsiveness and communication. Where information flows easily in both directions we should expect that high levels of trust and high levels of responsiveness exist. A lack of responsiveness to pressure is likely to reduce upward flows of information, including any sense of urgency (pressure) associated with such information.

In figure 15.3 we show a result similar to figure 15.1 except that the curves are now fat, which means they take into account the inert area bounds surrounding the demand for performance and the supply of performance. The actual performance may occur inside the intersecting area. The actual performance point will be somewhere in between the supply boundaries. Two influences are likely to determine that point: the extent to which the individual is responsive to the demand and the associated pressure; and the extent to which the performance point is adjusted for peer-group pressures, which usually imply some degree of adherence to an effort convention.

Note that there is no need for the supply of performance to equal the demand for performance. Whether this situation is stable or not

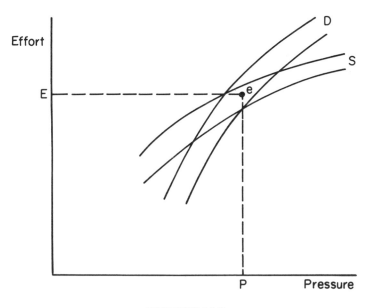

FIGURE 15.3

will depend on whether the demand and supply points are inside the inert area bounds. If they are, nothing further happens. If they are not, the one who demands performance may attempt to do something about it, such as putting on further pressure. If the latter does not work then this would imply widening of the inert area bounds. Note that there is no reason for the pressure obtained from the external environment and transmitted internally to be that pressure which equates demand for performance and its supply.

Two types of horizontal commitments have to be distinguished: cooperative commitments for productive purposes; and cooperative commitments for adversarial purposes. In the former case people at the same level cooperate to increase output. In the latter case adversarial feelings exist between levels and those at the same level have a tendency to support and foster these feelings among themselves, as well as to reduce their effort levels.

In many situations a number of subordinates are responsible to a given superior, and the extent to which subordinates cooperate among themselves on production goals will be an important factor in determining the level of responsiveness. Under highly productive horizontal cooperation coworkers are likely to influence each other to be more responsive vertically than would otherwise be the case. In cases in which such horizontal cooperation does not exist we would expect lesser degrees of vertical responsiveness depending on particular relations between the superior and different subordinates. In the cases in which cooperation is clearly for adversarial purposes we would expect the influence to be toward the maintenance of lower effort levels than otherwise. Also, in such circumstances, effort conventions based on upper-bound sanctions are likely to be the major determinants of output.

We have thus far assumed that the pressure-effort functions were smooth curves. However, once we take the inert area idea into account we should surround the relationships by inert area bounds. This is illustrated in figure 15.3. Any point in the intersection of the two inert areas represents consistent behavior for both parties. For the superior it fulfills the requirement for performance. Also, it meets the expectation of what is believed, by the subordinate, to be an adequate response. The nature of the subordinate's effort depends not only on his desire to respond to the demand, but in nonunique situations, on the effort of similarly placed peers; that is, on whether or not the situation is covered by an effort convention. In the latter circumstance the effort produced is likely to fit the existing convention. The width of the inert areas are likely to be smaller where vertical and horizontal productive relations are simultaneously cooperative, and larger where vertical relations are adversarial and the horizontal relations are cooperative for adversarial purposes.

It is interesting to look at two contrasting cases. The first is a commitment structure that leads to a highly elastic response to pressure, and the second is one that leads to a highly inelastic response. Consider the case in which the network commitment structure is strongly vertical and is supported by horizontal productive commitments. Assume that the enlarged mutual commitments are open. In this case the pressure is likely to be transmitted from higher levels to lower levels. Also, assume there are no breakpoints. As a consequence, the pressure will go down as far as necessary. The strong horizontal production commitments imply a lack of property rights to particular jobs, or a lack of narrow job definitions. The result should imply a relatively low level of free riding and narrow inert areas. Hence, the absolute level of effort should be closer to the optimal than otherwise.

In considering enlarged commitments we made the point that this in turn *depends on* commitments being supported by a sense of identity with the firm and a sense of common objectives. However, keep in mind that a high level of mutual commitment, if spread fairly uniformly throughout the enterprise, also *helps to create* a sense of identity and a sense of common objectives.

The situation just considered represents a type of vertical and horizontal structure that is close to ideal. We can more readily see the possibilities for inefficiency if we examine the obverse case, where the commitment structure leads to a highly inelastic response. In this instance the network commitment system is vertically adversarial, and contains gaps in the connections, while at the same time firm members are cooperative for adversarial purposes.

The lack of vertical connections is likely to create a situation in which there is a relatively high degree of free riding. Effort free riding will be limited only by effort conventions. Thus, the effort level will depend on the past history of effort in the enterprise. At the same time we should expect relatively wide inert areas. Furthermore, conventions are likely to be such that individuals do not respond very much to pressure for effort. Indeed, given adversarial relations we should expect firm members at a given level to find various ways to shelter themselves from vertical pressure.

The lack of horizontal cooperation for production is likely to lead to a situation where there are narrow job descriptions. This, in part, will be associated with a fear that a positive response in helping others productively will result in requests for greater effort in the interest of others. The general, independent, relatively isolated atmosphere does not promise or provide incentives for internal entrepreneurship, and creates a sense that others would not support internal entrepreneurial efforts. All in all, we would expect that under such circumstances the effort level would be relatively low, and the effort-pressure slope, while possibly positively inclined, would be rather shallow.

A Diagrammatic Treatment of the Model

We now turn to a diagrammatic treatment of the overarching relationships between variables. The critical relations we have just considered between pressure, hierarchy, and effort are one important aspect of the somewhat larger picture we will consider here. It is convenient to think of the relations as drawn for the average levels of the basic variables for the firm as a whole. A few simple diagrams help to illustrate the connections among these relationships.

As emphasized earlier, we postulate that the basic relations are imbedded in inert areas. This holds also for the relation between internal pressure and pressure reaction. Thus, if the hierarchically translated external pressure and the pressure reaction have overlapping inert areas, then the firm is in equilibrium.

First, consider the pressure-translation problem. Real pressure exists "out there" in the performance of somewhat similar firms, and in observable market conditions and other market signals. But such market information has to be perceived by the hierarchy and translated into pressure inside the firm. It has to be translated into pressure *on* members of the firm in order to influence their performance. In figure 15.4 we show three possibilities. The outside pressure may be translated accurately, that is, along the 45-degree line, or it may be translated "optimistically," introducing less pressure to the inside than exists outside, say on the basis of the 30-degree line. The final possibility is to introduce a pessimistic bias, say on the basis of the 60-degree ray. In figure 15.4, internal pressure *O* reflects the optimistic interpretation, *R* the realistic one, and *P* the pessimistic one.

Apart from pressure translation, the basic variables and their relations to each other are illustrated in figure 15.5. Consider first the optimal situation. We start with Quadrant I and then move counterclockwise.

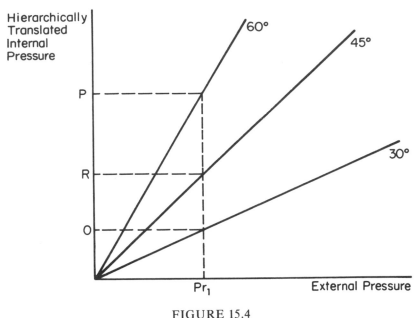

FIGURE 15.4

In the optimal situation pressure is accurately perceived by the hierarchy, and furthermore, it is the optimum amount of pressure Pr_0, as shown on the abscissa in Quadrant I. Note that the pressure-effort relation PE is based on the Yerkes-Dodson curve. The optimum pressure, at the peak of the Yerkes-Dodson curve, leads to the optimal effort level E_0. Effort translates into costs and revenues in Quadrant II. The effort-cost relation EC is drawn to reflect the idea that the greater the effort the lower the cost. The effort-revenue relation ER reflects the idea that the greater the effort the greater the revenue. We can use the cost and revenue points determined by the effort level to select the appropriate constant-cost ray in Quadrant III, and given the revenue and the related cost ray we obtain the performance level. In Quadrant IV the performance level translates into a pressure reaction, $f(Per)$, that is consistent with the internal pressure level, which of course accurately reflects the external pressure.

In most real situations neither the initial external pressure nor its translation by the hierarchy will be optimal. Thus, we can visualize nonoptimal solutions. Start with nonoptimal pressure Pr_1. This leads to nonoptimal effort E_1. Moving counterclockwise, nonoptimal effort leads to nonoptimal cost C_1, and nonoptimal revenue R_1 in Quadrant II.

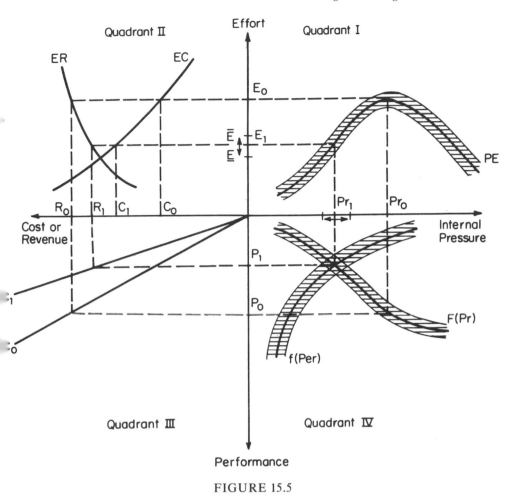

FIGURE 15.5

Nonoptimal performance P_1 in Quadrant III may lead to a pressure reaction response consistent with internal pressure Pr_1 in Quadrant IV. Thus, a nonoptimal equilibrium exists. Note that nonoptimal equilibria are facilitated by inert areas surrounding internal pressure and the pressure reaction function, as well as the translated internal pressure. The shading in the diagram indicates the inert areas that surround the basic relationships.

In Quadrant IV we show two functions, performance as a function of pressure $F(Pr)$, and pressure as a function of performance $f(Per)$. The intersection of these functions yields the equilibrium performance and pressure levels. The point (Pr_1, P_1) is shown as an equilibrium in figure 15.5, while (Pr_0, P_0) is not. Note that the function $F(Pr)$ is derived from the relations in the other three quadrants and is not an independent function. To indicate the consequences of a superior organization would imply a different performance-pressure function $F(Pr)$, that is, one that reflected greater performance for the same pressure. A superior organization may or may not impose more pressure in response to a given performance level. This would depend on the particular nature of the improved organization. Such functions for an improved organization are not shown in the diagram.

What may appear as indeterminate parts of the solution, because of the inert areas, are in fact made determinate by conventions. These are shown as particular points inside the inert areas. Thus the effort level E_1 could exist at any point between $\underline{E}$ and $\overline{E}$, but it ends up at E_1, which is the particular effort convention determined by past history and current informal sanctions. As already indicated, E_1 leads to the cost and revenue levels which, in their turn, are the main components of the performance level. The point is to show that one can get a consistent, inefficient internal equilibrium with respect to a given market and/or environment, and the pressure on the firm that they reflect. Furthermore, note that since the equilibrium is surrounded by inert areas it is a "loose equilibrium," which is likely to be more stable than the tight equilibrium of standard micro theory (see Chapter 9).

Sources of Inefficiency

The ideas developed in the previous chapters and the theory outlined here suggest some possible sources of internal inefficiency. Some are more readily seen in terms of individual behavior, while others can be better appreciated as aspects of organizational behavior. The two are always interrelated.

We turn first to consider the following possible sources of inefficiency in individuals' behavior: (1) nonoptimal decision making, (2) effort free-riding, (3) behavior in accordance with suboptimal conventions, (4) insufficiently motivated effort, (5) inability to overcome procedural gaps or obstacles, and (6) behavior in response to a low-motivational procedural system.

Since nonoptimal decision making is part of our overall decision scheme, we suggest that nonoptimal decisions by individuals on behalf of the firms for which they work are likely to be a source of inefficiency.

One reason for nonoptimal decisions is the transmission of nonoptimal pressure to individuals through the hierarchy. This may involve insufficient or excessive pressure. Under low pressure, why should we expect individuals to do better if there is no pressure to make really good decisions? Of course, there is a great variety of nonoptimal decision-making behavior, some of which has already been examined in detail. Recall that nonoptimal decision making by following conventions is in part the saving grace of the system since individual maximization would lead to the Prisoner's Dilemma solution.

A major source of inefficiency is effort free riding. There are various ways in which free riding with respect to effort manifests itself. Among the most important of these are: lower pace of work, lower quality of effort (which transmits itself into a lower-quality product), negligence with respect to various aspects of work, absenteeism which may not only reduce the effort of the individual but also the effort level of others (depending on the absentee), nontimeliness of effort, and noncooperativeness (such as a lack of responsiveness to reasonable requests). All of these are compared to some optimal level.

Some individuals may be willing to put forth greater effort levels in response to appropriate incentives. Thus, a poor matching between the motivations of individuals and the incentives provided becomes a source of internal inefficiency. Note that the firm supplies incentives, while individuals possess motivations that create the *demand* for suitable incentives for performance. The incentives supplied and those demanded by the individual's motivational system need not match.

Some individuals may manage well with a given procedural system while others are insufficiently motivated to overcome the gaps and obstacles in the system. A poor match between individuals allocated to certain jobs and the procedural gaps and obstacles most pertinent to these jobs can be a critical source of inefficiency. To remedy the situation may require a reallocation of people to different organizational units or a change in the procedural system, but most likely a change in both.

The procedural system may be adequate in the sense of having few gaps or obstacles, but some individuals may find it unpleasant or onerous to use certain procedures. Thus, their motivations lead them to ignore certain procedures or to use roundabout, less-optimal procedures. This lack of motivation may be a source of inefficiency.

Some individuals may have rather wide inert areas so that they make no attempts to change when change would be in the interest of the objectives of the firm. Their failure, because of inertia, to adjust to changes in the independent variables when appropriate turns out to be a source of inefficiency. Individuals at relatively high hierarchical levels who fail to adjust may induce a chain of inefficiencies down through the hierarchy.

Finally, some individuals may find it easy to relate to peers but difficult to relate to either superiors or subordinates. Their vertical relationships may become obstructions to the vertical flows that are necessary for the smooth operation of the hierarchical system.

Of course, these sources of inefficiency viewed from an individual behavioral viewpoint are hardly likely to be independent of each other. Some forms of inefficiency are likely to support others, and their interactions as they spread through the vertical and horizontal commitment system lead to greater inefficiencies than would otherwise be the case.

Among the organizational sources of inefficiency the following are likely to be of importance: (1) adversarial relations, (2) low-effort conventions, (3) hierarchical flow obstructions, (4) inadequate hierarchical flow relations, (5) inadequate hierarchical consensus procedures, (6) gaps and obstacles in the procedure set, (7) wide group inert areas, (8) inefficiently arranged procedures, and (9) wages and working conditions poorly matched to effort conventions.

A firm's culture and history may have developed adversarial relations between management and labor, or between some more narrowly defined hierarchical levels. These adversarial relations are likely to interfere with vertical cooperation, and thus to encourage restrictive practices that adversely affect output or quality (that is, effort free riding). Thus, underlying potential conflicts are a source of internal inefficiency even if they erupt infrequently into more open forms of conflict.

The history of the firm and the relations between individuals at different levels, especially strong peer-group relations, are likely to determine the effort conventions, which in turn determine output levels. Probably one of the most significant sources of internal inefficiency is the deviation between actual effort conventions and optimal conventions.

Various internal inefficiencies occur because of obstructions in hierarchical flows in both directions. For instance, it may be difficult or impossible to introduce improvements without getting approval from one or more persons at higher levels, or there may be limited access for those below to suggest improvements. In the other direction, it may be difficult or impossible for some employees to get subordinates to cooperate in carrying out certain tasks because of constraints or limits to the downward flow of information.

A more subtle type of hierarchical flow that leads to inefficiency is the relations between people at different levels that involve degrees of commitment. Four important components of this type of relation can be distinguished by the following questions: (1) Are the desires of the superior consistent with the objectives of the firm? (2) Is the subordinate committed to the perceived desires of the superior? (3) Are there open and augmented mutual commitments between subordinates and superiors? and (4) Does the chain of mutual commitments go up to all levels in the hierarchy or are there breaks in the commitment chain? If these commitments are nonexistent or weak, or there are gaps in the chain, then these will be sources of internal inefficiency. All this is aside from the question as to whether commitments to individuals do not turn out to be commitments to the organization because of differences in individual and organizational agendas.

Of course, commitment may not be sufficient if there is a lack of agreement, especially among vertically related individuals, about what has to be done in the interest of the organization. A major form of disagreement frequently exists *between* vertical groups that have different agendas. This is the classic case of factionalism, which can be costly because it uses effort and other resources that can be better employed in the unified interests of the firm. Conflicting or unresolved stances about what has to be done are obviously a source of problems. Thus, a lack of a consensus-creating machinery or a lack of an adequate use of such mechanisms will be a source of inefficiency.

Almost every procedural system is bound to possess some gaps or obstacles or both. Such gaps and obstacles become sources of inefficiency in two ways. (1) Because of gaps and obstacles unnecessary, roundabout methods of doing things develop which are less efficient than more direct alternatives. (2) In addition, the gaps and obstacles may make it difficult or impossible to handle some unanticipated requests either from within the firm or from the market.

It is not only what people do, but also failure to change when appropriate that may be a source of inefficiency. Hence, when decision procedures are bounded by wide inert areas for individuals and groups, this can lead to inadequate responses to circumstances requiring changes.

Closely connected with wide inert areas is an inadequate transmission of pressure from outside the firm to those inside. This can occur whether pressures are initially received at the highest levels of the hierarchy or by specialists lower down. If pressure is not transmitted internally, either because of flaws in the hierarchical flow mechanism or flaws in the perception or receipt of information from outside the firm, then inefficiency can result. What we have in mind is not only directives or information, but also the transmission of a sense of urgency to attend to certain problems or else face consequences to the organization. The greater the pressure outside, the greater the likelihood that priorities will have to be changed inside. Clearly, breaks in pressure transmission are likely to lead to inadequate organizational responses to market or other environmental conditions.

Finally, the internal distribution of rewards may be out of synchronization with the gross revenue of the firm, which in turn may be a source of inefficiency. If the commitment of wage and working-conditions costs is too high relative to the effort level and the revenues generated by effort, then losses will result. Such losses may eventually create further inefficiency by influencing morale, or by making it difficult to carry out appropriate personnel replacements. In addition, excessive payments to those at higher levels at the seeming expense of those at lower levels is likely to influence the attitudes and the degree of commitment of subordinates to their superiors. At the same time this may involve a poor distribution of rewards lower down the hierarchy so that superiors at various levels find it difficult to create the incentives needed to obtain adequately open and sufficiently augmented commitments from subordinates.

Efficiency Wages

An important inefficiency is the inability to adjust to market conditions, especially in labor surplus cases. This affects the firm in question, but since it involves unemployment it also affects the economy as a whole. Keynesian macroeconomics requires rigid wages without giving an explanation of wage rigidity itself. In recent years the efficiency-wage theory has been advanced by a number of economists as an explanation of rigid wages and hence of unemployment.[3] The theory requires that

---

3. See Akerlof and Yellen (1986), Stiglitz (1984), and Katz (1986) for reviews of the literature. My own previous contributions to efficiency wage theory are contained in Leibenstein (1957) and Leibenstein (1974).

wages be connected to productivity and that lower wages may induce lower productivity. Thus, it is possible for employers to fear lower wages because productivity may fall more than proportionately, and wages per unit of output, or per effort unit, will rise. In this section we plan to show how the ideas developed earlier are consistent with the efficiency-wage thesis. However, we do not argue that the efficiency-wage doctrine is the sole explanation of unemployment.

The explanation involves two elements: the existence of rigid money wages, and efficiency wages as a support for wage rigidity. Consider the first element. We have argued earlier that many aspects of the employment contract will depend on conventions. This is likely to be true not only of effort, but of various understandings about working conditions. One of these conventions is that the existing wage will not be lowered, at least in nominal terms. This is part of a larger convention, which is that the job and the employment contract have a continuing relationship. That is, the terms are not renegotiated every day. This is likely to imply that there are limits to the extent to which employers can be arbitrary with respect to wages. Thus, being employed on the same terms on a day-to-day basis implies a non-lower-wage convention.

We now turn to explain the relationship between wages and productivity. To start with, note that if wages are related to effort then they are likely to be related to productivity. Not only does less effort imply lower productivity if nonwage inputs remain constant, but lower effort is also likely to lower the productivity of other inputs. For example, less effort applied to machine maintenance will result in greater frequency of breakdowns and hence lower productivity attributable to capital. By and large, the wage-effort relation will be in the same direction as the wage-productivity relation, so it will be sufficient for our purposes to consider wage-effort relations.

We now turn to the question of whether there exists the *possibility* of an effort reaction to a wage reduction. Keep in mind that some degree of effort discretion exists on the part of every firm member. Furthermore, we have earlier emphasized the voluntary effort postulate: that to a considerable degree the highest effort levels, both in terms of quantity and quality (especially quality), are usually unmonitorable and obtained through freely given voluntary effort. It would seem clear on the face of it that a significant aspect of effort is voluntary, and if effort discretion is seen to exist, then the possibility of reducing effort in response to some inducement and stimulus must exist.

A critical question is whether a wage reduction is likely to operate as an inducement to lowering effort. Here, keep in mind that a non-lower-wage convention usually exists.[4] Thus, any attempt to lower the wage of existing employees violates this critical convention. It clearly operates as a threat to the living standards of current employees. Furthermore, because a convention is involved, employees can count on similarly placed others also feeling that the convention has been violated, and that they face a common threat. It is likely that the latent adversarial relationship, which is normally suppressed, comes into play as a result of the convention violation.

A question that arises is the possibility of a dual wage system under which new employees are paid a lower wage than current ones. This involves some of the insider-outsider relations considered by Lindbeck and Snower (1986) who argue that insiders may have poor relations with new employees and choose to engage in disruptive activities to induce the firm not to hire new employees, and generally not to co-operate with new hires. Note that hiring new employees at a lower wage threatens existing employees with replacement. Existing employees may reason that the firm would not keep them since they are more costly, and that at any time some pretext may be used to replace them with cheaper new employees. One way for existing employees to show their displeasure is by lowering voluntary effort. In addition, the new employees have to follow some effort convention, which they in a sense "learn" from the existing employees. In this way all employees develop a lower effort standard than before the introduction of the dual wage system.

Also, note that the nature of the job has now been changed since the non-lower-wage convention is seen to be either violated or threatened by the new employees hired at a lower wage. Similarly, the new employees can visualize themselves being replaced at a still lower wage as they become relatively more expensive in the marketplace. Such internal threats are likely to be inconsistent with the maintenance of a predetermined effort convention under which the non-lower-wage convention holds.

Two reactions to breaking the non-lower-wage convention are possible. One is a strike of some sort, and the other is lowering effort. In fact, both involve lower effort levels, at least temporarily. There is likely to be a general expectation that peer agreement will exist to support such a reduction of effort. In extreme cases employees can also

4. The exception to this rule is where workers are hired each day separately, or in the case of a significant bonus system tied to performance. In this connection see Freeman and Weitzman (1986) on the Japanese bonus system.

count on sanctions against deviant employees to enforce some effort reduction all around. As argued earlier, relaxing the maximization postulate helps to explain why people will take up the imposition of sanctions on others even when it may be irksome to do so. Thus, in general we can see that the structure of the model developed earlier is consistent with effort reductions in response to wage reductions. Furthermore, management is likely to be aware of the convention, of the latent adversarial feelings that could be aroused by such actions, and of some possible consequences.

There is an exception to this argument. The notion that conventions are surrounded by inert areas implies that under some circumstances that go beyond the inert area bounds people may accept a violation of the convention, such as an unusual wage reduction. This involves situations in which everyone feels they are in the same boat and only wage concessions all around can save the enterprise from failure and can save jobs all around (for example, Chrysler in 1979). In other words, a wider sense of vertical identification with others in the firm, and a sense of potential loss sufficient to pierce the inert area bounds, can lead to a sense that the convention *should not* hold under these circumstances. This, in turn, can allow the acceptance of lower wages without a reduction in effort.

Nevertheless, deviations such as those just described, of which there are a number of recent examples, do not change the fact that by and large the non-lower-wage convention will be taken seriously where the external circumstances do not threaten the enterprise as a whole. Under such circumstances employers may fear the lower-effort reaction. This, in turn, will support relatively rigid money wages for a considerable portion of the economy. Thus, the wage level can come down if employees in firm after firm gradually begin to recognize that their own enterprise may be threatened unless they accept lower wages at the same effort level. However, the point is that such a wage reduction process is likely to take place rather slowly. Wages will be "sticky." The essence of the argument is that within cyclical aggregate demand fluctuations such gradual wage reductions could take place too slowly to guarantee a full-employment equilibrium.

Some Concluding Remarks

Our focus in this book has been on sources of internal inefficiency. We have not attempted to provide a design for an optimally efficient organization, although some suggestions indicating characteristics of an optimal organization were put forth. There are at least two reasons why it would be difficult to design an optimal organization. First, conventions and invisible human relations (that is, the company culture) depend on history. We cannot change the history of an existing firm, which might be of a nature that would prevent an optimal organization from developing. Nor for that matter can we design an initial organization that will be guaranteed to have an historical path leading to optimality. That is because conventions and invisible relations arise from the voluntary actions of people vis-à-vis each other. Second, for purposes of analysis and policy determination it is probably more important to understand sources of *in*efficiency rather than to focus on the characteristics of an ideal organization.

An important point is that productive efficiency is not the same as efficiency under which individual welfare is taken into account. It is easier to consider inefficiency in terms of output rather than welfare. It is possible to conceive of an organization that produces a maximum output, or near-maximum output, but is not a maximum welfare organization. Pressure for production may be so strong that some employees may prefer less pressure, less output, and lower wages and working conditions, but they may be caught up in a set of conventions, vertical relations, and short-run incentives that do not allow them to *individually* choose a less pressured working environment. Some scholars have suggested that the Japanese Management System as it operates in some firms ends up in situations of this sort.

It is useful at this juncture to keep in mind that our relaxation of the maximization postulate turns out to be helpful toward understanding suboptimal performance of firms, and for assessing the options that each individual firm has to improve or worsen its own performance. It meant that we are able to recognize that from the wide range of performances that are possible we end up with a half-full glass. The half-full interpretation is suggested because the convention solution avoids the almost-empty glass, Prisoner's Dilemma outcome. Of course, from another point of view the glass appears half empty, that is, internally inefficient to some degree, with room for improvement.

Finally, as stated in previous work, the theory of X-efficiency is an expansive set of ideas. Many people are researching many aspects of the problem, from a variety of viewpoints, including empirical tests of the theory.[5] There is still much work to be done.

5. Roger R. Frantz, in a forthcoming book (1987), reviews over fifty published empirical studies that either measure the degree of x-inefficiency that exists in various situations, or empirically test the implications of the theory.

Appendix

References

Index

Language, Choice, and Nonoptimization

In most disciplines the possibility of nonoptimal choices appears well accepted, but this is not the case in economics. Part of the problem has to do with the history of the profession, and part with the way language is used. The main burden of this chapter is to argue that words must not be used in such a way, or in such contexts, as to deny any essential parts of their meanings. If a concept or word has a *comparative* meaning, then the comparative nature of the term must not be denied or contradicted by the use of the term in certain contexts, or by postulates that lead to the denial of essential comparisons. These rather broad ideas will be clarified by example as we proceed.

It is important to emphasize that what follows is not an argument against the employment of the maximization postulate in various theories, rather I am arguing in favor of considering a system of analysis that allows for suboptimal decisions. The basic suggestion is that by some measure, whether phrased in terms of money, short-run utility, or long-run utility, there is a reasonable sense under which an inferior option remains an inferior option, and that such options can under some circumstances be "chosen." Furthermore, there is nothing in the general sense of decision-making processes that would not allow for a decision process that would result in a net loss, unless this possibility was assumed away at the outset.[1] These ideas will be clarified later.

---

1. There is a growing literature on the possibility and the fact of nonrational decision making. Probably most important is the fairly large body of work developed by Tversky and Kahneman (1981), and others who have followed their lead. This research suggests that the way a question is framed can determine the responding choice of options entirely apart from the content of the options involved. Thus, the response to the desirability of two types of medical treatment depends on whether the option is stated in terms of "one-third of the people will survive," or "two-thirds of the people will die." Some research reports that describe nonmaximizing behavior are reviewed in two recent papers by Amitai Etzioni (1986, 1987). A recent paper by Robert H. Frank (1987) presumes that occasional nonmaximizing behavior is a fact of life, and contains additional examples. Recent work by Akerlof and Yellen (1985) is also based on the assumption that there are lapses from rationality. There thus appears to be some tendency for economists to consider the problem of lapses from maximization, and its consequences.

For those who readily accept the idea of occasional nonoptimal choices, much of this appendix will appear as though I am pushing through an open door. Thus, if the idea of relaxing the usual mainstream maximization postulate to include nonoptimal decisions is congenial, what follows can be ignored. For those who find the idea of *some* nonoptimal decisions, or any deviation from maximization, difficult to accept, what I have to say here may be helpful. What follows is based in part on a number of discussions with graduate students and faculty members both at Harvard and a number of other universities in the United States, Japan and Europe. American economists appear to exhibit somewhat more uniform responses than those abroad. In writing this appendix I have attempted to distill the most frequent arguments that have come up, and to present my own view.

Economics cannot avoid the use of language. But language has a certain imagery. Technical terminology may attempt to restrict this imagery but cannot eliminate it, nor can it always restrict its public meaning. This is especially true in economics where ordinary words frequently are used in a special sense. But this creates problems. The question always arises, in whose special sense? There is usually no way of avoiding a multiplicity of interpretations. In addition, where there are a multiplicity of interpretations ambiguity can arise. Technical terminology may attempt to restrict such ambiguities but it will not necessarily eliminate them.

At the same time language creates consistency problems. If there is a concept fundamental to the primary meaning of a word and to all its connotations, then the definitions of the word do not allow usage that contradicts that fundamental concept, nor arguments that contradict the concept. These ideas will be used in the analysis of such terms as "maximization," "optimization," "choice," and "technical efficiency."

Some economists have argued one way or another that nonmaximization is unthinkable or close to unthinkable. Both students and distinguished economists have made points of this sort. Frequently initial reactions to the idea that we will employ postulates that allow for nonmaximizing decisions are extreme puzzlement on the part of some, as if the possibility of describing and accounting for a nonmaximizing decision is not or cannot be understood. Individuals who think of nonmaximizing behavior as unthinkable appear to be involved in a system of internal reasoning that is circular and does not allow them to think of nonmaximizing possibilities. Probably different individuals are hung up mentally in different ways on this question. It is clear that there is something like a "single loop" system of reasoning that makes it difficult for people to think of nonmaximizing behavior. To those who think outside the loop, nonmaximizing instances appear as obviously reasonable, but once inside the loop it no longer appears that way. Clearly this involves a certain type of mental fixity.

Thus, those who believe nonmaximization is unthinkable are, in part, misled by an incorrect use of language, and in part, stuck with certain reactions as to how to interpret possible instances of nonmaximizing or suboptimal behavior. In what follows we will consider both the linguistic problems and the lines of reasoning followed in response to the assertion of such instances, and especially the relations between language, consistency, and reactions.

Now, we cannot always tell from the context what mode of reasoning underlies the discussion. This is especially true when the context uses language that has more than one possible interpretation, and when the context itself does not make any arguments about maximization or nonmaximization. Since in most discussions in economics arguments of possible suboptimal behavior are not entertained one way or the other, although maximization as a postulate of one form or another is usually stated or implied, it becomes difficult or impossible simply from a given text to infer the use of language and mode of reasoning that are involved. Thus, I will argue against a certain type of reasoning about maximization, but I do not assert that all use of language necessarily implies the mode of reasoning to be considered.

Let me make it clear that I am in no way arguing against the maximization postulate in standard micro theory. There is nothing wrong in assuming that economic agents maximize or optimize. But there exist possibilities for alternative modes of reasoning in which some suboptimal decisions are allowed. Thus, what follows should be viewed as an argument for allowing for suboptimal decision making as developed in earlier chapters.

There are modes of analysis in which the decision postulate is not an issue. This is true of many macroeconomic models. But in micro theory a decision postulate is usually spelled out. The basic arguments to be presented are as follows. The nature of the language of maximization, optimization, and choice is comparative. These concepts imply that some entities are to be compared and from among those entities an optimum is to be chosen. Our emphasis is on the *comparative* aspect. If the concept is comparative then this implies the *existence* of one or more nonoptimum options, where some options are of unequal value. There are two modes of reasoning that appear to deny the existence of suboptimal options. These are: the revealed preference argument; and the argument that emphasizes a misspecification of the objective function. We shall examine these modes of reasoning and try to show that in both cases the comparative nature of the initial language is denied.

The nub of the objection is that the argument presumes that whatever is chosen is optimal and hence it really says nothing more than what is chosen is chosen and we call that optimal. The result of this mode of reasoning is that a nonoptimal choice cannot be made. Of course our basic argument is that a nonoptimal choice can be made.

Comparative Language Problems

Is it possible for an individual to choose a nonmaximum? The concept of maximization would seem to imply a choice procedure involving situations in which there are both maximum and nonmaximum options, and the individual is presumed to choose in a way such that the maximum is chosen. There are three possible situations. The first is the case in which there is only one option. The second is the case in which there are many options, but all have the same valuation or utility. These are trivial cases and can easily be ignored in what follows without any loss to the validity of the general argument.

We shall be concerned with the nontrivial cases in which there are many options and in which at least some of the options have different valuations or utilities associated with them. If the values associated with three options, A, B, and C, are 8, 4, and 1, then a maximizer would choose A, the one associated with value 8, and a nonmaximizer would choose B or C. However, maximization cannot take place if it is assumed that whatever is chosen has the value 8. In this case, the choice procedure denies the possibility of choosing anything with value 4 or value 1. In other words, the comparative nature of the options and the fact that there are differences is eliminated by the *postulate* that whatever is chosen will be assumed to have the value 8. Under this latter assumption, nonoptimal choices cannot be made. It is as if nonoptimal values cannot be associated with the options of choice. Thus, any decision procedure that does not permit nonoptimal choices denies the essential meaning of the word "optimization," that is, the necessarily comparative element involved. The comparative nature of the term implies that inferior options exist. If inferior options exist one such option can be chosen by some decision procedure. In other words, such a process is not unthinkable.

A somewhat more complicated argument involves the term "choice." The imagery of choice implies that the chooser can compare and select. Furthermore, he can select whatever option he pleases, without restriction. Thus, the idea of a choice suggests a comparative element and the possibility of inferior options.

But the imagery of the word "choice" gets in the way of seeing the possibility of a decision in favor of an inferior option. "Choice" suggests a highly conscious and deliberative process. Under such circumstances it is hard to see why anyone would ever want to choose an inferior option. But I will argue that this is a narrow view of the problem. Earlier in this book we substituted the words "decision procedure" for the word "choice." In other words, there are procedures and circumstances under which an inferior option *gets* to be selected.

Ex Ante versus Ex Post Arguments

An argument frequently put forward depends on the distinction between ex ante and ex post. Basically the argument suggests that all decisions are optimal ex ante. However, ex post they may not turn out that way because of mistakes, unanticipated circumstances, or some other aspect that cannot have been foreseen. From this point of view the intent is to make an optimal decision.

While the ex ante/ex post distinction may account for observed deviations from optimal decisions under some circumstances, it is a mistake to think that it is always applicable. This main point of the ideas presented in Chapter 2 is that there are decision procedures or decision occurrences that frequently do not include ex ante versus ex post considerations. Keep in mind some of the procedures mentioned: habits, conventions, rules of thumb, standard operating procedures, and the emulation of others. Deviations between ex ante intentions and ex post results often simply do not enter as part of such decision procedures. Consider habits. Habit is a noncalculated procedure. You just do things that way, and ex ante intent simply does not cross one's mind. The same holds frequently for conventions, rules of thumb, and standard operating procedures. Similarly, a decision may be carried out by the emulation of others without concern as to whether that is the best way of doing things.

The main point is that many decision procedures do not require any ex ante intent of any kind, nor do they require an intent toward optimizing behavior.

Even if a calculated procedure is used it may be carried out sloppily or not as carefully as possible. In some cases the person may know that he did not do as well as he possibly could have done. This may be true even if the person has told others his intention is to perform optimally. By observing behavior others may be able to determine that the real intention in a particular instance was to perform at less than the person's best ability. In other words, the real intent was something other than optimization.

The relation between the intent to optimize and decision procedures is far from simple. Four possibilities come to mind. (1) There may be no conscious sense of intention to optimize, and hence procedures are chosen without that intent. (2) There may be an intent to optimize and this may determine the actual procedures. (3) There may be an intent to optimize but other considerations turn out to be stronger and hence some emotion may overwhelm the intention and may rule the situation. (4) Finally, there may be a conflict of intentions. After all, the intention to optimize is just one intention. An individual may have a variety of other intentions, some of which may conflict with the intent to optimize.

We have already considered the idea that the intent to optimize may not enter as a concern. Also, no arguments need be presented that the intent to optimize may dominate the situation. However, items three and four require some elaboration. Consider the case of smoking, in which a person may know the adverse results of smoking and yet not give it up. Here the intent may exist, but other emotions connected with smoking may overwhelm the situation so that smoking continues despite the recognition that this is a nonoptimal decision. In such a case it is possible that the intent is not really as strong as would be required to behave optimally. Similar arguments can be made about diets, exercise, and so on. Finally, individuals have a variety of intentions. Many of these are unrelated to optimization. For example, an individual may intend to do as well as possible, and simultaneously intend to do harm to some other individual out of some emotional need. Carrying out the second intention may lead to a nonoptimal outcome (such as going to prison) despite the other intention.

Some of the decision procedures considered, such as habits, conventions, rules of thumb, or standard operating procedures, are historically determined, in essence. But historically determined procedures can be nonoptimal. A major conclusion from standard economics is that optimizing behavior requires that people recognize that bygones are bygones. An optimal decision usually requires that one consider the future flow of benefits and the future flow of costs from the time of the decision. Past benefits and past costs are not relevant to the making of rational decisions. The past must not determine the future since repeating past actions can be inconsistent with optimizing. Thus, as long as the procedures used depend on history then bygones are not bygones, and nonoptimal procedures may be employed. Clearly, historically determined procedures need not require any ex ante intent toward optimizing. On the whole we can readily see that raising the possibility of ex ante concerns does not eliminate the possibility of suboptimal decision procedures.

The Revealed Preference Case

A related approach is to argue that we start the analysis with the postulate that preference is known by how people choose. Thus, if given two options, A and B, and if the chooser should happen to pick A, then we assume that A is preferred to B. Similarly, if the chooser should pick B, then we assume that B is preferred to A. Starting with this idea of a revealed preference, and all preferences are assumed to exist only in terms of how they are revealed in real-choice situations, it follows that no nonoptimal choice could be made. In this case, one might say that nonoptimal choices are literally unthinkable. In other words, they go outside the system of choice and the system of the valuation of preferences that we start with.

Something is surely wrong here in the use of the words involved. The word "choice" by itself is a comparative notion. If all options are not equally good, then there must be the possibility of choosing an inferior option. We cannot be said to have choice if we cannot choose an inferior option where all options are not equally good. Moreover, the word "prefer" does not really depend on how we choose. In normal use "preference" is independent of choice, and has to do with comparative feelings *internal* to the one choosing.

Defining preference by choice implies that what is chosen is chosen. It really tells us nothing about preference as an internal feeling of the chooser, nor does it tell us anything about the capacity of an individual to choose a lower-valued option. Here, too, it would seem to be that part of our problem is linguistic. We get involved in procedures, or we start with postulates, that deny the essential normal language meaning of some of the words we use. In this particular case, the procedure of assuming that preference is determined by actual choice contradicts the meaning of preference as a feeling internal to the individual. It also denies an essential aspect of the meaning of choice, that is, the idea that it is possible for an individual to choose a lower-valued option, whether or not in practice he would actually do so. If we are really free to choose, then we must be free to choose a lower-valued option.

If an individual is assumed not to be able to make any lower-valued choice, then it follows that all choices are valued equally, or else that he changed his preferences very quickly over the period of time. In other words, this could imply the possibility of extremely unstable preferences. The main point is to argue that systems of ideas that do not allow for nonoptimal choice deny the comparative essence of our basic concepts.

Note that we do not suggest that there is anything wrong with the maximization postulate as long as it is used in a way such that it is conceivably falsifiable. The view taken here is that the maximization postulate must not be used in a tautological or self-immunizing sense. By this we mean that both the statement of the postulate and the mode of reasoning used allow for the possibility of the observation that non-maximizing choices could occur whether or not they in fact do occur. In other words, we must allow mental experiments under which they occur even if in real experiments they do not occur. Whether or not such occurrences take place is, of course, a purely empirical matter and ought to be determined by the results of experiments, observation, or other types of empirical research. Thus, the argument being made is about the way in which the postulate is to be interpreted. The significant point is that the only correct interpretation allows for an alternative postulate under which nonmaximization occurs, or for a more complex postulate that combines both maximizing and nonmaximizing possibilities.

On Objective Function Misspecifications

Other ways of denying the comparative essence of optimization come to mind. One is to argue that if a nonoptimal choice appears to be chosen, all this implies is that there was a misspecification of the objective function. The nature of what is involved can be seen if we consider a dialogue between two protagonists, Adam and Bill, such that

Adam believes in the possibility of nonoptimal choices, and Bill does not. Adam argues that he knows of a situation in which an individual could have earned a certain profit but instead chose an option with a lower profit. Bill comes up with a counterargument that what the individual was really choosing was a combination of profit and leisure, so that while the choice made involved lower profit, it involved a higher value for leisure. Thus, the total choice was the best possible. If Adam finds an example of a choice in which both profit and leisure are inferior, then Bill searches for some other variable, say, the possibility of long-run growth, and argues that given the belief about the possibility of long-run growth, this last counterbalanced the other elements, and hence an optimum choice was made.

There is no end to a dialogue of this sort. If the variables and objective function can be checked and examples found to show that they involved choices inferior to those that could be made, then it is always possible to think of an additional variable, frequently one that has not yet been checked, and could not be checked, to counterbalance the inferiority of the other choices. Thus, in this manner you can always postulate a respecification that denies the power of the example of an inferior choice argued by Adam.

It is important to observe that the procedure that involves finding a respecification for every assertion of a nonoptimal choice is itself a denial of the meaning of optimization. What is behind the procedure is the idea that *every* nonoptimal choice involves a misspecification of the objective function. Hence, what is really being said is that no matter what choice is made it can be interpreted as an optimal choice of a more complicated objective function in which all the objectives are known. Anybody who persists in this matter, that is, in finding more and more complex objective functions against any instance of non-maximization, is essentially denying the *possibility* that nonoptimal choices exist, and hence is simultaneously denying that the word "optimization" is meaningful. In other words, it is denying the existence of the options B and C mentioned earlier and their associated values of 4 and 1.

A story told by my colleague, Daniel Bell, is appropriate here. It seems that a general visiting a small town in tsarist Russia was very much impressed by the marksmanship displayed on various barn walls. In every instance a bullethole was found through the center of the bull's-eye. "I must meet this exceptional shot," exclaimed the general. "We have much to learn from him." Though the general was told that the marksman was the village idiot, he persisted until a meeting was arranged. "Tell me," the general commanded, "how do you do it? How do you always put the bullet through the bull's-eye?" The village idiot explained. "Oh, Excellency, it's not so hard. First I shoot, then I paint the bull's-eye."

Are Nonoptimal Choices Always Translatable?

Let us now consider a slightly different argument—one that suggests that the same results are always achievable by translating or reinterpreting nonoptimal results into optimal ones. The procedure is somewhat as follows: suppose the options are A and B, and the economic agent selects A; an observer argues that this is a suboptimal choice since the profits under A are less than that of B; that is, $\Pi\,(A) < \Pi\,(B)$. Furthermore it is reasonable to presume that $U(A) < U(B)$. Thus, either from a profit or a utility measure viewpoint the agent made a suboptimal choice. The translator's mode of thought is that behavior is always described by optimization. Thus, the translator adds another variable, say leisure, L, and then "translates" behavior as follows:

$$U(A + L) \geqq U(B)$$

that is, the combined utility of option A plus the utility of leisure (L) is greater than the utility of B. Of course, the additional variable need not be "leisure." It could be transaction cost, or the cost of decision making, or something else. The point is that it is an *unmeasured* factor and that it is inserted *after* the fact. To generalize, let us call it the Unidentified and Unmeasured factor F (a "fudge" factor). This approach says

$$U(A + F) \geqq U(B)$$

that is, the utility of A plus the previously excluded factor F is greater than or equal to the utility of B. Note that there is no information whether the fudge factor really exists. Clearly, there is a strong similarity between this approach and some of the other arguments presented. Since everyone is especially used to thinking in maximization or optimization terms, such translations almost always come to mind, and they will essentially be made in the mind or in the writings of the maximizing believer involved. But in fact this is exactly the same mode of reasoning as that involved in the objective function misspecification argument.

Another closely related mode of reasoning is frequently used.

Consider the case of sacrifice. Suppose someone gives money to someone else without receiving anything in return. Is this a nonoptimal form of behavior? The essence of the argument that this is not the case is to suggest that money is not the relevant currency of calculation or is not relevant to the utility of the person who acts in this way. Thus, there is a shift from ordinary money as the basic counter to utils. In terms of money there is clearly a loss, but this is not the case in terms of utils, because the person somehow gets satisfaction by carrying out a charitable act. In other words, the utility of money foregone is less than the utility gained by the act of charity. This may indeed be the case. Or it may not be the case. We do not know this simply by carrying out the translation. All we are concerned with here is the nature of the argument that shifts accounting from one form, money (for example, profits), to utils.

Another translation technique is similar—an act that appears to involve a loss of utility in the short run is asserted to involve a net *long-run* gain in utility. This may be viewed as a shift from short-run utils to long-run utils.

Nevertheless, there must be a sense in which we can see that sacrificing behavior is possible, and in which such behavior involves a net loss. All the various translation attempts discussed above do not change the fact that inferior options exist. Thus, in some sense, whether we phrase the matter in terms of money, short-run utility, or long-run utility, there is some ultimate measure in which an inferior option remains an inferior option. There is nothing in any general sense of decision making that would not allow for decisions which result in a net loss, unless this possibility is assumed away at the outset.

The Disutility of Maximization

Another interesting possibility involves the argument that an individual may maximize a utility function that includes the disutility of maximization as one of its arguments. The function may be written as follows:

$$U(x, \text{disutility of maximization}),$$

where x is a general variable to be manipulated. This is an extreme case because the disutility of maximization is stated baldly and explicitly. In other cases this may be hidden behind some vague phrases such as the inconvenience costs of maximization. However, when the matter is put baldly, it becomes clear that there is a basic contradiction.

Several aspects should be considered here. The first is the cost of calculation and information. Obviously, the time and equipment cost of calculation can be a real phenomenon. Where it is, it should be taken into account, just as any other cost would be. One should have no problem with this as long as it is a real cost. However, it is important to distinguish between real costs that are necessary to make an optimal decision, and any feelings an individual may have toward making decisions, or associated with the decision process that interfere with making an optimal decision.

Real costs of decision making, such as telephone costs to gather information, are costs that have to be taken into account in any calculation as to which option yields maximum utility. Feelings a person associates with the decision process do *not* enter into the assessment of the preference ordering of options. This point is crucial enough to deserve elaboration. The essence of the argument is that we have to separate two sets of considerations: (1) those elements concerned with the preference ordering of goods and the fact that a decision is suboptimal; and (2) the reason that a suboptimal decision may have been made. The following (artificial) example will help indicate the exact nature of the distinction.

A buyer considers two commodities, A and B, and he has determined that he prefers A to B. Either A or B is purchased each morning and consumed in the afternoon. The afternoon's consumption experience confirms the validity of the preference. Now suppose that on two of the mornings the buyer takes a pill that makes him irritable and impatient. Instead of purchasing A he purchases B, because he spots B on the shelf first. What the buyer does not do is take into account the effects of the pill on his purchasing decision. The effects of the pill are short-run and do not last beyond the morning. On the two afternoons in question he consumes B and regrets the purchase. He would have preferred to consume A. His preference ordering has not changed at any time in the process. Clearly, on these two occasions a suboptimal purchasing decision was made. The characteristics of A and B, and the preferences between A and B are not connected with the taking of the pill. The taking of the pill helps us to understand why a suboptimal decision occurred. But, whatever the feelings associated with or consequent to the taking of the pill, they do not change the fact that a suboptimal decision was made. If such feelings, (irritability, impatience, and the like), arose spontaneously without the pill taking and B was purchased instead of A on those occasions, the same argument holds, especially if the buyer did not take these feelings into account in making his decision. The feelings may help us to understand *why* a suboptimal decision was made but would not change the fact that a suboptimal decision occurred.[2] Feelings that interfere with making an optimal decision are separate from the preference determination of *A* over *B*.

The essential point can be made in the following way. An inferior option in the preference ordering is one that is neither as good as, nor preferred to, one or more alternatives that could be chosen. It seems reasonable to define a nonmaximizing decision as one that uses a decision procedure (rule of selection) that results in the choice of an inferior option, for a given preference ordering. Now, suppose that initially a rule of selection is employed that leads to an optimum, and a change in the environment generates emotions that result in a different procedure being used, without changing the preference ordering. If the new procedure results in the inferior option, then this represents nonmaximizing behavior. Note that emotions may induce but do not necessitate following the inferior procedure. A decision maker *could* follow the superior procedure when feeling impatient, even though in many instances he may not.

The idea of the disutility of maximization is very similar if the feeling involved is a *taste* against making maximizing decisions. It seems obvious that if an individual is not making maximizing decisions because of a taste against making them, then maximization is not taking place. Nothing is achieved by attempting to translate that into the view that he is maximizing a utility function in which the disutility of maximization is an argument. He cannot be maximizing if he is not making maximizing decisions *because* he dislikes making them. Here clarity and simplicity would call for referring to this behavior as nonmaximizing decision making. There is no point in using roundabout ways of saying things if in essence it is nonmaximizing behavior that is really involved. Whether feelings reduce the quality of decision making or lead to

2. An incident that occurred while I was teaching in Berkeley in the 1960s is a case in point. Emotion can interfere with optimizing behavior. Aldous Huxley, who was a visiting professor one year, was rather proud of the claim that he had overcome his extreme myopia by doing certain eye exercises and he refused to wear glasses. The cashiers at a local supermarket knew he sometimes brought some seemingly bizarre items to the checkout stand. On one occasion when Huxley might have been preparing for a trip, my wife noticed him coming to the stand with two items, a toothbrush and a tube of anchovy paste. The cashier said, "Professor Huxley, that's anchovy paste." Huxley replied, "Of course I know it's anchovy paste. I am not blind." He paid and walked off with his toothbrush and anchovy paste.

avoidance of decision making, they only explain why a suboptimal decision is made. Such feelings do not change the preference ordering of the options.

Inertia, Inert Areas, and Utility

We should consider whether utilities attributed to the concept of inertia are of the same type, or involve the same universe of discourse, as those attributed to other domains of economics. My argument is that this is not the case. We start by distinguishing between mental phenomena inside the individual and entities outside the individual, and the relations between them.

When we apply the utility calculus to exchange we are really concerned with the establishment of a preference ordering for goods that are outside the individual. In other words, using utility ideas, we are concerned with the connection between certain feelings (that is, utilities) and different quantities of objects (or services) we refer to as goods. Here, where the goods are obviously outside of the individual, attributing utility to these goods causes no basic difficulty. This is the standard way economics looks at things.

A category that is somewhat more subtle involves an individual's relationship to the effort he or she puts forth. The effort involved in deciding whether to move from one point to another is itself a feeling internal to the mental states of an individual. Any disutility associated with this feeling of effort is unconnected with the utility of the goods that will be chosen as a consequence of this decision.

More generally, the mental state of the decision maker while making his decisions does not determine the relative optimality of the choices made. Mental or emotional states that distract or divert the individual from making the best decision possible do not change the utility of the choices available or the utility of the choices made.

To argue in favor of the possibility of nonoptimal behavior in cases where inertial forces are at work involves the need to separate what goes on within a person, and the choices made by such a person. The argument is roughly as follows: suppose that G_1 is the optimal choice and G_2 is the nonoptimal choice. G_1 and G_2 are bundles of goods outside of two individuals alpha and beta. The ordering of these bundles is the same for both individuals. Now, if alpha chooses G_1 and beta chooses G_2 we would call alpha a maximizer and beta a nonmaximizer. Why alpha and beta chose as they did is a very different and not directly relevant question compared to the fact that we classify them on the basis of the way they chose; that is, alpha is classified as a maximizer and beta as a nonmaximizer.

Now, consider the case in which the utility of bundles G_1 and G_2 depend on some environmental variables, say the weather. Suppose that both alpha and beta initially chose G_2, but that the weather changes so that G_1 is now superior to G_2. Suppose further that alpha shifts out of G_2 into G_1 and beta does not. The outcome and conclusions are exactly the same as before.

Now, we could examine the personalities and thought processes of alpha and beta. However, what goes on in their minds when they make their choices, so to speak, does not change their preferences or the fact of the way they chose.[3] Most relevant is what went on in beta's mind, the nonmaximizer. Almost anything could have gone on in his mind. Beta may have been distracted or influenced by certain strong emotions, or he may have felt he did not want to make the effort to decide which option was now superior, or he may have wanted to do what he happened to have been doing without interruption, or he may have been preoccupied with other thoughts and oblivious to the need to make a decision, and so on. Understanding beta's mental and emotional states may or may not help us understand why he chose G_2. Nevertheless, as long as he did not change his preferences it does not change our classification.

Now suppose we attribute utilities to beta's mental state. Suppose previously, as a consequence of inertia, he was choosing G_2 period after period. Suppose we attribute a certain utility to the feeling of the absence of decision making effort in the case of staying with G_2, and a disutility to the feeling of effort that accompanies the decision making that leads to shifting to another choice. All this would tell us is how the individual feels about the effort of making decisions where he considers staying versus shifting. It explains why the person called beta chose nonoptimally, but it does not change the fact that he did choose in a nonoptimal fashion. The U(the feeling of no effort) and the U(the feeling of effort that accompanies decision making) do not influence the utilities attributable to different bundles of goods, that is, the pref-

---

3. Of course, real costs associated with determining if the preference ordering is still valid would have to be taken into account. For example, the prospective costs of telephone calls to determine if G_1 has certain climatic characteristics is part of the cost of G_1, and should be taken into account in determining the reassessment of the preference ordering.

erence ordering. Hence, knowing why an individual chose a certain way does not change the fact that he chose nonoptimally. In other words, the utilities of the mental states simply tell us something about the different personalities of alpha and beta but do not tell us that they have different preferences for G_1 versus G_2, or the fact that one chose an optimal bundle and the other did not.

A true universal maximizer would always have a zero utility associated with the feeling of effort entailed in making the decision to either stay or shift. In other words, he would always move to a new bundle of goods (that is, a new option) if the change in certain parameters altered the most preferred bundle of goods. Those who do associate a positive utility with the absence of the feeling of effort that accompanies decision making may not move even if staying in that position makes them worse off (when any real costs of decision making are included) than would otherwise be the case. Moreover, a true maximizer would always resist being distracted or diverted from the optimal decision procedure by mental or emotional states.

Let us summarize the positions we have taken. First, we agree that we can attribute utility or disutility to staying in a given position and to shifting to a new position, add these to the utilities of the bundle of goods chosen and presume that the sizes of the attributed utilities are such that decision makers are always maximizing. But we argued that this is a tautological approach and one that does not really help us to understand behavior.

Second, we argued that we want a system of analysis that allows for nonmaximizing behavior. Within such a system we include the inert area concept and, in that case, most points in the inertial set would be nonoptimal points. It is to be noted that in using this approach we do not specify why inert areas operate the way they do. We simply postulate their existence.

Third, if we do not take the tautological approach, we can still obtain suboptimal nonmovement within inert areas. Sometimes nonmovement will occur through calculating behavior and sometimes on the basis of decision procedures that do not involve calculations. Thus, nonmovement may occur rationally as well as nonrationally. On the whole it seems best to allow for the existence of inert areas because inertia is a widespread fact of life. At the same time, there is no need to explain the existence of inertia by presumedly universal calculating behavior.

Decision Making: Individuals versus Groups

Thus far the argument has been concerned with individual decision making. Of course, a great many decisions are made by groups such as committees, parliaments, and the like. Various types of voting and agenda setting are involved in group decision making. It is well known, especially as a consequence of Kenneth Arrow's work (1963), that ordinary voting can lead to nontransitive results. Furthermore, results may be skewed if some members of the committee attempt to vote strategically. That is, they vote in such a way as to anticipate the outcome, and vote in accordance with such expectations rather than in terms of their actual preferences. In addition, the position of items on the agenda, which will frequently determine the length of discussion around the given item, the persuasiveness of different arguments because of time constraints, the number of people voting, since some may leave a meeting before the agenda is completed, can lead to results that do not accurately reflect preferences. Without going into detail, it seems clear that in such circumstances various types of nonoptimal decision making can take place.

Some of the physiological and psychological literature suggests that different cognitive inputs come from different areas of the brain and hence something like a committee voting arrangement within individuals may be involved. In addition, various emotional forces can skew the results. In any event, both of these sets of considerations for individuals and groups argue for permitting the introduction of some suboptimal decisions.

Language and the Concept of Technical Inefficiency

The concept of technical inefficiency has been used in the literature in a way similar to the way I have used the term X-inefficiency. For contexts in which these two terms mean the same thing there may be no point in arguing in favor of a certain term. This is particularly true where the subject matter concerns econometric techniques for measuring this type of inefficiency, or for processing data in order to test the extent to which such inefficiency exists.

However, for purposes of developing theory of the kind I have been concerned with in the past, and of the type presented in this book, the imagery of the language used is of some significance. The imagery of the word "technical," is very different from other elements inside the organization that may lead to some type of "internal" inefficiency. In a book on labor productivity, Yankelovich and Immerwahr (1983) used the concept of discretionary inefficiency. While this may be superior to the bland concept of X-inefficiency, it still does not capture all the elements involved. At least three elements of "internal" efficiency come to mind: (1) an individual discretionary element, (2) organizational aspects, and (3) motivational elements. In other words, an individual may have discretion within a certain area and may wish to decide in a certain way, but organizational obstacles may prevent such a decision, and motivational considerations may result in a lack of persistence in putting the decision into effect. There appears to be nothing technical about these matters, so it seems desirable, if possible, to avoid the concept of technical inefficiency in this area.

Summary

The main point of the previous sections is to argue in favor of being allowed to develop and present decision models under which occasional suboptimal behavior occurs. The view taken is that such behavior is not impossible. Hence, we argued against the views that suboptimal decisions are unthinkable. I attempted to show that modes of reasoning in defense of the unthinkability (or impossibility) of suboptimal decisions usually violated the comparative implications of the concept of either maximization or optimization, or the related concept of choice.

References

Abegglen, James C. and George Stock, Jr. 1985. *Kaisha, the Japanese Corporation*. New York: Basic Books.

Aitken, Hugh G. J. 1960. *Taylorism at Watertown Arsenal: Scientific management in action, 1908–1915*. Cambridge, Mass.: Harvard University Press.

Akerlof, George A., and Janet L. Yellen. 1985. Can small deviations from rationality make significant differences to economic equilibria? *American Economic Review* 75:708–720.

———, eds. 1986. *Efficiency wage models of the labor market*. New York: Cambridge University Press.

Alchian, Armen A., and Harold Demsetz. 1972. Production, information, costs, and economic organization. *American Economic Review*. 62:777–795.

Aoki, Masahiko. 1984. *The cooperative game theory of the firm*. Oxford: Oxford University Press.

——— 1986. Horizontal vs. vertical information structure of the firm: An approach to U.S.-Japan comparison of industrial organization. *American Economic Review* 76:971–983.

———, ed. 1984. *The economic analysis of the Japanese firm*. New York: North Holland.

Arrow, Kenneth J. 1963. *Social choice and individual values*. New York: Wiley.

Atkinson, John W., and David Birch. 1978. *Introduction to motivation*. New York: Van Nostrand.

Axelrod, Robert. 1984. *The Evolution of cooperation*. New York: Basic Books.

Barkai, Haim. 1977. *Growth patterns of the kibbutz economy*. (Contributions to Economic Analysis 108). New York: North-Holland.

Beckmann, M. 1977. Management production functions and the theory of the firm. *Journal of Economic Theory* 14:1–18.

Befu, Harumi. 1971. *Japan: An anthropological introduction*. Tokyo: Charles E. Tuttle.

Broadbent, D. E. 1971. *Decision and stress*. London: Academic Press.

Calvo, G., and S. Wellisz. 1978. Supervision, loss of control and the optimum size of the firm. *Journal of Political Economy* 86:943–952.

Chandler, Alfred D., Jr. 1956. *Henry Varnum Poor, business editor, analyst and reformer.* Cambridge, Mass.: Harvard University Press.

———. 1962. *Strategy and structure: Chapters in the history of the American industrial enterprise.* Cambridge, Mass.: MIT Press.

———. 1977. *The visible hand: The managerial revolution in American business.* Cambridge, Mass.: Harvard University Press.

Chandler, Alfred D., Jr. and Herman Daems, eds. 1980. *Managerial hierarchies: Comparative perspectives on the rise of the modern industrial enterprise.* Cambridge, Mass.: Harvard University Press.

Christopher, Robert C. 1983. *The Japanese mind: The goliath explained.* New York: Simon and Schuster.

Clark, Rodney. 1979. *The Japanese company.* New Haven: Yale University Press.

Coase, R. H. 1937. The nature of the firm. *Economica* 4:386–405.

Comanor, William S., and Takahiro Miyao. 1985. The organization and relative productivity of Japanese and American industry. *Managerial and Decision Economics* 6 (June):88–92.

Cornell, Alexander. 1980. *The decision-maker's handbook.* Englewood Cliffs, N.J.: Prentice-Hall.

Day, Richard H. 1984. Disequilibrium economic dynamics: a post-Schumpeterian contribution. *Journal of Economic Behavior and Organization* 5:57–76.

Doi, Takao. 1971. *The anatomy of dependence.* Tokyo: Kodansha International Company.

Don, Yehuda. 1985. Industrialization in the Israeli kibbutz: An economic appraisal. Department of Economics, Bar Ilan University, Israel. Unpublished.

Eden, Dov, and Uri Leviatan. 1974. Farm and factory in the kibbutz: a study in agrico-industrial psychology. *Journal of Applied Psychology* 59:596–602.

Edwards, W. 1956. Reward probability, amount and determinants of sequential two-alternative decisions. *Journal of Experimental Psychology* 52:177–188.

Etzioni, Amitai. 1986. Rationality is anti-entropic. *Journal of Economic Psychology* 7:17–36. North-Holland.

———. 1987. How rational are we? *Sociological Forum* (in press).

Frank, Robert H. 1987. Passions within reason: prisoner's dilemmas and the strategic role of emotions. Unpublished.

Frantz, Roger R. 1987. *X-efficiency: Theory, evidence, and applications.* New York: Kleuwer-Nyhoff.

Freeman, Richard B., and Martin L. Weitzman. 1986. Bonuses and employment in Japan. Unpublished.

Frey, Bruno S., and Klaus Foppa. 1986. Knowing the possible: human behavior. *Journal of Economic Psychology* 7:137–160.

Gilad, Benny. 1985. Complexity and disequilibrium: how creativity, entrepreneurship, and the economy come together. In *Proceedings of the Second Annual Symposium on Creativity, Entrepreneurship and Productivity*. Washington, D.C. (March).

Gilad, Benny, and P. Levin. 1986. A behavioral model of entrepreneurial supply and its impact on corporate formation. *Journal of Small Business Management* 24:45–53.

Halberstam, David. 1986. *The reckoning*. New York: Morrow.

Hayek, F. A. 1945. The use of knowledge in society. *American Economic Review* 35:519–530.

Hayes, J. L. 1979. Review of *The visible hand: The managerial revolution in American business* by Alfred D. Chandler, Jr. *Journal of Economic Literature* 17:93–96.

Hébert, Robert F., and Albert N. Link. 1982. *The entrepreneur: Mainstream views and radical critiques*. New York: Praeger.

Helman, Amir. 1979. Lectures given at Hotel Hilton, Jerusalem, September. Ruppin Institute, Haifa University, Israel.

———. 1980. Income-consumption relationship within the kibbutz-system. In *Integrated cooperatives in the industrial society,* Bartolke et al., eds., pp. 131–146. Assen, The Netherlands: Van Gorcum.

Hess, James D. 1983. *The economics of organization*. New York: North-Holland.

Imai, Masaaki. 1981. *16 ways to avoid saying no: An invitation to experience Japanese management from the inside*. Tokyo: Nihon Keizai Shimbun (Japanese Economic Journal).

Ishida, Eiichiro. 1974. *Japanese culture: A study of origins and characteristics,* translated by Teruko Kachi. Tokyo: University of Tokyo Press. First published in Japan in 1968 under the title, *Nihon bunka ron*.

Katz, Lawrence F. 1986. Efficiency wage theories: a partial evaluation. National Bureau of Economic Research Working Paper No. 1906. April.

Kelly, John E. 1982. *Scientific management, job redesign and work performance*. New York: Academic Press.

Kirzner, Israel M. 1973. *Competition and entrepreneurship*. Chicago: University of Chicago Press.

———. 1979. *Perception, opportunity, and profit: Studies in the theory of entrepreneurship*. Chicago: University of Chicago Press.

Lange, Oskar, and Fred M. Taylor. 1948. *On the economic theory of socialism.* Minneapolis: University of Minnesota Press.

Leibenstein, Harvey. 1957. The theory of underemployment in densely populated backward areas. In *Efficiency wage models of the labor market,* ed. George A. Akerlof and Janet L. Yellen. New York: Cambridge University Press.

———. 1974. Efficiency wages, X-efficiency, and urban unemployment, In *Economic development and planning: Essays in honour of Jan Tinbergen,* ed. Willy Sellekaerets. London: Macmillan.

———. 1976. *Beyond economic man.* Cambridge, Mass.: Harvard University Press.

———. 1978. *General X-efficiency theory and economic development.* New York: Oxford University Press.

———. 1984. The Japanese management system: an X-efficiency-game theory analysis. In *The economic analysis of the Japanese firm,* ed. Masahiko Aoki. New York: North-Holland.

Lerner, A. P. 1934. Economic theory and socialist economy. *Review of Economic Studies,* vol. 2 (October).

Lewis, David. 1969. *Convention: A philosophical study.* Cambridge, Mass.: Harvard University Press.

Lindbeck, Assar, and Dennis J. Snower. 1986. Wage setting, unemployment, and insider-outsider relations. *American Economic Review* 76:235–239.

Litterer, J. A. 1961. Scientific management: The search for order and integration. *Business History Review* 35:472–474.

Macneil, I. R. 1974. The many futures of contracts. *Southern California Law Review* 47:691–816.

Maital, Shlomo. 1982. *Minds, markets, and money: Psychological foundations of economic behavior.* New York: Basic Books.

McClelland, David C. 1961. *The achieving society.* Princeton: D. Van Nostrand Co.

McClelland, David C., and Douglas G. Winter. 1969. *Motivating economic achievement.* New York: Free Press.

Miron, D., and David C. McClelland. 1979. The impact of achievement motivation training on small businesses. *California Management Review* 21:13–28.

Morishima, Michio. 1982. *Why has Japan 'succeeded'?* New York: Cambridge University Press.

Nadworny, Milton J. 1955. *Scientific management and the unions.* Cambridge, Mass.: Harvard University Press.

Nakane, Chie. 1973. *Japanese society.* London: Penguin Books.

Nelson, Daniel. 1974. Scientific management, systematic management, and labor, 1880–1915. *Business History Review* 48:479–500.

Nelson, Richard, and Sidney G. Winter. 1982. *An evolutionary theory of economic change*. Cambridge, Mass.: Harvard University Press.

Patrick, Hugh and Henry Rosovsky, eds. 1976. *Asia's new giant: How the Japanese economy works*. Washington, D.C.: Brookings Institution.
Pears, David. 1986. *Motivated irrationality*. New York: Oxford University Press.
Peleg, Dov. 1986. The kibbutz economic model. Kibbutz Sa'ar, Israel. Unpublished.

Rapaport, Anatol. 1962. The use and misuse of game theory. *Scientific American* 207 (December):108–118.
Ronen, Joshua. 1983. Some insights into the entrepreneurial process. In *Entrepreneurship*, ed. J. Ronen, pp. 137–173. Lexington: D. C. Heath.
Rosner, Menachem. 1984. The factory of the future and the typical kibbutz factory. International Conference on the Factory of the Future. Tel-Aviv.
———. 1986. New technologies in kibbutzim. *Jerusalem Quarterly* 39:82–89.

Sansom, G. B. 1981. *Japan: A short cultural history*. Rutland, Vt.: Charles E. Tuttle Co.
Schelling, Thomas S. 1960. *The strategy of conflict*. Oxford: Oxford University Press.
Schonberger, Richard J. 1982. *Japanese manufacturing techniques: Nine hidden lessons in simplicity*. New York: Free Press.
Schotter, Andrew. 1981. *Economic theory of social institutions*. Cambridge: Cambridge University Press.
Schumpeter, Joseph A. 1951. *The theory of economic development: An inquiry into profits, capital, credit, interest, and the business cycle*. Cambridge, Mass.: Harvard University Press.
Siegal, S., and D. A. Goldstein. 1959. Decision-making behavior in a two-choice uncertain outcome situation. *Journal of Experimental Psychology* 55:150–155.
Simon, Herbert A. 1976. From substantive to procedural rationality. In *Method and appraisal in economics*, ed. S. J. Latsis. Cambridge: Cambridge University Press.
———. 1978. Rationality as process and as product of thought. *American Economic Review* 68 (May):1–16.
Smiles, Samuel. 1860. *Self-help: With illustrations of character and conduct*. New York: Harper & Bros.
Smith, Adam. [1776] 1937. *An inquiry into the nature and causes of the wealth of nations*. New York: Modern Library.
Stark, Oded. 1986. Cooperating adversaries. Harvard Institute of Economic Research Discussion Paper 1211, February 1986.

Stiglitz, J. E. 1984. Theories of wage rigidity. National Bureau of Economic Research Working Paper no. 1442. September.

Storry, Richard. 1960. *A history of modern Japan*. Baltimore: Penguin Books.

Strongman, K. T. 1978. *The psychology of emotion*, 2d ed. New York: Wiley.

Taylor, Michael. 1976. *Anarchy and cooperation*. New York: Wiley.

Tversky, Amos, and Daniel Kahneman. 1981. The framing of decisions and the psychology of choice. *Science* 211 (January):453 458.

Ullman-Margalit, E. 1977. *The emergence of norms*. New York: Oxford University Press.

Von Neumann, John, and Oskar Morgenstern. 1947. *Theory of games and economic behavior*. Princeton: Princeton University Press.

Waley, Arthur, trans. 1935. *The tale of Genji*, by Lady Murasaki. New York: Houghton Mifflin Co.

Weiss, Howard M., and Daniel R. Ilgen. 1985. Routinized behavior in organizations. *Journal of Behavioral Economics* 14, symposium (Winter):57–67.

Williamson, Oliver E. 1967. Hierarchical control and optimum firm size. *Journal of Political Economy* 75, no. 2 (April):123–138.

———. 1975. *Markets and hierarchies*. New York: Free Press.

———. 1985. *The economic institutions of capitalism*. New York: Free Press.

Wintrobe, Ronald, and Albert Breton. 1986. Organizational structure and productivity. *American Economic Review* 76:530–538.

Yankelovich, Daniel, and John Immerwahr. 1983. *Putting the work ethic to work: A public agenda report on restoring America's competitive vitality*. New York: Public Agenda Foundation.

Yerkes, R. M., and J. D. Dodson. 1908. The relation of strength of stimulus to rapidity of habit-formation. *Journal of Comparative Neurology and Psychology* 18:459–482.

Index